FIRM INTERESTS

A VOLUME IN THE SERIES

CORNELL STUDIES IN POLITICAL ECONOMY

edited by Peter J. Katzenstein

A list of titles in this series is available at www.cornellpress.cornell.edu.

Firm Interests

HOW GOVERNMENTS SHAPE BUSINESS LOBBYING ON GLOBAL TRADE

CORNELIA WOLL

Cornell University Press ITHACA AND LONDON

First published 2008 by Cornell University Press

Printed in the United States of America

Library of Congress Cataloging-in-Publication Data

Woll, Cornelia.
    Firm interests : how governments shape business lobbying on global
trade / Cornelia Woll.
        p. cm. — (Cornell studies in political economy)
    Includes bibliographical references and index.
    ISBN 978-0-8014-4609-2 (cloth : alk. paper)
    1. Corporations—Political activity.   2. Free trade.   3. Trade
regulation.   4. International trade.   5. Lobbying.   6. Service
industries.   7. Business and politics.   I. Title.   II. Series.

    HF1713.W653 2008
    382′.3—dc22   2007042823

Cloth printing   10 9 8 7 6 5 4 3 2 1

To my parents

Contents

Figures and Tables

Figures

Tables

Preface

Firms do not always know what they want from trade negotiations. Business contacts with governments regarding trade policy are as much about defining preferences as they are about influencing the stances defended by negotiators. However, we know little about the ways in which firms determine their goals. This is all the more striking since business interests are a core element of the literature on international political economy (IPE). If we want to know how firms develop a position on trade, the obvious way to find out is to go and ask them. Because we already have useful predictions about material interests from economic theory, however, scholars tend to shake their heads at researchers who naively interview business representatives about their firms' preferences. Over forty years ago, Bauer, Pool, and Dexter experienced this skepticism when they undertook a nine-hundred-interview poll on the trade policy stances of American firms:

> When we inaugurated this study, one prominent economist told us that we were wasting our time. "Tell me what a businessman manufactures," he said, "and I will tell you where he stands on foreign trade." (Bauer, Pool, and Dexter, 3)

The economist's opinion was indicative of the theory-building on international trade negotiations that followed. As a consequence, some of the most interesting findings of Bauer, Pool, and Dexter's ten-year study were largely ignored in trade policy models. For example, not just big and competitive firms, but also medium and small ones supported reducing most tariffs in the 1950s, despite the fact that the latter were supposedly vulnerable to foreign competition. For Bauer et al., policy stances were as much affected by communication and the new norm of trade liberalization as they were by material conditions, which is why size and competitiveness did not play a role in interview responses in the mid-1950s. But why should norms affect policy stances? To the skeptics, support for liberalization appeared as a simple public relations strategy of firms. Firms might claim to be in favor of reducing tariffs, but behave quite differently once the issue becomes a reality. After all, these critics argued, every firm knows that too much competition can be detrimental if its factors of production are not mobile. Norms or communication are irrelevant for firms, since their profits depend crucially on the distributional consequences of trade policies. In this way, economic theory centered on material benefits claims to serve as a guideline for predicting the lobbying behavior of firms on trade policy.

I argue that such a perspective is insufficient for explaining the evolution of policy stances. In a world where actors and economic stakes are clearly defined, material interests may be obvious. Quite often, however, the reality of trade negotiations refuses to fit simple models. In complex settings, it is impossible to impute an economic interest simply by looking at what a firm produces. Many firms maintain multiple operations and cannot easily be categorized into a particular sector of activity. Trade policies that hurt one part of their activities may help another. In addition, firms have to choose among competing ideas about how to manage international operations in order to remain profitable. Put differently, firms may be faced with a multitude of sometimes contradictory material incentives. Even though firms are acutely aware of material realities, they have to determine which economic interests to pursue in a given context. The understanding of complex cases necessitates studying how firms mediate between their different options. We need to pay attention to the microfoundations of economic behavior to know under what conditions traditional models of trade policy lobbying are valid.

Through a study of service trade liberalization, I address this blind spot in the IPE literature. Service trade was a radically new issue for many of the firms affected by multilateral or bilateral liberalization, so it is possible to observe the evolution of their behavior from initial confusion to confident lobbying. Contrary to formal models of trade policymaking, the case studies presented here show that firm behavior and the goals that actors pursue are socially embedded. Shaped by regulatory and political arrangements, the identities of the firms studied, the beliefs they held about international

operations, and the opportunities they found in their interaction with policymakers profoundly affected what they actually lobbied for. As a consequence, business lobbying differs fundamentally across sectors and
countries, even when a focus on economic incentives would suggest that
we should observe similar behavior.

In particular, the book focuses on the liberalization of telecommunication services in the framework of the World Trade Organization (WTO)
and the partial liberalization of international air transport. As is often the
case, my interest in these sectors has a personal dimension. Living between
two continents during my formative years made me acutely aware of changing prices for air travel and telecommunication. When I was in high school
in the United States, I remember how costly it was to fly home to Germany
and how I only talked to my family once every Sunday for fifteen minutes,
with my parents getting quickly nervous about prolonging our conversa-
tion. Only a few years later, we talked several times a day without watching
the time. Today, I commute between Germany and France by air with
flights starting at 19€ a ticket. Before I began this study, I thought that the
telecom firms and airlines must surely not have been as enthusiastic as I
was about these dropping prices. Old European network monopolies were
probably being forced into liberalization by the demands of user groups,
or maybe by international institutions. I assumed that the winners from
market opening were competitive American firms or new market entrants,
while the former public service companies in Europe must have been the
losers in these recent developments.

During my first exploratory interviews, I found a different reality. Many
European firms declared that they were very happy about the WTO Basic
Telecommunications Agreement and had actively supported it during the
1990s. European airlines turned out to be quite critical of the existing
framework for international aviation and proposed ways to liberalize it and
make airlines act less like protected and privileged government partners
and more like normal businesses. I was surprised: firms with such important home markets were against protection and in support of market opening? Surely this must be a perfect example of dishonest interview partners
who tried to make a past defeat look less humiliating. At best, I was dealing
with a case of false consciousness. And yet I was puzzled. The more I talked
to business representatives, the less I felt that they were being disingenu-
ous. Yes, they had not liked the liberalization project in the beginning, they
admitted, but things had changed. I wanted to get to the bottom of this.
What had changed? Why had preferences evolved so decisively over such

a short period of time? What did it take to make a business actor move from protectionism to support for liberalization?

My aim in this book is to embed existing answers to these questions in a more general framework of preference evolution. To understand how firms make sense of their interests, we have to take their own answers to these questions seriously. While this may sound like an anthropologically oriented research posture, I seek to engage the traditional IPE literature on its own terms. This is an uncomfortable exercise. In many workshops and reviews, economics-oriented critics have let me know that big concepts such as norms and identity only obscure what could be an interesting case analysis. If trade theory is insufficient for predicting the observed behavior, I was told, network economics or theories of foreign direct investment might be more adequate. For many, I was concentrating on the wrong data.

I learned tremendously from these conversations, but I continued to be frustrated. The search for an explanatory mechanism seemed to require an ever more detailed breakdown of the incentive system firms faced. If I was unable to assemble all this information into a coherent prediction of the behavior I expected, how were firms supposed to do the same, consciously or unconsciously, when choosing their lobbying strategies?

The constructivist IPE literature provided a broader perspective that allowed me to work on the politics of trade without neglecting the often surprising behavior of the actors who are actually involved. However, many of my colleagues in Europe did not see the point of engaging the international relations literature at all. Constructivism, to them, was merely a fashionable word tagged to the sociological study of international politics, producing little more than shallow concepts that were already well known to most social scientists. If I was truly interested in the role of ideas, they argued, then I should invest much more time and effort into a satisfactory treatment of their evolution and much less into economic theories.

Some readers will find themselves in one or other of these camps. However, the book was written with the conviction that we need a dialogue between social theory and political economy, if we do not want an increasing divergence between approaches to understanding and predicting world events.

Acknowledgments

This book owes much to the discussions I have had with those who did not like it, but it would never have come into being without the support of those who did. Above all, I thank Wolfgang Streeck for his encouragement and support during the years he invited me to spend as a doctoral and postdoctoral fellow at the Max Planck Institute for the Study of Societies. Everything I have written has benefited greatly from the extraordinary intellectual environment and the constant exchange with my friends and colleagues in Cologne. My dissertation advisors, Richard Balme at Sciences Po Paris and Wolfgang Wessels at the University of Cologne, have accompanied this project from its very beginning and I thank them as well as André Kaiser, Yves Surel, and Patrick Messerlin for their insightful remarks on my work in its various stages.

My research, involving extensive travel to capitals and business centers, was made possible by the generous funding of Sciences Po Paris, the Max Planck Institute in Cologne, the European Commission's EUSSIRF fellowship for a short stay at the European University Institute in Florence, the DAAD fellowship at the American Institute for Contemporary German Studies of Johns Hopkins University, and the BMW Center for German and European Studies at Georgetown University. In the years following, I was fortunate to receive a scholarship from the Max Planck Institute and from the Berlin-Brandenburgische Akademie der Wissenschaften, and to be hosted by the Centre d'études européennes at Sciences Po Paris. My current home institution, the Centre d'études et de recherches internationales at Sciences Po, proved to be a perfect place for finishing the manuscript.

My deep gratitude goes to all of the business and government representatives who have granted me interviews, and to my colleagues and friends who have discussed my ideas with me. I will not be able to name all of them, but I would like to thank those who have read and commented on parts of this manuscript or different versions of its chapters: Alvaro Artigas, Sabina Avdagic, Jens Beckert, Dirk de Bièvre, Pieter Bouwen, Helen Callaghan, David Coen, Holger Döring, Andreas Dür, Steffen Ganghof, Catherine Hoeffler, Martin Höpner, Sigrun Kahl, Daniel Kindermann, Nikitas Konstantinidis, Alex Kuo, David Levi-Faur, Frédéric Mérand, Andrew Moravcsik, Pierre Muller, Abraham Newman, Britta Rehder, Fritz Scharpf, Susanne Schmidt, Tobias Schulze-Cleven, Marc Smyrl, Wolfgang Streeck, Yves Tiberghien, Christine Trampusch, Raymund Werle, and Josh Whitford. Jan Rutger toe Laer of KLM Airlines and Allen Mendelsohn from the U.S. Department of State have given extensive feedback on my early writings on international air transport. Emiliano Grossman and Armin Schäfer have spent much time discussing written and unwritten ideas with me and cheering me up when I got stuck. Nicolas Jabko has read the entire manuscript, parts of it several times. His support and feedback during the last phases of the revisions have contributed significantly to the final shape of this book.

At Cornell University Press, I thank Peter Katzenstein for his unfaltering interest in the project and his detailed comments on the manuscript, and Roger Haydon for his insightful suggestions and his enthusiasm.

For parts of chapter 3, I draw on material first published in a joint article with Alvaro Artigas, "When Trade Turns into Regulatory Reform: The Impact on Business-Government Relations in International Trade Politics," *Regulation and Governance*, 1 (2), 2007, 121–38. Chapter 4 expands my article "From National Champions to Global Players? Lobbying by Dominant Providers during the WTO's Basic Telecom Negotiations," *Business and Society*, 46 (1), 2007, 229–52. Parts of chapter 5 have appeared in "The Road to External Representation: The Commission's Activism in International Air Transport," *Journal of European Public Policy*, 13 (1), 2006, 52–69, and parts of chapter 6 in "Trade Policy Lobbying in the European Union: Who Captures Whom?" in David Coen and Jeremy Richardson (eds.) *Lobbying in the European Union: Institutions, Actors and Issues*, Oxford University Press, forthcoming. I thank the publishers for allowing me to use these materials and the various anonymous reviewers for their helpful remarks.

The article whose elaboration has contributed most to this book, however, has never been published. Starting as a summary of my main argument, it has gone through three years of revisions, rejections, resubmissions, and reformulation with nearly twenty reviews from eleven different scholars. By the time the paper was finally in shape to get published, the book manuscript had supplanted the article. Still, the article reviews proved to be essential guides in the revisions of the book manuscript, and I thank all of their authors for the detailed feedback, as well as Robert Falkner of the *European Journal of International Relations* for his interest and patience.

The faith and inspiration necessary for writing has come from my family. My husband, Morgan Després, patiently accompanied me on this long journey and has always accepted to read through long passages of political science jargon to help make them more accessible to readers. My sister Bettina was constantly available for emergency phone calls across several continents. Finally, without the often incompatible perspectives of my parents on socio-economic issues, I would never have become interested in most of the questions in this book in the first place. For their wise counsel, loving support, and inspiring disagreement, this book is dedicated to Artur Woll and Irene Woll-Schumacher.

FIRM INTERESTS

1

Free-Marketeers despite Themselves?

In the late 1970s, American Express encountered difficulties with its international card operations. James D. Robinson III, then chief executive officer of American Express, was searching for a policy solution to overcome restrictions abroad and asked Harry L. Freeman, his vice president in charge of strategic planning and government affairs, if there was a lever in trade policy. The two men knew little about trade, so in 1979 they bought a book by Kenneth W. Dam called *The GATT.* They challenged each other to read the work in order to see every morning who had gotten further and what they had learned about the international trading system.[1] When they had finished the book, they were determined to make the General Agreement on Tariffs and Trade (GATT) apply to service operations to help them overcome the obstacles to their international operations.

Trade in services had become an issue debated within the U.S. government during the 1970s, and firms such as Pan American Cooperation and the American International Group actively supported a possible expansion of the GATT to services.[2] Yet there was little momentum for such an ambitious project. Once financial service companies like Citigroup and American Express backed the U.S. trade representative, however, the issue gained in salience. In the early 1980s, the coalition of financial service companies began what they called a "strategy of illumination": they gave hun-

---

1. Interview in Washington, D.C., April 2003.
2. Yoffie and Bergenstein, "Creating Political Advantage," 31.

dreds of speeches to underline the need for and feasibility of a multilateral agreement on services. In 1982, company representatives were quoted almost weekly in the *New York Times, The Economist,* and *Fortune.*[3] Service trade became the political cause of American Express throughout the 1980s and during the negotiations leading to the Uruguay Round, which concluded with the signing of the General Agreement on the Trade of Services (GATS) in 1994.

Is this just another story of powerful businesses influencing trade policy to serve their objectives? Indeed, the important role of American financial service companies in the promotion of a service trade agreement is often cited as a proof of business power in international trade.[4] The observed behavior corresponds to popular beliefs and theoretical models of business-government relations: large companies determine where their interests lie and then push for the policy most advantageous to the pursuit of their goals.

The lobbying by American Express, Citigroup, or American International Group may not be surprising, but these companies were not the only ones to support the liberalization of service trade. In fact, many of the firms whose sectors were affected by the GATS spoke out in favor of market opening. In telecommunications, service providers such as MCI, AT&T, Sprint, and ComSat lobbied for a sectoral agreement on basic telecommunications in the 1990s. But even network operators such as the U.S. Regional Bell Operating Company (RBOC) NYNEX started following the multilateral negotiations and turned to support liberalization.[5] Similarly, European operators declared in favor of a multilateral agreement. Deregulated telecom companies such as British Telecom and Sweden's Telia were quickest to support international liberalization, but these pioneers were eventually joined by traditional monopolies such as France Télécom, Deutsche Telekom, and Telefónica.

Similar behavior can be observed in other service sectors. Lobbying to advance service trade liberalization was even undertaken by companies that were not directly affected by multilateral negotiations. In air transport, which was largely excluded from the reach of the GATS, airlines started to support bilateral liberalization through open sky agreements in the 1990s,

---

3. Ibid.
4. Sell, "Big Business and the New Trade Agreements"; Wesselius, "Behind GATS 2000."
5. NYNEX merged with Bell Atlantic in 1997. In 2000, the company bought General Telephone and Electronics and transformed into Verizon. For the historical discussion, I refer to it as NYNEX, while some interviewees refer to it by its current name.

despite initial resistance. European carriers later joined forces to develop a more ambitious plan from transatlantic liberalization and turned to the European Union to push for a liberal multilateral aviation agreement with United States. Why did all these companies support service trade liberalization? Since when do national monopolies lobby for the opening of their home markets? What do multinational service providers, large user companies, and former public service companies have in common that could explain these converging policy stances?

It is true that these firms did not all have the same motives or engage in the same amount of lobbying activities. The most determined and aggressive ones were first movers such as American Express, Citigroup, Time Warner, and MCI, which saw important opportunities in foreign market access. Others turned supportive of liberalization under certain conditions only. These ambiguous activists included NYNEX, which supported liberalization but insisted simultaneously on the need to protect the home market investment of incumbents threatened by new competition. Similarly, many airlines advocated liberalization, but only if it came with certain control mechanisms to protect their interests. Former public service companies in Europe remained conspicuously absent from WTO talks during most of the 1990s. It was only in 1996, barely one year before the signing of the WTO agreement, that EU telecom operators mobilized in favor of liberalization, which makes them late starters to say the least. Does the difference between first movers, ambiguous activists, and late starters indicate that the true interests of these companies lay elsewhere? Why then did they decide to pay lip service to liberalization? Since lobbying in support of liberalization has far-reaching consequences, it is important to understand what motivated the policy stances of these companies.

My aim in this book is to explain the surprising business support for service liberalization in the United States and the European Union. By comparing the complex evolution of firm preferences across sectors and countries, I show that the preference formation of economic actors is socially embedded. We have no single theory about the stances we should have expected from these firms, because they faced a variety of economic incentives among which they had to arbitrate. How these decisions where made, I argue, depended much more on regulatory and political arrangements than the pure material structure of the issues and the distributional consequences of trade liberalization. This was true as much for first movers as it was for late starters. As a consequence, it is misleading to say that business simply dictated policy. This book demonstrates that the content of corporate policy demands is shaped by the political interactions of firms.[6] Firms may influence policy outcomes, but policies and politics in turn influence business demands.

At a theoretical level, I dispute policy models that assume that the activities of economic actors are materially determined. In retrospect, it is always possible to reconstruct the economic rationality that firms were apparently pursuing. The successful signing of the GATS seemingly explains why American Express pushed for service trade with such fervor: liberalization provided new markets to the multinational company that allowed it to become a leader in international financial services, a success which was worth all the time and effort invested in lobbying activities. But even if American Express had long-run concerns about restrictions on its services operations overseas, other policy concerns were of much greater significance and far more pressing, in particular tax issues and financial deregulation questions in the United States.[7] Why did the company not invest its efforts into these immediate goals? More importantly, what was the benefit of enlarging the question to include all services? By tackling financial service liberalization through the prism of a service agreement in the GATT framework, American Express embarked on a political investment that took nearly twenty years before it came to fruition. In the business world, which concentrates on next quarter's profits, such a time horizon is equivalent to eternity: hardly a sound strategic decision! We could also ask why network providers in Europe turned supportive of liberalization over the course of the GATS negotiations. For companies with high and often immobile investment in their home markets, this is hardly what theory would have predicted. Maybe the telecom bubble of the 1990s made foreign markets a real stake for network providers, even in formerly protected markets, and firms chose to give up their privileged home position if this enabled them to obtain foreign market access. But at what tipping point should we expect such a reorientation?

The narrative of the preference evolution in service trade provided here shows that the definition and redefinition of political stances happened as a result of interaction with competitors and government representatives. Rather than being a function of economic incentives that automatically created a corporate response, trade preferences crucially hinged on ideational and strategic conditions. In particular, the identities of firms, which

6. This extends similar arguments made about European politics. See Grossman, "Bringing Politics Back In."

7. Yoffie and Bergenstein, "Creating Political Advantage."

in some cases moved from public service providers to competitive or global players, the beliefs they held about their international operations, and the strategic opportunities they found in interaction with their governments turned out to be determining. Once firms have defined their objectives, they behave in a perfectly rational manner by trying to maximize their goals. However, since identities, beliefs, and political opportunities depend on the political and regulatory contexts, business lobbying varies between cases, even when material conditions would indicate that behavior should be similar.

Studying Service Trade

International service liberalization was an unusual trading issue, because it was such a radically new idea. Traditionally referred to as "invisible transactions," service exchanges across borders did not fit the regular trade language and not even governments knew whether they should support or object to integrating services in the GATT framework.[8] How then did firms determine where their interests lay?

The study of business lobbying on service trade liberalization offers an exceptional opportunity to assess the ways in which firms respond to a changing political environment. In confronting a trading issue with distributional consequences, firms should behave as trade theory specifies: a wealth of theories lay out when and why firms mobilize in support of protectionism or liberalization. However, many implicit conditions of trade policy models are not given in this new context and the models are therefore of limited use. In particular, economic actors have to act in a context of great uncertainty. They not only lack information about the most likely costs and benefits of liberalization, they do not even know what liberalization actually means for their particular sector. Hence it is necessary to explore how firms assemble this information and what informs their anticipations and eventually their political demands.

In particular, I have chosen to compare service trade lobbying in the United States and the European Union, focusing on the liberalization of telecommunication markets through the Basic Telecommunications Agreement of the World Trade Organization (WTO) and the partial attempts to liberalize international aviation through open sky agreements and subsequently through a transatlantic aviation agreement. Both sectors are simi-

---

8. Drake and Nicolaïdis, "Ideas, Interests, and Institutionalization."

lar network service industries dominated by large, often national firms, which we can assume to have important ties to their government representatives. Interestingly, while telecommunication firms generally supported multilateral market opening through the WTO, airlines were more reserved about complete multilateral liberalization. The cases studied here thus make it possible to analyze a variety of policy stances in a changing environment and to compare what sectoral conditions weigh on firm preferences.

Comparing the United States and the European Union permits an analysis of lobbying in two different political systems. Moreover, both governments work with private actors in the pursuit of their political strategies and they are important trading partners with considerable leverage over the course of trade negotiations.[9] Firms in the United States and the European Union are thus encouraged to speak out for their policy preferences, first because their demands will be considered and second because convincing their trade delegations may well make a difference in multilateral negotiations.

The case studies draw on qualitative research from 2001 to 2007, with the majority of interviews carried out between 2002 and 2003. They are based on policy statements, public documents, and around eighty interviews with representatives of large service firms, governments, and business associations in the United States and the European Union, who all worked on the issue of service trade liberalization in telecommunications and international air transport.[10] The interviews supplied information when official documentation about business-government relations was patchy.[11] However, the analysis of lobbying behavior does not rely on the information given by the firms alone, but was instead cross-checked with government or competitor information to assure credibility. In essence, interviewing allowed me to reconstruct the ways in which firms positioned themselves, understood the stakes of international liberalization, and engaged on the issue of service trade. It helped me to illustrate the confusion that prevailed during initial negotiations on service sector liberalization and to trace what events and cues triggered important changes in the companies' demands.

9. See Shaffer, *Defending Interests.*

10. Representatives of several smaller firms were interviewed as well. However, since they often decided not to mobilize on trade policy issues, they were not studied systematically, but served instead as counterexamples.

11. A complete list of interviews can be found in the appendix. To ensure the anonymity of the interviewees, direct citations do not indicate the person or the company represented. Interview transcripts are available upon request.

Some readers may feel that service trade is a very specific issue that has little in common with trade in goods. Can we learn anything about trade policy lobbying in general by studying such a unique case? One could argue that predictions stemming from trade theory should not apply to service trade, because they were formulated for a different context. I contend that the more interesting question, and the one I seek to answer in this book, is *why* traditional models fail to explain service trade dynamics. What elements turn out to be essential for firms to behave in a way that we can predict with reference to trade theory?

Constructed Rationality

To answer this question, we have to consider economic action under conditions of uncertainty, a central theme in the field of economic sociology.[12] Max Weber drew attention to the fact that economic action is nothing but a particular type of social action, characterized by its narrow focus on utility.[13] The rational action model that underlies current political economy analyses maintains that actors coherently pursue those strategies that help them to maximize their utility. What utility actually consists of depends on the valuation of the individual. Jon Elster therefore distinguished between "thin rationality," which only requires that an individual's actions are consistent with the objectives he or she hopes to attain, and "thick rationality," which requires making assumptions about the valued ends of the individuals studied.[14] Since thin rationality gives little indication about the expected behavior of actors as long as we do not know what they value, current political economy literature has converged on a materialist understanding of utility. In economic contexts, utility is thus most often equated to welfare, be it income for an individual or profit for a firm. Behavior that deviates from the welfare-maximizing assumption is considered irrational and treated as an exception.

Although examples of irrational behavior are common, economic sociologists concede that they either involve little cost or frequently fall outside of the realm of the economy.[15] For economic actors such as firms,

---

12. Granovetter, "Economic Action and Social Structure"; Beckert, "What Is Sociological about Economic Sociology?""

13. Weber, *Wirtschaft und Gesellschaft,* chap. 2, 3–4. Swedberg, *Max Weber and the Idea of Economic Sociology.*

14. See Elster, *Sour Grapes.*

15. Frequently cited examples are voting, donations, and tipping in a restaurant that one will never return to.

striving to maximize welfare is indeed necessary in well-functioning markets, if they do not want to be wiped out by competition. For Jens Beckert, this points to "systemic limitations for the possibility of irrational behavior on the part of the firm." According to him, the difference between sociological and economic approaches is not the assumption of irrational or rational behavior respectively. Economic sociologists content that actors intend to maximize their welfare in economic settings, but they question whether these actors can in fact deduce their behavior from a clear preference ranking, especially in complex and uncertain situations. In essence, a large number of studies in economic sociology thus focus on "how intentionally rational actors reach decisions under conditions when they do not know what is best to do."[16]

This is indeed the focus of this book. In line with the economic sociology literature, I do not claim that firms behave in ways that conflict with their economic self-interest. Rather, how firms make sense of their economic interests in a complex setting depends on the historical and structural embeddedness of the relations they maintain with governments and competitors.[17] The political and regulatory context each firm has to act in proves to be a crucial indicator of the material conditions firms concentrate on, and of the beliefs they develop about relationships between means and ends and the political feasibility of their different options. In a context of uncertainty, analysis of social relations allows us to gain a far more meaningful insight into the content and timing of business demands than consideration of mere material conditions. This insight in turn leads to the conclusion that firms are intentionally rational actors, but that the content of this rationality is socially constructed.[18]

The condition under which analysts will be able to study how this rationality operates is uncertainty. Indeed, "neo-classical economic theory provides us a robust normative theory for the prediction and explanation of behavior of actors in economic settings *under the condition of perfect markets and complete knowledge.*"[19] Uncertainty has been well studied in economic

16. Beckert, "What Is Sociological about Economic Sociology?" 804.

17. Embeddedness refers to the ways in which the decision-making of individuals is enabled and constrained by culture, cognition, power, and the structure of social networks. See Zukin and DiMaggio, "Introduction." The concept of embeddedness dates back to Karl Polanyi's work, but has since changed its meaning. Cf. Beckert, "The Great Transformation of Embeddedness."

18. DiMaggio, "The New Institutionalisms," 700. This argument is quite similar to the concept of "interpretive rationality" developed by Albert S. Yee, "Thick Rationality and the Missing 'Brute Fact.'"

19. Beckert, "What Is Sociological about Economic Sociology?" 817 (emphasis in the orig-

theory and has given rise to several subfields such as transaction cost economics, signaling theory, and search theory. The fact that firms are confused about potential future costs and benefits therefore does not surprise economists. They suggest that we should simply expect a time lag in the mobilization of firms on trade issues, during which firms assemble information about their interests and potentially correct their behavior accordingly. After this period of information updating, economic actors should then behave as predicted.

This points to a fundamental divergence in the understanding of uncertainty between neoclassical economics and economic sociology, which has been underlined by Beckert and more recently Mark Blyth.[20] For neoclassical economists, uncertainty concerns the actual costs or benefits and the likelihood that an anticipated event will actually occur. For economic sociologists, it refers to lack of knowledge about relationships between means and ends. Moreover, not only is gathering information costly, but the marginal utility of an investment in the search for information can also not be determined. Beckert reminds us that these two types of situations have previously been distinguished by Frank Knight as situations of risk and situations of uncertainty. Risk refers to changes in the economy to which probabilities can be assigned, while uncertainty describes situations where the economic actor has no information on which to base a calculation of probabilities.[21]

Even though this distinction was accepted by the Austrian school of economics and by John Maynard Keynes, it was subsequently supplanted by an understanding of uncertainty as risk only. In a critique of the stylized assumptions of general equilibrium theory, economists started working on asymmetrical information and the existence of multiple equilibria. With the use of Bayesian probabilities for the determination of expected utilities, uncertainty can even be dealt with if we do not have objective, but only

inal). For Beckert, the correspondence between neoclassical economic theory and actual economic behavior in a context of certainty is due to "the institutionalization of instrumental behavior orientation and systemic mechanisms that discourage deviations from instrumental rationality in market contexts" (ibid., p. 818).

20. For a detailed discussion of the historical evolution of the concept of uncertainty in economic theory and its sociological critique, see Beckert, *Beyond the Market*, 36–50. For the difficulties uncertainty poses to theory-building in political science, see Blyth, "Great Punctuations."

21. Knight actually distinguishes several types of probability judgments from situations where "there is no possibility of forming in any way groups of instances of sufficient homogeneity to make possible a quantitative determination of true probability," which he calls true uncertainty. Since the business world has developed probability techniques to deal with risks, he stresses that "measurable uncertainties do not introduce into business any uncertainty whatsoever." Knight, *Risk, Uncertainty and Profit*, 231–32.

subjective probabilities. Agents are assumed to rationally anticipate the choices of other agents using information they have acquired from the observation of past behavior. Provided that actors share the same information and the same subjective probabilities, "Bayesian rationality" thus allows the computation of risks in a context of uncertainty. In other words, an economic agent will always find a rational strategy and one that other actors can anticipate. Several economists therefore reject Knight's distinction between risk and uncertainty altogether and prefer speaking of subjective probabilities.[22] This reinterpretation of uncertainty as a mere computational challenge of risk assessment is mirrored in the writing of Douglas North or Herbert Simon, who acknowledge the difficulties individuals have in determining the most suitable choice of action, but speak of "problem solving software"[23] or limits to cognitive processing.[24] Despite the complexity of situations, the fundamental interests actors pursue are apparently evident.

Conceptualizing the content of rational behavior as socially constructed, by contrast, suggests that the ways in which actors make sense of their self-interest result from interactions with their social surroundings. These interactions are not only indicative of the most likely future behavior of strategic partners or competitors, they also establish, maintain, or transfer ideas about how means are connected to ends and which means are the most appropriate ones to pursue in a context of constraint. In essence, a constructed rationality approach states that the assumption of self-interested maximizing behavior will be devoid of content and therefore underdetermined if we do not consider the social and historical embeddedness of individual actors.[25]

This perspective is at the heart of the actor-centered institutionalism approach developed by Renate Mayntz and Fritz Scharpf, who refer to it as "intentional action."[26] In order to analyze how actors make choices in a setting of uncertainty and institutional constraints, Mayntz and Scharpf propose to combine the rational actor model common in neoclassical economics with the sociological insight that action under uncertainty is only possible because humans create routinized behavior and achieve "a social

22. E.g. Hirshleifer and Riley, *The Analytics of Uncertainty and Information.*

23. North, *Instititutions, Institutional Change and Economic Performance,* 25.

24. Simon, *Models of Bounded Rationality.*

25. A similar critique of the underdetermination of narrow rational choice models has been made forcefully within the economic literature by Sen, "Rational Fools."

26. Mayntz and Scharpf, *Gesellschaftliche Selbstregelung und politische Steuerung;* Scharpf, *Games Real Actors Play.*

construction of reality" that assures the convergence of cognitive orienta-
tions.[27] Although the two perspectives disagree on many points,[28] they are
not mutually exclusive, according to Scharpf:

> While the rational-actor paradigm may capture the basic driving force of
> social interaction, its information content with regard to the operative in-
> tentions of human actors outside of the economic field is close to zero—
> unless we are able to resort to institution-specific information for the spec-
> ification of actor capabilities, cognitions and preferences.[29]

Combining action-theoretical insights from sociology and neoclassical economics for the analysis of economic behavior allows achieving a better fit
between theoretical predictions and the empirical reality of changes in
the political economy which are driven by purposive actors. Mayntz and
Scharpf's contention mirrors the theoretical ambition of Granovetter, who
stresses that a broad formulation of rational choice, which does not insist
on atomized individuals and purely material goals, has much in common
with his approach. Unlike alternative approaches, the embeddedness perspective "makes no sweeping predictions of universal order or disorder but
rather assumes that the details of social structure will determine which
[one of the two] is found."[30] In other words, the perspective seeks a middle ground between predicting and understanding behavior. It concedes
that certain regularities exist and orient the behavior of economic actors,
especially in times of stability. Uncertainty, however, can create profound
divergences from expected behavior in ways that will be impossible to understand *ex ante*, without knowledge of the content and structure of social
relations.[31]

   The difference between uncertainty as calculable risk and Knightian uncertainty has empirically observable consequences. If economic actors can
overcome uncertainty by updating information and verifying whether
their assigned probabilities correspond to empirical development, we
would merely expect a time lag between the moment of change and the
corresponding behavior of economic actors. Firms that are initially hesi-

27. Berger and Luckmann, *The Social Construction of Reality*.
28. The ontology of social forms is one of the most important differences. Narrow economic rationality presupposes that the economic environment will be perceived in the same
way by the actor and the scientific observer, while sociologists consider social realities to be
highly contingent and intersubjective.
29. Scharpf, *Games Real Actors Play*, 21–22.
30. Granovetter, "Economic Action and Social Structure," 493.
31. See also Blyth, "Great Punctuations."

tant about lobbying, but eventually do so in ways that we would have predicted, have simply undergone a period of risk assessment. In a situation of Knightian uncertainty, however, firms will rely on social devices to reduce uncertainty, such as traditions, networks, institutions, and the use of power. These devices will become an important selection mechanism between several competing pathways to maximize self-interest. By looking at the content of social relations and constraints, we will understand how firms define and redefine their interests in ways that would have been impossible to determine *ex ante*. For the politics of trade liberalization, I suggest that regulatory and political arrangements contain the information most relevant to the reorientation of actors' preferences. Accordingly, we should expect variation between sectors and countries that are independent of material incentives.

The Constitution of Interests

The sociological critique of neoclassical economics corresponds to the constructivist critique in comparative politics and international relations. In particular, this book contributes to the recent literature on preference formation that seeks to provide a more complete empirical understanding of the "interests" actors pursue in the policymaking process.[32]

In much of the political science literature, it has been common to assume that interests are given and change little.[33] This postulate has been particularly successful since the decline of functionalist and structuralist analysis in the 1970s, because it provides a convenient entry point for policy analysis focused on the agency of individual actors. If interests are given exogenously, then it becomes possible to study how the demands of individual or collective actors are aggregated by institutions and potentially mediated by ideas to produce policy outcomes.

However, successive research programs on interests, institutions, and ideas in contemporary political science have oftentimes juxtaposed expla-

32. Within that literature, it has been common to oppose constructivism and rationalism, which is a mistake. A social theory of the preference formation of economic actors does not imply that they are not intentionally rational; it merely indicates that material factors do not elicit a direct response. Material determinism may be implicit in a large number of rational choice models, but the two are not inevitably linked. Constructivism is thus the opposite of material determinism, not rationalism. See Adler, "Constructivism and International Relations."

33. See Stigler and Becker, "De gustibus non est disputandum," for the canonical statement. For a historical perspective on the study of interests, see Hirschman, *The Passions and the Interests* and Swedberg "Can There Be a Sociological Concept of Interest?"

nations based on these three factors as if they were strict alternatives. As Peter Hall has argued, understanding interests, institutions, and ideas as competing variables obscures the study of preference formation, which requires an exploration of how the three interact.[34] In opposition to rational choice institutionalism, the literature on historical institutionalism has highlighted the need to endogenize preferences into policy analysis.[35] Although the studies within this literature differ in their approaches, they are all concerned with the question of temporality and the weight of historical contexts on successive events. Most importantly, they investigate the effect of institutional conditions not only on actors' strategies within a given context, but also on the goals that actors pursue. Ellen Immergut explains this attention to the political construction of interests:

> Much confusion has been caused by efforts of historical institutionalists to endogenize the political construction of interests to their models. This does not mean that institutions radically re-socialize citizens in a revived version of social determinism or that norms dictate to actors what should be their behavior. . . . Instead, institutions act as filters that selectively favor particular interpretations either of the goals towards which political actors strive or of the best means to achieve these ends.[36]

Historical institutionalism thus acknowledges that intentional action requires an interpretation of goals and an understanding of the best way to achieve them. This is one of the central tenets of the constructivist literature. In opposition to the material assumptions that underlie many treatments of interests as exogenously given, constructivists insist on the role of ideas in shaping the goals and the behavior of actors. However, there is a divide in the literature between those who consider ideas as variables that are analytically distinct from interests and those that argue that the two are interconnected. While the former focus on the causal role of ideas, the latter are interested in the constitutive role of ideas.[37]

34. Hall, "Institutions, Interests and Ideas in the Comparative Political Economy of Industrialized Nations"; Hall, "Preference Formation as a Political Process: The Case of European Monetary Union."

35. See Steinmo, Thelen, and Longstreth, *Structuring Politics;* Pierson and Skocpol, "Historical Institutionalism in Contemporary Political Science." For a recent attempt to merge rational and historical institutionalism for the study of preference formation, see Katznelson and Weingast, *Preferences and Situations.*

36. Immergut, "The Theoretical Core of the New Institutionalism," 20.

37. Wendt, *A Social Theory of International Relations,* 77–89. It is important to be clear about this distinction because the two imply different research methodologies: causal arguments necessitate variable testing, while constitutive arguments require process tracing. See Hall, "Aligning Ontology and Methodology in Comparative Research."

Focusing on the causal role of ideas, Judith Goldstein and Robert Keohane have theorized a minimalist position. Although they insist that interests and ideas interact, they treat them as analytically separate and propose categories to evaluate the impact of ideas. Starting from a null hypothesis where policy outcomes can be explained entirely by factors other than ideas, they seek to show that ideas are crucial to explaining "empirical anomalies."[38] In other words, ideational explanations serve only as residuals after the impact of material interests has already been determined. Similarly, Craig Parsons investigates when ideas cut across lines of material interests to demonstrate how much ideas matter independently.[39] Distinguishing between worldviews, principled beliefs, and causal beliefs, Goldstein and Keohane suggest that ideas can affect policy (1) by providing road maps; (2) by orienting strategies toward a common goal when there is no unique equilibrium solution; and (3) by becoming embedded in institutions, which then work to constrain actors. In line with these propositions, several authors have investigated how ideas have affected the policy choices of actors who were trying to pursue a given set of goals.[40]

Those who argue that ideas are in fact constitutive of interests refuse such a separation. According to Mark Blyth, the analytical distinction between ideas and interests should not lead us to assume a synthetic one, "which holds that ideas and interests are *in fact different things* in the world."[41] Similarly, John Campbell suggests that interests are merely a particular type of idea.[42] Scholarship interested in the social construction of interests has thus tried to specify which ideas contribute to the selection of goals actors choose to pursue. In particular, they have pointed to the role of identities, to the constitutive role of beliefs, and to the relationships between ideas and strategic interactions.

Identities, defined as continuous self-categorizations, shape interests because they provide information about the normative expectations addressed to an actor, and because they specify the social unit on whose

38. Goldstein and Keohane, *Ideas and Foreign Policy*, 6.

39. Parsons, "Showing Ideas as Causes"; Parsons, *A Certain Idea of Europe.*

40. E.g. Garrett and Weingast, "Ideas, Interests and Institutions"; Berman, *The Social Democratic Moment.*

41. Blyth, *Great Transformations,* 18 (emphasis in the original). See also Woods, "Economic Ideas and International Relations"; Finnemore, *National Interest in International Society;* Finnemore and Sikkink, "International Norm Dynamics and Political Change."

42. Campbell, *Institutional Change and Globalization,* 91. Even the Utilitarian writer Jeremy Bentham acknowledged that interests require the "constant imagining of the future" through which "commensurables have to be constructed and balanced," according to Engelmann, *Imagining Interest in Political Thought,* 3.

behalf a goal will be pursued. As Scharpf has stressed, "it is in terms of identity that actors perceive opportunities and threats, set goals for strategic behavior, assess the appropriateness of particular strategies and tactics, and evaluate the intended and unintended outcomes of their actions."[43] In international relations, identity research has stressed that state identity is an empirical question: we need to know how popular identities fashion the ways in which states conceive of themselves and others in order to understand what interests they are likely to pursue. According to Ted Hopf, identities imply interests that are social cognitive products.[44] Following the pioneering work of Alexander Wendt and Peter Katzenstein,[45] a broad literature currently grapples with this research agenda.[46] In particular, it has proven difficult to move beyond descriptive analysis of state identity, which makes it hard to specify what type of identity will lead to a particular choice of action.[47] In parallel, empirical analysis in comparative political economy shows that governmental decision-making is affected either by the professional identities of political decision-makers or by a sense of national identity.[48] Even management research now considers identities as important elements in the formation of corporate political strategies.[49]

Beliefs, understood as sets of normative and causal ideas about means-end relationships, equally influence the goals actors pursue, as several studies of economic policymaking have highlighted.[50] New economic paradigms not only provide road maps for action, as Goldstein and Keohane have shown, they also have an indirect effect on preference formation by specifying causal and normative relationships relevant to a particular choice of action. For example, independently of the pecuniary benefits individuals can derive from social policies, individuals who believe that social mobility provides a faire opportunity to all citizens to rise above poverty are more likely to oppose redistribution, especially in countries where indi-

43. Scharpf, *Games Real Actors Play*, 61–65.

44. Hopf, *Social Construction of International Politics*, 16–17.

45. Wendt, "Anarchy Is What States Make of It: The Social Construction of Power Politics"; Wendt, "Collective Identity Formation and the International State"; Katzenstein, *Cultural Norms and National Security;* Katzenstein, *The Culture of National Security.*

46. For discussion, see Abdelal et al., "Identity as a Variable."

47. For overviews, see Hopf, "The Promise of Constructivism in International Relations Theory"; Finnemore and Sikkink, "Taking Stock." For a critical review, see Zehfuss, "Constructivism and Identity."

48. Ziegler, *Governing Ideas;* Campbell, Hall, and Pedersen, *National Identity and the Varieties of Capitalism.*

49. E.g. Wilts, "Identities and Preferences in Corporate Political Strategizing."

50. Hall, *The Political Power of Economic Ideas;* Sikkink, *Ideas and Institutions;* McNamara, *The Currency of Ideas;* Blyth, *Great Transformations.*

vidual effort has a high normative value.[51] Put more abstractly, what an actor wants depends crucially on beliefs about the ways in which his choices and the choices of the people around him are related to ends, because these beliefs influence the normatively acceptable set of alternatives and prescribe the most appropriate behavior.

Finally, constructivist scholars have underlined the relationship between ideas and political strategies. Strategies, defined as activities employed to achieve one's goals, are a central element of the rational choice literature: depending on political feasibility, actors are assumed to trade off ranked preferences in order to get as close to their desired outcome as possible.[52] What is politically feasible, however, can depend on more than just institutional constraints. In particular, building necessary policy coalitions requires a shared analysis of the issues, as Kathleen McNamara has shown in her study of European economic and monetary union, which only became possible once policymakers agreed on new monetary ideas.[53] Actors therefore employ cognitive frameworks strategically to facilitate policy agreement.[54] Nicolas Jabko goes even further, arguing that actors need not even share a diagnosis, as long as they can find an objective that allows them to work towards their separate goals simultaneously. Driving policy change thus requires constructing a leitmotiv that brings together otherwise heterogeneous policy actors. This "social constructing of strategy" is contrary to the classic idea of strategy as a utility-maximizing tool, as Jabko demonstrates, since actors neither control the long-term effects of their cooperation, nor do they know whether they have indeed chosen an appropriate strategy.[55] The feedback effects of these socially constructed strategies are diverse. Actors can be forced to adhere to past rhetorical commitments, even if they would have preferred other policy options.[56] More profoundly, strategic coalition building can affect the preferences of actors, who incrementally adjust to the common objective in ways they would not have done in the absence of a coalition. Bruno Palier, for example, shows that

51. See for example, Feldman, "Economic Self-Interest and Political Behavior"; Alesina and La Ferrara, "Preferences for Redistribution in the Land of Opportunities"; Linos and West, "Self-Interest, Social Beliefs, and Attitudes to Redistribution."

52. For an overview of strategy in international relations, see Lake and Powell, *Strategic Choice in International Relations*.

53. McNamara, *The Currency of Ideas*.

54. For example, Sell and Prakash, "Using Ideas Strategically."

55. Jabko, *Playing the Market*, 29–32.

56. Schimmelfennig, "The Community Trap"; Schimmelfennig, *The EU, NATO and the Integration of Europe*.

the French state, trade unions, and employers agreed on the diagnosis that past welfare state policies had failed, which led them to cooperate on "new" policy approaches. Initially, these solutions were only possible because they were sufficiently "ambiguous" to allow aggregating the often opposed objectives, but nonetheless created an incremental cumulative transformation that Palier characterized as "third order" paradigmatic change.[57] Put differently, understanding strategy as a social construction highlights that strategic choices have feedback effects on the preference formation of the actors involved.[58]

Emphasizing that interests are constituted by ideas about identity, means-end relationships, and strategies has contributed considerably to our understanding of the goals actors pursue. However, recognizing that interests are intrinsically bound up with ideas is of little analytical value if scholars cannot specify when and how these mechanisms operate and what this implies for an understanding of policy change. As Mark Blyth reminds us, "the danger is simply to move from a materialist reductionism to an ideational essentialism, which would be a mistake."[59] The objective here is therefore not just an analysis of how service firms redefined their interests, but also when they did so and why.[60]

The framework proposed here indicates what ideational changes reorient the material objectives firms pursue in ways that we will not be able to predict *ex ante*. As Alt et al. have written after a comprehensive summary of the materialist IPE literature,

> We admit that each model is in some way correct depending on the circumstances. . . . We will never have a single model that explains most of what we want to understand about international trade.[61]

Looking at the patterns that affect the context of economic rationality helps to understand this variation. My premise is that it is crucial to conceive of preference formation as a complex process in order to think about these "circumstances" more systematically. This approach helps us to recognize cases where materialist assumptions are unproblematic and signals what elements will lead to unexpected variation. By doing so, it can provide guidelines that help analysts to choose which predictions will most

57. Palier, "Ambiguous Agreement, Cumulative Change."
58. See also Jabko, "The Importance of Being Nice."
59. Blyth, *Great Transformations,* 270.
60. Pierson, "Not Just What, but When."
61. Alt et al., "The Political Economy of International Trade," 714.

likely apply to their case. Understanding cases thus goes hand in hand with efforts to predict outcomes.

Overview

The study of how firms determined what they wanted in the radically new context of service trade leads to three basic conclusions. First of all, traditional trade models are more appropriate for tariff negotiations in the trade of goods than for the study of new trade issues such as service trade or regulatory harmonization. For the latter, the question is no longer whether or not to liberalize trade but how to liberalize trade in a given sector. In this context, business-government relations are much more characterized by mutual learning than they are by firms exerting pressure in the pursuit of a predefined goal. In particular, business interests will be difficult to predict by looking at the distributional effect of trade when the logic of international exchange is not evident or when firms operate in regulatory contexts that do not require them to act as competitive players.

Second, many assumptions about business-government relations in trade come from the study of the United States and do not transfer well to the European context. Most importantly, analysts tend to underestimate the strategic constraints created by multilevel decision-making in the European Union and the pivotal role of the European Institutions. By rendering a variety of policy demands politically infeasible, the European Union system forces firms to embrace positions that we would not expect in the U.S. context. Since the political system in which firms have to lobby and the regulatory arrangements that govern a particular industry have an impact on preference formation, such variation between countries will be systematic and needs to be taken into account for comparative trade policy research.

Third, because policy contexts affect business preferences, a demand-side conception of business-government relations in trade policymaking is misleading. Firms and other societal actors do not simply dictate a series of policy options, so that governments have to do little more than arbitrate. Indeed, most observers of service trade liberalization acknowledge the presence and involvement of large service companies, but argue that this does not explain the policy evolution: government strategies and new ideas were much more decisive.[62] Understanding that the elaboration of policy

62. Drake and Nicolaïdis, "Ideas, Interests, and Institutionalization"; Young, *Extending European Cooperation;* Crystal, "Bargaining in the Negotiations over Liberalizing Trade in Services."

preferences is socially embedded helps to explain why: business demands result as much from government action as policy decisions respond to business demands.[63]

In the following, chapter 2 reviews the literature on the role of firms in policymaking in comparative and international political economy. Discussion of the trade policy literature shows that the deduction of firm preferences from economic theory offers insufficient insight into the behavior of economic actors in a context of uncertainty. Integrating constructivist insights into the study of preference formation provides a conceptual framework that indicates what type of changes will have consequences for the goals firms pursue in trade. Chapter 3 turns to the issue of service trade and lays out why traditional trade interest hypotheses do not transfer well to this area. It then presents the history of and the issues involved in service trade and introduces the sectoral comparison between telecommunication services and air transport. The next two chapters are the heart of the empirical study. Chapter 4 discusses the evolution of business preferences regarding the negotiation of the Basic Telecommunications Agreement of the WTO. Chapter 5 analyzes the policy demands of airlines concerning the liberalization of international aviation and, in particular, the negotiation of a transatlantic open aviation area. Both chapters begin with an historical overview of the policy issues to clarify the political and regulatory contexts in which firms are embedded. Following the conceptual model, interview data then demonstrate the evolution of business preferences with respect to identity, beliefs, and the strategic environment. Chapter 6 summarizes the comparative lessons and demonstrates how ideational changes interact with strategic ones. Playing a crucial constitutive role, ideas explain how firms reorient their policy demands, while strategic changes trigger often profound transformations of firm preferences. In the European Union in particular, this interconnection explains how governmental action shapes the economic interests of firms. A comparison between services, textiles and clothing, and agricultural lobbying demonstrates that the same mechanism operates in EU trade policymaking whether firms seek liberalization or protection. The conclusion revisits questions of influence and power of firms in trade policymaking and discusses the implications of this study for a normative debate about democratic decision-making and accountability in international trade negotiations.

63. See Drezner, *All Politics is Global.*

2

Business Interests in Political Economy

Firms have moved to the center stage of research in political economy. In the field of international political economy, business lobbying has been considered a central element of economic policymaking ever since E. E. Schattschneider's classic study of the Smoot-Hawley bill.[1] Comparative political economy preoccupied with the structure of capitalism had long focused on class conflict and stability created by institutional path-dependencies.[2] Increased understanding of the patterns of change in socio-economic governance, however, showed the limits of labor-centered theories and led to a revival of interest in the political role of business.[3] Much of the literature in the 1990s attests to the centrality of employer associations and industry groups in the shaping and remaking of socio-economic institutions.[4] In line with this perspective, Peter Hall and David Soskice state that the fundamental contribution of their edited volume on the varieties of capitalism is "to bring firms back into the center of comparative political economy."[5]

1. Schattschneider, *Politics, Pressures and the Tariff*. For an overview, see Milner, "The Political Economy of International Trade."

2. See especially the welfare state literature: Korpi, *The Working Class in Welfare Capitalism;* Korpi, *The Democratic Class Struggle;* Esping-Andersen, *Politics Against Markets;* Korpi, "Contentious Institutions."

3. Thelen, "Beyond Corporatism."

4. For example, Crouch and Streeck, *The Political Economy of Modern Capitalism;* Hollingsworth and Boyer, *Contemporary Capitalism;* Kitschelt et al., *Continuity and Change in Contemporary Capitalism;* Streeck et al., *Governing Interests.*

5. Hall and Soskice, *Varieties of Capitalism*, 4.

The analytical choice of concentrating on firms begs the question what motivates firms when they engage in politics at the national or international level. Despite agreement on the centrality of firms, few scholars have focused their studies on how firms determine what goals to pursue in economic policymaking, especially in international political economy.[6] The main effort to understand preference formation has recently come from studies in comparative political economy and it is illuminating to review this debate before turning to the literature on trade policy lobbying.

In their respective studies of employer preferences, Peter Swenson and Isabela Mares have criticized the traditional literature for simply assuming preferences based on capital-labor cleavages. Rather than opposing labor demands in the shaping of socio-economic institutions, employers have actually contributed to creating these institutions in order to ensure benefits such as wage restraint, labor peace, and investment in labor skills.[7] Since employers had to arbitrate between several competing objectives, there was a much greater room for cross-class alliances and the actual positions taken by firms need to be explained as a result of these strategic alliances. Similarly, Hall and Soskice insist that firms are embedded in specific institutional settings. The corporate strategies firms develop will be those that "take advantage of the institutional support available for particular modes of coordination."[8] National institutions matter because they condition strategic interactions. The behavior of firms will therefore differ according to their domestic institutional contexts and this explains the persistent divergence of different types of capitalism, which are defended by firms that hope to benefit from "comparative institutional advantage" in international competition.

Despite this attention to historical and institutional settings, the action-theoretical assumptions at the heart of these firm-centered studies are less evident. Many authors apply a simple rational action model of welfare maximization, but some are careful to avoid such general conclusions and point to less material factors. The extensive introduction to Hall and Soskice's edited volume is an instructive example of the unresolved ambiguities arising from these two perspectives. The authors announce that they will adopt a "relational view of firms," which relies heavily on insights from microeconomics, and that they "construe the key relationships in the political economy in game-theoretical terms."[9] This seemingly implies that

6. But see Bauer, Pool and Dexter, *American Business and Public Policy.*
7. Swenson, *Capitalists against Markets;* Mares, *The Politics of Social Risk.*
8. Hall and Soskice, *Varieties of Capitalism,* vi.
9. Ibid., 5.

institutions define the stakes and the rules of the game, within which firms then act strategically. Indeed, the authors consider the most relevant institutions to be those that "reduce the uncertainty actors have about the behavior of others and that allow them to make credible commitments."[10] This is a typical coordination problem, or risk in Frank Knight's sense, not a true case of uncertainty.

However, Hall and Soskice then turn to institutions in coordinated market economies and underline that these show the importance of institutions that provide firms with "a capacity for *deliberation.*" Indeed, institutions allow a "common diagnosis" of external shocks and "an agreed response." This is highly relevant to cases of Knightian uncertainty: "In many instances, what leads the actors to a specific equilibrium is a set of shared understandings about what actors are likely to do, most often rooted in a sense of what is appropriate to do in such circumstances." History and culture matter beyond formal institutions, Hall and Soskice argue with reference to the work of March and Olson and of DiMaggio and Powell, from which they borrow an understanding of culture as "a set of available 'strategies for action' developed from experience" analogous "to the cognitive turn" taken by sociology.[11]

This deliberative perspective is neither particularly game-theoretical nor rooted in microeconomics. One may speculate that the contrasting views reflect a certain action-theoretical disagreement between the two authors. In his other writings, David Soskice consistently employs a materialist understanding of economic preferences. In his work with Torben Iversen on social policy, for example, he postulates that citizens support or oppose welfare state policies as a function of their investment in labor skills. Social policy preferences are thus a simple function of human capital investment.[12] Similarly, he explains preferences for electoral institutions with reference to the nature and geographical distribution of economic interests, which are either class- or asset-specific interests in welfare distribution.[13] Even women's career choices are explained as a function of the economic incentives created by different models of capitalism.[14] Peter Hall, by contrast, has published widely on the importance of economic

10. Ibid., 10.

11. Ibid., 11–12 (emphasis in the original). See March and Olson, *Rediscovering Institutions;* Di Maggio and Powell, *The New Institutionalism in Organizational Analysis.*

12. Iversen and Soskice, "An Asset Theory of Social Policy Preferences."

13. Cusack, Iversen, and Soskice, "Economic Interests and the Origins of Electoral Systems."

14. Soskice, "Varieties of Capitalism and Cross-National Gender Differences."

ideas for the orientation of policy decisions.[15] Preference formation in particular, he argues, is a deeply political process, where actors interpret their interests in response to an unfolding set of experiences and interactions with others.[16] Understanding institutional change in contemporary capitalisms requires therefore analyzing what leads "key groups to adjust their interpretations of their interests."[17] David Soskice's and Peter Hall's perspectives are emblematic of an ontological divide between scholars in comparative political economy. While some consider economic interests as a function of the objective distribution of material benefits within given institutional contexts, others believe that interests reflect intersubjective beliefs about personal advantages.[18]

Despite these disagreements, the comparative political economy literature has contributed significantly to our understanding of the role firms play in the shaping and maintenance of socio-economic institutions and has drawn our attention to the effects of institutional settings on firm preferences. Corporate strategies across nations are assumed to display systematic differences that parallel the overarching institutional structure. However, *how* institutional context induce behavioral differences has not been categorically resolved, and this disagreement has given rise to an explicit ontological debate. Peter Hall, for example, argues that contemporary political economy is "gripped by a neomaterialism even more reductionist than that of Marxist analyses of the 1960s and 1970s."[19] In order to move beyond this reductionism, historical institutionalists and rational choice institutionalists have begun to investigate the historical and social origins of preferences.[20]

The emergence of such a debate shows that comparative political studies are slowly moving toward a dialogue between political economy, historical analysis, and economic sociology. This is much less the case in international political economy, where especially trade policy analysis re-

15. Hall, *The Political Power of Economic Ideas;* Hall, "Institutions, Interests and Ideas in the Comparative Political Economy of Industrialized Nations."

16. Hall, "Preference Formation as a Political Process."

17. Hall, "Stabilität und Wandel in den Spielarten des Kapitalismus."

18. Hall and Soskice suggest in a particularly vague manner that firms "gravitate towards strategies that take advantage of [institutional] opportunities," (*Varieties of Capitalism*, 15). Whether this gravitation is due to the structural forces of a material incentive structure or to the socialization induced by collective action within these institutional settings is left up to the imagination of the reader.

19. Hall, "Preference Formation as a Political Process," 129.

20. Katznelson and Weingast, "Intersections Between Historical and Rational Choice Institutionalism."

mains quite resistant to interdisciplinary perspectives.[21] In contrast to the paradigmatic clashes in other areas of international relations, scholars in the field of IPE claim to have "approached consensus on theories, methods, analytical frameworks, and important questions" in the last twenty years.[22] As a consequence, the study of business preferences on international trade is currently marked by a materialist orthodoxy. Implicitly or explicitly, most trade policy scholars follow an analytical model in which politicians confront pressures from economic actors and the broad public. Understanding trade policy outcomes therefore proceeds in three analytical steps: (1) identifying the economic interests at stake; (2) studying the organization of these interests; and (3) investigating how such organized interests are mediated through political institutions.[23]

The economic interests of firms are held to be evident, because of the important distributional consequences of trade policy. Studies that do consider the effect of ideas on preferences in IPE concentrate on state interests, not firms.[24] Bauer et al.'s important study is an exception, but their findings have had no effect on theory-building in IPE.[25] The opening or closing of markets has such immediate effects on the welfare of firms that assigning utility is considered unproblematic. Some scholars even define the field as "all work for which international economic factors are an important cause or consequence."[26] Here, material determinism is more than just an assumption; it is the definition of half of the field. Almost by consequence, the field is dominated by a perspective in which developments are determined by changes in material conditions. As Jones points out,

21. In a general review, Abdelal, Blyth, and Parsons note: "while constructivism swept through international relations like wildfire, its impact on the field of international political economy has been marginal." Abdelal, Blyth, and Parsons, "Constructivist Political Economy." For exceptions, see Ford, *A Social Theory of the WTO;* Duina, *The Social Construction of Free Trade.*

22. Frieden and Martin, "International Political Economy: Global and Domestic Interactions," 118. The "consensus" arose when IPE developed into an established subfield of international relations in American political science in the 1970s, and does not apply to historical studies on trade policy nor to European and in particular British perspectives on IPE. For an overview of contributions from both sides of the Atlantic, see Jones, "International Political Economy"; Watson, *Foundations of International Political Economy,* chap. 1. See also Wæver, "The Sociology of a Not So International Discipline."

23. According to Frieden and Martin, "International Political Economy," 126–27.

24. Goldstein, *Ideas, Interests, and American Trade Policy;* Ford, *A Social Theory of the WTO.*

25. Bauer, Pool, and Dexter, *American Business and Public Policy.* For another exception and an argument very similar to the one made in this book, see Crystal, "What Do Producers Want?"

26. Frieden and Martin, "International Political Economy," 118.

[Material] determinism haunts IPE like a spectre at a family feast. The idea that important developments necessarily follow from, or are driven simply and directly by, a relatively simple set of basic factors or forces is far more common within political economy in general, and international political economy in particular, than is often supposed.[27]

The implicit material determinism of IPE studies translates into an explicit treatment of preferences as exogenously given. Moreover, there is a broad consensus that it is analytically most satisfying to deduce business preferences on trade from economic theory. Investigating preferences through observation, so the argument goes, has serious shortcomings, because it collapses behavior and actors' underlying interests.[28] Instead, deducing interests from theory posits that the distributional outcomes of a policy create material incentives that best help to predict an actor's behavior. The literature has thus worked to produce a variety of preference maps that indicate what lobbying behavior we should expect firms to adopt in different circumstances.[29]

This chapter surveys the literature on the trade preferences of business actors in international political economy in order to specify the preference maps that will be relevant for our case studies. In order to study evolving preferences, I present a nuanced conceptualization of business interest in international trade that takes into account ideational and strategic changes induced by firms' political and regulatory interactions. In this way, I hope to address what Matthew Watson has criticized as the "seminal absences" in the explanatory accounts of IPE. In particular, Watson underlines the absence of a historicized conception of economic relations, of all challenges to a rationalist ontology, of a theory of individual and social action.[30] In order to move beyond the "bounded political worldview" of traditional theories, I propose pragmatic ways for combining empirical accuracy and generalizability in research on trade policymaking.

Trade Preferences in the IPE Literature

A large area of research within IPE deals with the domestic politics of foreign economic policy. Concerning trade policy, the central question of this

27. Jones, "International Political Economy," 822. See also Hall, "Preference Formation as a Political Process."
28. Frieden, "Actors and Preferences in International Relations."
29. For overviews, see Alt et al., "Political Economy of International Trade"; Milner, "The Political Economy of International Trade"; Hiscox, *International Trade and Political Conflict.*
30. Watson, *Foundations of International Political Economy*, 32–43.

strand is how national policymaking shapes the international trading system.[31] More concretely, why and when do governments decide to engage in free trade or protectionism?

Answers to these questions typically center either on the strategies pursued by states and policymakers or on the demands expressed by societal actors. Thomas Oatley distinguishes between state-centered and society-centered approaches.[32] However, if one adopts the three-step approach mentioned above, it becomes possible to consider both. Determining the societal interests at stake comes first, but their expression depends on the organizational capacities of different groups and may fail due to collective action problems. Once we know all relevant economic interests and how they are organized, we can study the mediation of these demands by political institutions. Policy demands do not necessarily translate into outcomes, when governmental actors are sufficiently insulated from these demands, for example through delegation of authority or the use of a multilevel strategy.[33] Variations in the observed outcomes are thus located at the level of political institutions and the organization of interest groups. This analytical framework leaves room for a great variety of different perspectives on trade policymaking. At one extreme, societal demands determine outcomes, because government is the passive supplier of policies; at the other extreme, government pursues a strategy of its own and ignores societal demands. In either case, however, it is most attractive to start by identifying the economic interests of societal actors, because they appear to be the most stable element of the analytical framework.[34]

Underlying this perspective is the idea that policymakers are confronted with a combination of pressures from special interest groups and the broad public. This "demand-side" conceptualization has its roots in the theory of economic regulation or, alternatively, in analytical Marxism.[35] Indeed, the work of economists working on the politics of trade decisions has had a lasting effect on theory-building in IPE. Asking why the optimal solution of free trade is so rarely put into place, economists and public choice theorists argue that regulation is the result of lobbying by rent-seeking indus-

31. For an overview, see Milner, "The Political Economy of International Trade."
32. Oatley, *International Political Economy*.
33. For examples, see Putnam, "Diplomacy and Domestic Politics"; Lohmann and O'Halloran, "Divided Government and U.S. Trade Policy"; De Bièvre and Dür, "Constituency Interests and Delegation in European and American Trade Policy."
34. The risks of this approach are discussed by Woodruff, "Commerce and Demolition in Tsarist and Soviet Russia."
35. Cf. Frieden and Martin, "International Political Economy," 127.

tries.[36] One of the critiques of this model was that government acted merely as the passive supplier of regulation without a will of its own. Hence, within the framework, it proved very hard to explain the introduction or abolition of regulation, or in the context of trade policy, the reduction of tariffs when producer interests did not change.[37] Critics of the model, most prominently Grossman and Helpman, have therefore postulated that government preferences for "political support" are endogenous to the policy process.[38] Institutional changes, they argue, can affect the government's willingness to protect particular sectoral interests. However, the assumption about the policy preferences of the constituents has not changed: they are taken to be exogenous to the model. In other words, interests of societal actors such as firms are considered to be stable over time given a fixed set of material conditions.

Within the framework, the question about business interests then becomes the following: what conditions external to the policy process help us to best predict where firms will stand on international trade? This question has led to a burgeoning literature on trade preferences, which deduces these from the distributional effects of the policy in question. The basic logic links preferences to income: policies that will lead to a gain in income should be supported, while policies that lead to a loss of income will be opposed. Scholars have therefore turned to international trade theory to predict the distributional effect of market opening or protectionism.[39]

Two theories have received particular attention: factoral models that focus on the distribution of labor, land, and capital endowment; and sectoral models that concentrate on different industries and the specificities of their assets.[40] Based on the Stolper-Samuelson theorem, factor endowment models predict that owners of factors of production that are scarce in a country will benefit from trade protection, while owners of relatively abundant productive factors will form free-trading coalitions. Specifically, labor in capital-rich countries and capital in labor-rich countries should be

36. Tullock, "The Welfare Costs of Tariffs, Monopolies, and Theft"; Stigler, "The Theory of Economic Regulation"; Peltzman, "Towards a More General Theory of Regulation"; Buchanan, Tollison, and Tullock, *Toward a Theory of the Rent-Seeking Society;* Magee, Brock, and Young, *Black Hole Tariffs and Endogenous Policy Theory.*
37. See Peltzman, "The Economic Theory of Regulation after a Decade of Deregulation."
38. Grossman and Helpman, "Protection for Sale"; Grossman and Helpman, *Special Interest Politics.*
39. For an overview, see Alt et al., "Political Economy of International Trade."
40. See Alt and Gilligan, "The Political Economy of Trading States."

protectionist. The second model is based on the Ricardo-Viner or specific factors approach and emphasizes comparative costs of foreign trade. It asserts that factors of production specific to import-competing industries will be affected most by international trade. Both perspectives yield testable hypotheses about the most dominant fault lines that we should expect to see between supporters and opponents of free trade: class conflict in the first, conflict between different industry groups in the second.[41] Hiscox recently bridged the two perspectives by specifying that class coalitions dominate trade politics only when factors are mobile, while group competition between different industries is likely when neither labor nor capital can shift their assets into a different industry.[42]

In addition, some scholars have pointed out the importance of economies of scale for the trade preferences of large firms. Firms with increasing returns to scale will be supportive of access to new markets. For Milner and Yoffie, these are typically large firms with considerable initial investments that require a growing sales volume to realize the minimum scale to break even.[43] Barriers to trade are costly to such firms, because they inhibit obtaining larger-than-national markets to exploit economies of scale. Similarly, firms with such technologies from small countries will be supportive of gaining access to a larger customer base than their home markets can offer.[44] Chase furthermore draws attention to the importance of production chains that extend beyond borders.[45] In sum, these predictions are in line with the intuitive sense that export-oriented firms, multinational companies, and firms that are engaged in production processes that already extend across borders are likely to support liberalization in order to benefit from increasing returns to scale.

Since we are interested only in business preferences and not in class conflict, the factoral model is least relevant to our study. The remaining hypotheses can be summarized as follows. We should expect firms to be protectionist if they (1) depend on specific factors, i.e. factors that are not mobile between industries; (2) have low returns to scale; and/or (3) are not engaged in production processes across borders. Conversely, firms

41. For evidence in support of the Stolper-Samuelson models, see Rogowski, *Commerce and Coalition;* Scheve and Slaughter, "What Explains Individual Trade-Policy Preferences?"; Beaulieu, "Factor or Industry Cleavages in Trade Policy?" On the Ricardo-Viner models, see Milner, *Resisting Protectionism;* Magee, Brock, and Young, *Black Hole Tariffs.*
42. Hiscox, "Class versus Industry Cleavages."
43. Milner and Yoffie, "Between Free Trade and Protectionism."
44. Casella, "Large Countries, Small Countries, and the Enlargement of Trading Blocs."
45. Chase, "Economic Interests and Regional Trading Arrangements."

should be supportive of means to gain access into new markets if they (1) are exporters; (2) have made high investments that require large markets to obtain sufficient returns to scale; (3) are based in countries that are too small to provide a sufficient consumer base; and/or (4) are engaged in production processes across borders that will be facilitated by reducing barriers to trade.

Limitations of Existing Trade Policy Preference Hypotheses

Taken together, these preference maps provided by the political economy literature constitute a useful toolbox for the analysis of trade policymaking. They all generate testable hypotheses that have helped to account for observed variation in trade policy stances of societal actors in different sectors and countries. Still, there is no agreement on the superiority of one particular model. According to Alt et al.,

> Each appears to explain some things that others do not, and the phenomena each emphasizes are likely to be at work to some degree. More soberingly, each seems to be contradicted in some significant way by the available data, and, even in combination, the models to not appear to entirely explain the observed variation.[46]

Indeed, it is not always clear which one of the hypotheses the analyst should apply to a particular case. Most trade policy observers would agree that an American automobile firm or a small German textile company will probably take a protectionist policy stance, while a multinational software company or a Japanese semiconductor firm will tend to support trade liberalization. But where should we expect to find firms that are hybrids of our ideal cases? How would we predict the policy preference of a large French textile company engaged in an integrated production chain beyond European borders or a small American software company with no international operations? How will the lobbying of a large German footwear firm compare to the lobbying of a large Swedish mining company? The study of specific business cases may tempt us to construct an economic explanation once we know the policy stance of the firm. If the large French textile company turns out to be protectionist, we will attribute it to potential losses from import-competition; if it supports liberalization, we will cite

---

46. Alt et al., "Political Economy of International Trade," 699.

intra-industry trade, returns to scale, and its international production chain. Put differently, why are the models we have all useful, but at different times and only in specific situations that we cannot seem to predict entirely? After so many years of research and studies of impressive breadth and scope, why are we still lacking a theory that accounts completely for trade preferences?

The answer proposed in this book points to the micro-foundations of preferences, which have so far been largely ignored in the trade policy literature. In a series of recent studies, Hiscox and his co-authors have shown that material incentives are insufficient to explain the trade preferences of individuals. Education turned out to have an important effect on attitudes towards trade: college-educated individuals are more likely to support liberalization than others, independent of whether they are in the active labor force or retired. Trade preferences are therefore not only the result of distributional concerns linked to job skills; exposure to economic ideas also seems to play a key role.[47] Moreover, responses of blue-collar workers varied considerably depending on the way questions were framed.[48] Finally, there is a curious gender gap in the support for trade liberalization that also seems to have no foundation in economic differences: independent of income, women are more opposed to trade liberalization than men.[49]

If education, framing, and social roles have an impact on individual preferences, why should they not operate when we turn to a composite actor: a firm? A proponent of the traditional approach might counter that the assumption of profit maximization is less appropriate for individuals, but has turned out to be very useful for firms. I contend that this is only true when the firm happens to employ the same cognitive frameworks for understanding the distributional consequences of a policy that the analyst posits for deducing its preferences. In cases of Knightian uncertainty, however, a firm can find it very difficult to determine the distributional effects of trade liberalization. Gilpin stresses that

> Contrary to economists' belief that economic activities everywhere are universal in character and essentially the same everywhere, the specific goals of economic activities are in actuality socially determined and differ widely over the face of the Earth.[50]

47. Hainmueller and Hiscox, "Learning to Love Globalization."
48. Hiscox, "Through a Glass and Darkly."
49. Hiscox and Burgoon, "The Mysterious Case of Female Protectionism."
50. Gilpin, *Global Political Economy*, 41.

As we will see in the case studies, firms often define, update, and redefine their policy preference in interaction with government representatives. It is difficult to see how ideational factors can be completely assumed away in these contexts.

I will therefore present a conceptualization of preference formation that helps to make sources of variation explicit. The advantage of a more nuanced concept of preference formation is that the analyst can adapt her assumptions to the requirements of a specific case. In a simple setting, research can be facilitated by taking preferences as exogenously given. In a complex setting, we can endogenize different levels depending on the potential sources that might cause variation.

Conceptualizing Preference Formation

In the following, interests will be defined as valued ends.[51] Preferences refer to the way in which an actor orders the value of possible outcomes of an interaction, while strategies are the means he or she employs to obtain the best possible outcome.[52]

Studying Interests and Preferences

Preferences are widely studied in the research on decision-making and are a central element of rational choice theories. Unfortunately, they come with an epistemological problem: the only thing a scientist can observe is an individual's behavior. One can thus only infer which preference an actor was pursuing with a certain behavior and only make assumptions about the degree to which such a preference corresponded to the actor's actual interest.

Two broad strategies exist for imputing interests to policy actors, which have been labeled "subjective" and "objective."[53] A "subjective" strategy means that the analyst accepts choices and behavior as revealed preferences of actors, or even further, as defining their interests. Lobbying in favor of trade liberalization would thus be an indicator that the firm has an interest in accessing foreign markets. Under an "objective" strategy, the analyst uses other systematic evidence or theories to make assumptions about

51. For discussion, see Hirschman, "The Concept of Interest"; Swedberg, "Can There Be a Sociological Concept of Interest?"
52. Cf. Frieden, "Actors and Preferences," 42–47.
53. Balbus, "The Concept of Interest in Pluralist and Marxian Analysis"; Connolly, "On 'Interests' in Politics"; Mansbridge, *Beyond Adversary Democracy;* Polsby, *Community Power and Political Theory.*

the real interests of actors. Both subjective and objective imputing strategies have difficulties: while subjective strategies confuse strategies with interests, objective strategies "substitute the analysts' choices for actors' choices."[54] Not only Marxist analysis, but also mainstream IPE theory tends to assume that interests are somehow "objective" and can be determined independently of an individual's revealed preferences.[55] Specific types of firms can thus always be assumed to be protectionist: if they lobbied in favor of open markets, the analyst will suspect a strategic maneuver or, in the worst case, false consciousness. Since it is almost impossible to decide which assumptions most accurately help to approximate the real interests of the policy actors, one can resolve to agree with Milton Friedman or Kenneth Waltz: the question about strong assumptions is not whether they are right or wrong, but rather whether they are useful or not.[56]

Difficulties of observing interests notwithstanding, these debates clarify that actors have profound interests and context-related preferences. We can assume that there is such as thing as a "basic interest," which needs to be translated into a preference and then into strategic behavior.[57] Distinctions between different levels are common in the social science literature, which acknowledges the difference between interests and preferences.[58] Rational choice theory has furthermore drawn attention to the difference between preferences and strategies.[59] The choices actors make often do not properly represent their preferences and it is important to understand the context in which an actor makes a decision in order to predict her tactical calculations.

Despite these theoretical advances, "sins of confusion" between interests, preferences, and strategies are common.[60] Indeed, one recurring problem of trade policy literature is the assumption that protectionism is a fixed interest of firms. In what follows, I will argue that it is only a means to achieve profitability, which in turn assures survival. To distinguish more

54. Polsby, *Community Power,* 224.

55. Frieden, "Actors and Preferences," 65.

56. Friedman, "The Methodology of Positive Economics"; Waltz, *Theory of International Politics.*

57. Mayntz and Scharpf, *Gesellschaftliche Selbstregelung,* 52–58; Ganghof, "Promises and Pitfalls of Veto Player Analysis."

58. See for example Milner, *Interests, Institutions, and Information;* Lake and Powell, "A Strategic-Choice Approach"; Vogel, "When Interests Are Not Preferences."

59. E.g. Powell, "Anarchy in International Relations Theory."

60. Frieden cites the concept of power in international relations literature, which is sometimes taken as an end in itself, although it is really only a means of achieving survival. Frieden, "Actors and Preferences."

clearly, it is helpful to identify the different levels of abstraction on which "interests" can exist.

Translating Interests into Strategies

When thinking about these interests, it is useful to distinguish between the basic concept of what I call "universal" or "general" interest, and its role-specific translation.[61] One of the most widely held assumptions about interests is that actors strive for their subsistence, so that "survival" would appear to be the most minimalist or universal imputation an analyst can make. However, this general interest is undetermined—and therefore not very helpful—as long as it does not apply to a particular unit of analysis. In essence, we need to specify: What needs to survive? A role-specific interest thus applies the general interest to the individual situation of a given actor: the survival of a nation-state is equivalent to the maintenance of sovereignty, the survival of a politician means that she has to remain an actor in the public sphere, the survival of a firm means that it has to be profitable. These fundamental values are the most basic objectives an actor can hold and are generally labeled "interests."

However, in order to be able to make strategic decisions, an actor has to have some set of beliefs as to how this desired end can be obtained. This requires deriving a means preference from the end the actor is interested in.[62] Deriving a means preference is a second role-specific translation process, which requires that the actor fixes an overall strategic goal for obtaining his interest. In the case of the nation-state, sovereignty might best be assured through power; politicians traditionally remain in the public sphere through reelection; and firms try to ensure high profits through reducing direct price competition. However, one can imagine other alternatives, even if the basic interest does not change. For example, firms can try to maximize profits through offensive rather than defensive business plans, and politicians can try to stay in power through corruption rather than reelection.

A final translation step requires adopting a concrete strategy for obtaining the strategic goal. A firm that prefers protectionism needs to develop a plan for obtaining closed markets: it can lobby for tariffs, quotas, or vol-

---

61. I would like to thank Fritz W. Scharpf for suggesting this terminology.
62. The difference between ends and means preferences echoes Krehbiel and Hall. Krehbiel distinguishes between preferences among "outcomes" and preferences among "policies," Hall between "fundamental" and "strategic preferences." Krehbiel, *Information and Legislative Organization;* Hall, "Preference Formation as a Political Process."

Table 2.1. From interests to preferences to strategy

	Types	Politician	Nation-state	Business
Interests	1. Basic interest/ assumed universal value	Survival	Survival	Survival
Preferences	2. Role-specific interest/ fundamental preference	E.g. staying in the public sphere	E.g. maintaining sovereignty	E.g. profitability
Strategy	3. Means preference/ strategic goal	E.g. reelection	E.g. power	E.g. protection
	4. Context-related policy preference/strategy	E.g. specific industry support	E.g. armament or alliance	E.g. tariffs or quotas

untary import restrictions, or try to develop other means to restrict market access. Sometimes labeled "policy preference," this political strategy entails choosing an instrument with which the actor hopes to achieve the strategic goal. Policy preferences are thus divided into preferences for policy objectives and preferences for policy instruments.[63] Instruments are the most strategic element: they might not reveal the true interests of the actors, but they help to distinguish actors from each other and permit them to form coalitions or oppositions.

Table 2.1 summarizes the different levels of objectives using common examples from political science research. As preferences become more and more concrete, the illustrative examples become increasingly variable and context-dependent. The first and the second types are most often referred to as "interests." They constitute values the actor is assumed to pursue as ultimate goals. The second, however, is role-specific: it is a translation of the universal value to the situation of the individual unit of analysis. By concretizing the most basic interest in this way, the role-specific interest is thus a first approximation of how to achieve the universal value, in this case survival. Types 2 and 3 are then approximations of 1, which may be grouped under the label "preferences." Type 2 is a fundamental preference, however, and should change little, while type 3 is already a relatively conscious means preference. Both are beliefs about how to achieve the basic value, but the second is the goal from which the third type derives. Yet this third type needs to be contextualized in order to become a concrete policy preference. Types 3 and 4 can therefore be grouped under the label "strategy."

63. This final distinction explains why I have chosen not to adopt Krehbiel's or Hall's terminology, which would risk merging the two final translation steps.

Type 4 is the most context-related strategy, highly dependent on the political context, structural and institutional variation, and the opportunity structures and resources of the actor in question.[64] Within each group (interests, preferences, or strategies), one step defines the goal and the other one the way to achieve this goal.

Sources of Variation

As goals become more specific, analytical imputation becomes more and more risky and we are likely to observe considerable variation in empirical studies. What are potential sources of such variation? Since we have specified how goals are translated into strategies through more and more concrete steps, we can spell out what we would expect to be the most important source of variation for each step.

First, in order to translate a general interest into a role-specific interest, the actor needs to define who or what he or she is. At this level, variation is most likely if the identity of the actor changes. A politician who decides not to run for reelection for health reasons has traded her identity as a public figure for her identity as a mortal human being. For a competitive firm, survival means that it needs to be profitable. For a public service company, by contrast, survival can depend on the way in which it fulfils its universal service obligations and maintains political support. Secondly, to decide on a means preference for obtaining a role-specific interest, an actor needs to adopt some set of beliefs that explain how the strategic goal will ensure the desired end. Here variation is most likely when causal or normative beliefs change. A country that wants to maintain economic growth will fix different strategic goals depending on whether it applies a monetarist or a Keynesian economic model, for example. Finally, the policy choices actors pursue in order to obtain their strategic goals depend on the constraints and opportunities in their strategic environment. Figure 2.1 represents the levels at which these different sources of variation are most important. Since all levels are connected, however, it is also possible that a lower-level source of variation affects preferences or interests at a higher level as well. As we will see in the empirical discussion, the lack of available policy options can affect the second translation step, simply because it reduces the cognitive frameworks that yield politically viable strategies.

Distinguishing what element of a preference translation one wishes to

---

64. The overlap of types is deliberate and illustrates why there has been a considerable amount of confusion in the literature.

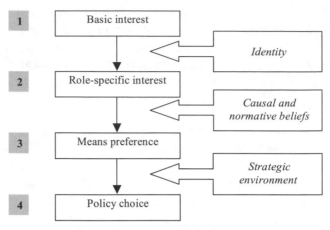

Figure 2.1 Sources of variation in strategic behavior

analyze is necessary to avoid an artificial juxtaposition of literatures that do not actually address the same question. In particular, it clarifies that constructivism and rational choice approaches are not necessarily competing explanations, but that they often just focus on different phases of the preference formation process. One needs to be explicit about the level of the translation process one wishes to consider. Furthermore, long-term analyses or comparisons of behavior across countries require dealing with several levels of abstraction in order to account for the observed evolution and to be able to make valid generalizations.

Making Translation Paths Explicit

Where studying business interests in trade policy is concerned, a conceptualization of the different translation steps helps to construct possible "translation paths," which allow us to trace or an observed change in strategic behavior to a more fundamental change in preferences. Translation paths are thus a heuristic tool for making a logical argument about preference changes that we cannot observe directly.

For business interests, we can identify a list of possible variations that might occur in the translation process. Let us begin by assuming that firms seek to survive. Traditionally, many authors suppose that an economic agent can only survive if it can be sure of being profitable, so its utility function will be profit maximization. Neil Fligstein, on the other hand, makes the case that firms are not only producers but also social organizations that need to operate in a stable environment in order to survive and therefore seek to ensure stability, for example through labor agreements or continuous supplier relations.[65] For empirical research, the principal question then becomes one of determining which identity is the dominant one in a specific context. A legal setting that facilitates hiring and firing and provides measures against strikes will foreground the competitive producer identity, a constraining institutional context the social organization identity of a firm.

Furthermore, role-specific interests can lead to a variety of means preferences depending on the beliefs that actors employ. A firm concerned with profitability might either seek to assure closed markets in order to benefit from protectionist measures, or it might anticipate making gains from expanding into new markets. Finally, firms have to determine which instruments are the most important strategic tools to obtain their preferred outcomes. Without claiming to present an exhaustive list, figure 2.2 represents possible variations in business demands for international trade graphically.

A reasonably well-constructed interest translation tree will help to clarify a claim about an—unobservable—change of preferences, i.e. changes at level 2 or 3 of the tree. Empirical observation can help to note changes in behavior only. With reference to these articulations, however, it becomes possible to argue that a rational firm with a preference for the status quo would not conceivably lobby for reciprocal trade liberalization, which often leads to radical reorganization of the market. In other words, if we find that a firm which has previously lobbied for import restrictions now lobbies for reciprocal trade liberalization, we can argue that it must have adjusted its means preferences from protection for profitability to expansion for profitability.

In the empirical chapters, I will use such explicit translation trees to connect observed policy stances with more fundamental goals that firms pursue in order to make an argument about the evolution of these unobservable preference changes. Being explicit about the ways in which I assume that abstract goals are connected to concrete stances thus encourages dialogue or counterarguments to claims that would otherwise not be falsifiable.

To summarize, the conceptualization proposed in this book stresses the

---

65. Note that this is not an either/or distinction; it is comparable to the multiple interests a person can have as a taxpayer, a mother, and a politician, for example. Fligstein, *The Architecture of Markets.*

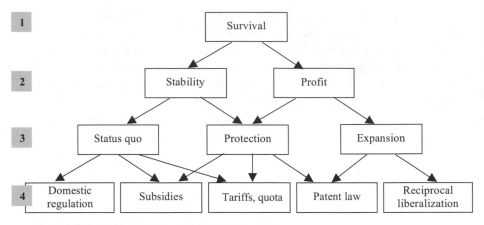

Figure 2.2 Possible variation in trade lobbying content

effect that changes in identity, causal and normative beliefs, and strategic environments can have on the policy stances communicated by economic actors. In many instances, these three items are stable and it is useful to work with a more parsimonious approach to studying business interests. The preference maps taken from studies on the domestic politics of international economic policy have proven particularly useful for this purpose. However, when we know that identities or beliefs are evolving, or when we are comparing business lobbying in two different strategic environments, it is important to adopt a more nuanced perspective. In the following chapters, I will demonstrate that existing IPE preference maps are insufficient to account for the policy stances pursued by American and European firms in the context of international service trade liberalization.

3

When Trade Turns into Regulatory Reform

International trade negotiations have evolved considerably over the last fifty years. Since the first rounds of talks under the GATT, stakes have moved from the reciprocal reduction of tariff barriers to include an increasing variety of nontariff barriers and even domestic issues with an impact on trade. The Uruguay Round led to the creation of the WTO in 1995 and expanded the coverage of the multilateral trading system to services and intellectual property rights.[1] Trade-related domains, such as environment or labor standards, competition or investment policies are also affected by the rules negotiated under the WTO.

Business lobbying takes different forms depending on the nature of the issues involved, and the dominant models we have to study business preferences—the factoral and the sectoral models—assume conditions that apply much better to the trade of goods than to the new trade issues. When trade negotiations deal not only with the reciprocal removal of barriers to trade, but also with the rules that govern international exchanges in a specific sector, businesses and government form relationships that are often based on the mutually beneficial exchange of information rather than just the exertion of pressure.

In the following, I will explicate how new trade issues differ from traditional ones and what this implies for business-government relations. I then

---

1. For further discussion, see Hoekman and Kostecki, *The Political Economy of the World Trading System;* Barton et al., *The Evolution of the Trade Regime.*

turn to the history of service trade and discuss the role private interests played in its conception. In preparation for the empirical chapters, I conclude by giving a quick overview of the sectoral comparison between telecommunication and air transport services and by laying out the central hypotheses framing the case studies.

The Changing Nature of Trade Negotiations and Lobbying Behavior

As early as 1989, Milner and Yoffie remarked that the study of business lobbying is trapped in a dichotomy between liberalization and protectionism.[2] In the tradition of David Ricardo, trade is imagined as the exchange of goods between two countries with competitive markets where production follows from each country's comparative advantage.[3] Under protectionism, a country raises the barriers to entry for foreign goods; under free trade, it lowers these barriers and exposes its firms to foreign competition. Multilateral tariff negotiations, the reason for which the GATT was created, ensure nothing more than the reciprocal reduction of external barriers and consequently the stakes for the affected firms are quite clear.[4] This assumption, however, holds true only if all countries have perfectly competitive internal markets on the inside and that they simply decide to open or close to foreign competition. This is not necessarily the case. Understanding how trade negotiations today can differ from the assumptions of our models is important for explaining different logics of business lobbying behavior. In particular, I distinguish between pressure lobbying posited by the literature on rent-seeking and business-government relations based on the exchange of information that characterize regulatory lobbying.

The Changing Nature of Trade Negotiations

David Yoffie argues in *Beyond Free Trade* that the nature of competition is very different depending on (a) whether there is a high or a low degree of industry concentration in a particular market and (b) whether government intervention in a sector is intensive or not. Yoffie summarizes the diverse nature of the global trading system as shown in table 3.1. According

2. Milner and Yoffie, "Between Free Trade and Protectionism," 239–40.
3. Ricardo, *The Principles of Political Economy and Taxation*.
4. The international trade regime used to be a simple coordination device. However, the extent to which this rational coordination can affect the preferences of the participants is discussed in Keohane, *After Hegemony*, 110–32.

Table 3.1. Drivers of international trade

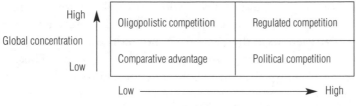

| | Low ——————————————————→ High |
| Government intervention | |

Source: Yoffie, *Beyond Free Trade*, 19.

to him, the classic trade model corresponds to the lower left-hand box. National markets have few imperfections and government has a small role, so that a large number of firms compete based on their comparative advantages once trade barriers are reduced. However, he also identifies three other forms of international competition: oligopolitistic competition between large firms in liberalized national markets, political competition between two different systems of government intervention, and regulated competition where both firm concentration and government intervention are high.

Service markets are most often characterized by considerable government intervention. Depending on the size of the firms in the sector, service trade should thus be considered regulated competition or political competition.[5] Yoffie's characterization corresponds to Cowhey and Aronson's analysis of global trade.[6] In their view, trade negotiations previously aimed exclusively at obtaining a "free trade regime" based on the free movement of goods and national comparative advantage. Today this logic has eroded. Investment has become coequal with trade, the boundary between services and goods is vanishing, and consequently the modes of trading have become more complex. Firms often maintain business operations in foreign countries but are unable to compete on equal footing with national producers due to product or process restrictions. The central question is no longer to what degree to allow trade with a foreign country, but how to ensure and maintain access to a foreign market. Instead of following universally applicable rules, "market access regimes" have to be nego-

5. This leads to the question whether competition between national regulatory arrangements leads to lower or higher regulatory standards. See for example, Vogel, *Trading Up.*

6. Cowhey and Aronson, *Managing the World Economy.*

tiated sector by sector, since the stake of a market access regime is the internationalization or the harmonization of domestic policies applying to a particular product or service market. While the classic literature has tried to include such restrictions in the concept of "nontariff barriers" to trade, they are often embedded in different domestic regulatory approaches or competition policy. Empirical analysis shows that domestic regulatory policies and international economic policies are no longer independent of each other, as previous models assumed.[7]

Considering the logic of service trade helps us to see this interdependence most clearly and clarifies how new trade themes can differ from the traditional stakes in the trade of goods. What does it mean to "trade" services? As the *Economist* famously noted, services are things that you can buy and sell "but not drop on your foot."[8] The specific characteristics of services have important implications for their exchange. Goods are simply sold to foreign nationals, and trade policy traditionally has addressed the price, number, and product standards of the items sold. In services, market exchange is more difficult and one needs to distinguish between different kinds of provision of services. In active service trade, the provider moves to the country of the buyer. In passive service trade, the buyer moves to the country of the provider, who remains in his home country. Correspondence services are traded without any movement of the provider or the buyer, as in the case of telecommunication or radio service, for example.[9] Finally, the provision of service might require the temporal movement of persons. The distinction of types is made in terms of the process through which the service is provided, not the product itself.[10] In the GATS, the different ways of trading services are dealt with as "modes," which are summarized in figure 3.1.

Because of these different forms of service provision, two issues are at the heart of service trade: access and the diversity of national regulation. Access simply describes the fact that the buyer must have the possibility to obtain the services offered by the provider. Barriers to active service trade are then discriminatory measures that prohibit the provision of a service in a foreign country by a national of another country. The diversity of na-

7. Ibid., 68.
8. "A Blind Eye to Invisible Trade," *Economist*, 11 July 1981, p. 72.
9. Cf. Snape, "Principles in Trade in Services."
10. Similarly, norms applying to the provision of services most often do not address the product; they regulate the production and provision process instead. The trade of alcohol, for example, will be framed in terms of its content, while the exchange of financial services across borders will be addressed in terms of liabilities and obligations.

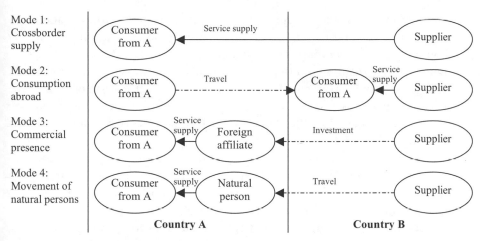

Figure 3.1 Synthetic view of modes of supply
Source: United Nations, et al., *Manual on Statistics of International Trade in Services,* 23.

tional regulation can also inhibit service trade. A construction worker, for example, might need to meet an accreditation requirement in order to work in a specific country, which will often be more difficult for foreign workers than for national ones.[11] The trade of services is thus tightly intertwined with the notion of regulation. Regulation commonly refers a great variety of standards throughout the provision process: from the accreditation of professional training to the supervision of the execution and enforcement of procedural standards. The core challenge of service trade is therefore to address the trade-restricting effects of regulation.[12]

On a semantic note, talking about regulation in the context of trade can lead to confusion. For the economists of the school of economic regulation, the term referred to all forms of government intervention and became the bipolar opposite of free competition.[13] For others, regulation refers to economic steering executed by independent administrative agencies. More generally, regulation often refers to a set of targeted rules. In

---

11. The first case is generally referred to as a discriminatory barrier to trade, while the second is called a nondiscriminatory barrier to trade.

12. Feketekuty, "Regulatory Reform and Trade Liberalization in Services"; Mattoo and Sauvé, *Domestic Regulation and Service Trade Liberalization.* For a discussion of the different regimes that can respond to these challenges, see Nicolaïdis and Trachtman, "Liberalization, Regulation, and Recognition for Services Trade."

13. Cf. Jordana and Levi-Faur, "The Politics of Regulation in the Age of Governance," 5.

the following, I will adopt a definition of regulation as "the promulgation of an authorative set of rules, accompanied by some mechanism . . . for monitoring and promoting compliance with these rules."[14] In multilateral trade talks, such rules are often procompetitive. They ensure that everybody can compete on an equal footing and are fixed in the form of sector-specific agreements, such as the basic telecommunications agreement and its reference paper.[15] At the domestic level, they concern product, production process, and provision standards.

Many of these domestic regulations cannot be undone simply by multilateral negotiations. In sectors where regulatory issues are salient, trade negotiations therefore attempt to harmonize or to internationalize regulatory standards. As we have seen, this typically applies to service trade negotiations, but even trade in goods poses the question of internationally applicable production and process regulation, such as environmental or labor standards. An increasing number of agreements therefore try to establish conditions for the exchange of goods, such as the Technical Barriers to Trade Agreement, the Sanitary and Phytosanitary Measures Agreement, and the Agreement on Trade-Related Aspects of Intellectual Property Rights of the WTO. In essence, a large part of debates revolve around what can be traded when. The question is no longer whether or not to liberalize trade but how to liberalize trade in a given sector. In sectors where the level of government intervention is high, multilateral trade negotiations have become equivalent to international regulatory reform.

Impact on Business Lobbying

For business actors, these new issues imply a very different type of engagement in international politics.[16] Previously, firms or associations tried to influence their government's decisions on lowering or maintaining barriers to trade. On regulatory issues, the stakes are less clear. Both government negotiators and firm representatives need to determine how to transnationalize or harmonize domestic regulation, preferably with the greatest possible benefit to the national economy (for government repre-

---

14. Baldwin, Scott, and Hood, *A Reader on Regulation,* 3.

15. In contrast to domestic rules, these international agreements do not necessarily lead to the establishment of independent regulatory agencies. Rather, implementation and compliance can be delegated to existing national agencies or simply be enforced through trade monitoring and the WTO dispute settlement procedures.

16. McGuire, "Firms and Government in International Trade."

sentatives) or a particular firm (for business representatives). Quite often multiple alternatives and a series of intricate details need to be evaluated and governments solicit industry input for doing so. Stakes are no more evident to firms, which often need a considerable amount of time in order to learn and evaluate the impact of a given set of negotiations.

How then should we understand business-government relations on multilateral trade? In the context of tariff negotiations, lobbying in trade policy was traditionally presented as "rent-seeking."[17] Firms were assumed to exert pressure on government in pursuit of their predefined goals: either protectionism or reciprocal trade liberalization. In response to the increasing importance of intra-industry trade, new trade theory abandoned the assumption of perfect competition and focused on increasing return to scale.[18] The search for exploitation of large economies of scale, in turn, leads to a greater variety of business demands.[19] While firms are still assumed to exert pressure, their political intentions have proven to be more complex than simple acceptance or rejection of increasing competition.

Indeed, research on lobbying strategies in the field of business administration has long moved away from the dichotomy between protectionism and liberalization.[20] Moreover, several authors have shown that national institutional contexts cause variation in the strategic behavior of firms, who seek to maintain technological innovation, foreign direct investment and intrafirm trade.[21] According to all of these business-centered studies, the stakes in international trade negotiations are foreign investment and market access relevant to the strategic positioning of firms. The shifting stakes reflect the distinction made by Yoffie and by Cowhey and Aronson. When multilateral trade negotiations are about the formulation of specific targeted rules that define market access and operation, business lobbying changes. On the one hand, firms have to influence the details of the rules in question, which requires closer cooperation than just pressuring for

17. Buchanan, Tollison, and Tullock, *Theory of the Rent-Seeking Society;* Magee, Brock, and Young, *Black Hole Tariffs.*

18. Helpman and Krugman, *Market Structure and Foreign Trade.*

19. Milner and Yoffie first underlined the importance of increasing returns to scale in the study of trade policy preferences. Milner and Yoffie, "Between Free Trade and Protectionism." See also Froot and Yoffie, "Strategic Trade Policies in a Tripolar World"; Chase, "Economic Interests and Regional Trading Arrangements."

20. See Rugman and Verbeke, *Global Corporate Strategy and International Trade Policy;* Dunning, *Governments, Globalization, and International Business.*

21. Pauly and Reich, "National Structures and Multinational Corporate Behavior"; Doremus et al., *The Myth of the Global Corporation.*

opening or closure of national markets. The transmission of information, and not just the provision of electoral or financial incentives, becomes an important part of trade policy lobbying.[22] On the other hand, governments need to negotiate the internationalization of domestic regulations, which requires knowledge about the constraints weighing on a particular market. Since trade negotiations aim at facilitating the operation of business, firms become privileged sources of information for government delegations.[23] Expertise thus proves to be an important resource for lobbyists trying to gain access to international trade talks.[24]

In other words, the transformation of multilateral trade negotiations has important consequences for the political activities of business actors, because it affects their political opportunity structure.[25] In simple matters like tariff reductions, economic interest groups can offer their financial or electoral support in exchange for decisions in their favor. In the case of regulatory issues, the exchange between business and government is based on technical expertise and legitimacy. This shift in resources is accompanied by a shift in constraints on lobbying success. Pressure lobbying is constrained political competition: many groups try to influence policymakers and have to prevail.[26] Regulatory lobbying rests on government solicitation for expertise, so the criteria for success or failure are different. Firms have to prove to the government that they are valuable partners, which requires credibility, reputation, and constructive cooperation.[27] When government delegations can shop around for business partners, they will privilege those that are perceived to facilitate the consultation process.[28]

In consequence, firms behave differently when engaging in pressure lobbying and regulatory lobbying. In regulatory contexts, firms are highly

22. For a discussion of informational lobbying, see for example Potters and Van Winden, "Modelling Political Pressure as Transmission of Information"; Austen-Smith, "Information and Influence."

23. Coglianese, Zeckhauser, and Parson, "Seeking Truth for Power." On the involvement of firms in the creation of global regulation, see Braithwaite and Drahos, *Global Business Regulation*.

24. See Radaelli, "The Role of Knowledge in the Policy Process."

25. "Political opportunity structure" refers to the configuration of resources, formal and informal institutional arrangements, and historical precedents that facilitates or constrains the access of nongovernmental actors to the policy process. For discussion, see, for example, Kitschelt, "Political Opportunity Structures and Political Protest," 58.

26. Stigler, "Economic Competition and Political Competition"; Becker, "A Theory of Competition among Pressure Groups for Political Influence."

27. Broscheid and Coen, "Insider and Outsider Lobbying in the European Commission"; Coen, "Business-Regulatory Relations."

28. Willman et al., "The Evolution of Regulatory Relationships."

Table 3.2. Two types of business-government relations

	Pressure lobbying on trade	Regulatory trade lobbying
Goal of multilateral negotiations	Opening/closing of domestic markets to foreign goods	Internationalization of regulatory regimes in order to facilitate trade and transborder operations
Typical means for achieving goal	Tariffs or nontariff barriers	Regulatory reform or creation of international regulatory standards
Stake for economic actors	Making demands for or against market opening	Participating in the elaboration of targeted rules specifying how to liberalize
Lobbying mode	Exerting pressure, consultation	Consultation, cooperation
Principal resource	Political support (financial or electoral)	Technical expertise
Principal constraint	Competition between groups	Dependence on government solicitation; complexity and uncertainty

aware that their access to decision-makers depends on signals that they are constructive consultants who can help increase the legitimacy of governmental decisions. This is done most effectively if firms are perceived to be not just self-interested, but to propose general solutions. As Broscheid and Coen have argued in the European context, lobbyists therefore have to strike a delicate balance between arguing for their immediate interest and making more general "public interest" arguments that will gain them access to the policy process.[29] Table 3.2 summarizes the two logics of business-government interactions.

Like most classifications, the table only highlights the ideal types of business-government relations on trade issues. In many contexts, we will find hybrid forms. Some actors might even use both means simultaneously, although a reliance on pressure can harm working relations on regulatory issues in the long run.[30] The central point of this juxtaposition is simply that the transformation of multilateral trade negotiations that has been observed by many authors has important consequences for the most likely types of business-government relations that will develop.

29. Broscheid and Coen, "Insider and Outsider Lobbying."

30. Despite the reliance on pressure in the first type of interaction and the use of cooperation procedures in the second, it is important to remember that both types of business activities should be considered as lobbying, i.e., attempts by private actors to influence the decision of political actors in their favor.

A Brief History of Service Trade

After this introduction to the theoretical issues of service trade, let us turn to its history. Since the two case studies in the following chapters are closely connected to the general transformation of service exchanges, it is helpful to understand how services were put on the agenda of international trade negotiators and the role that private actors played in this process.

The Emergence of Multilateral Service Trade

Traditionally the invisibility and temporariness of services had contributed to their neglect in trade affairs: at best they were considered a derivative of goods, at worst entirely unproductive. Since service exchanges are difficult to measure and categorize, governments dealt with them as part of the "tertiary sector" which included everything that was not manufacturing or agriculture. Transactions concerning services between countries showed up in national accounts under the broad label "invisibles."

With shifts in economic structures, the growth of service sectors, and the increased international activities of large multinational service companies, this conception began to change. In their account of the transformation, Drake and Nicolaïdis distinguish three periods: (1) a period of issue identification, which began with a meeting organized by the Organization for Economic Cooperation and Development (OECD) in 1972 on "trade in services"; (2) a period of issue consolidation from 1982 to 1986, when services were taken up in the GATT meetings as a new trade matter; and (3) a period of multilateral negotiations beginning in 1986 with the launching of the Uruguay Round.[31] Since 1986, participants in the GATT negotiated what was to become the GATS, a new international regime on service trade. In April 1994, the signing of the Marrakech agreement established both the GATS, and the WTO as an umbrella organization, as of 1 January 1995.[32] In the years that followed, members of the WTO undertook a variety of sectoral negotiations, many of which are still being continued, updated, or complemented today.

The GATS aims to bring service exchanges under the same trade regime as the exchange of goods under the GATT.[33] In order to understand how

31. Drake and Nicolaïdis, "Ideas, Interests, and Institutionalization."

32. For an in-depth treatment of the Uruguay Round negotiations, see Croome, *Reshaping the World Trading System;* Stewart, *The GATT Uruguay Round: A Negotiating History;* and Stewart, *The GATT Uruguay Round: The End Game.*

33. Often cited as the predecessor of the WTO, the GATT was not formally an international organization. This changed with the establishment of the WTO in 1995, which was created as a formal body administrating the GATT as well as several new agreements: the GATS, trade-related aspects of intellectual property rights (TRIPs), and all other agreements concluded

the GATS works, one needs to consider the GATT rules for trade in goods. The ambition of the GATT was to lower tariffs through negotiations between countries. An initial multilateral round specifies the agreed targets or formulas, which are then followed by bilateral negotiations on specific requests and offers between countries. The most important principal requires that once country *A* lowers a tariff on the goods of country *B,* it has to extend the same offer to all other countries as well. This principle is called the most-favored nation (MFN) principle and constitutes the first article of the GATT. Under specific conditions, countries may make exceptions to the MFN principle.

The GATS agreement of 1994 lays out the rules that govern the application of this procedure to services, with the exception of government services and most air transport services. It specifies that commitments on the trade of services should apply equally to services and service providers from all countries (MFN—Article II); and that regulation should not restrict foreign services or service providers ("market access"—Article XVI) or discriminate against them in a manner that is inconsistent with the binding GATS commitments ("national treatment"—Article XVII). Furthermore, the implementation of these principles has to be the subject of negotiations (Article XIX), of which the results have to be bound in national schedules (Article XX).[34] To make the new framework acceptable to the negotiation partners, the GATS provides a great amount of flexibility in claiming MFN exemptions for specific sectors and items. In contrast to the GATT, national treatment only applies to those services that countries specifically committed to. Overall, the GATS is therefore a much softer arrangement than the GATT.

By upholding the principles of market access and national treatment, the GATS framework agreement prohibited the use of discriminatory barriers to the trade in services. However, nondiscriminatory barriers based on regulatory diversity were much harder to address. The agreement therefore provided for the continuation of negotiations along sectoral lines. The aim of these negotiations was to negotiate the implementation of the GATS principles, to reduce the MFN exemptions taken, and to address regulatory issues that went beyond the direct denial of market access and national discrimination.[35]

---

during the Uruguay Round. Before the creation of the WTO, the participating countries were merely called contracting parties. After 1995, they became actual "members" of the WTO.

34. See Messerlin and Sauvant, *The Uruguay Round.*

35. For further information, see Hoekman and Kostecki, *Political Economy of the World Trading System,* chap. 7.

The Role of Business Actors

The emergence of service trade was not simply a technical project of international organizations or an issue for intergovernmental negotiations. It was above all a political issue shaped critically by the continued participation of business actors. Especially in financial and professional services, companies saw important market access opportunities in a service agreement and lobbied heavily for a strong U.S. proposal.[36] According to David Hartridge, former director of the WTO Service Division, "without the enormous pressure generated by the American financial services sector, particularly companies like American Express and CitiCorp, there would have been no services agreement."[37]

For large U.S. financial companies, service trade became an issue in the late 1970s. Trying to develop global financial service offers, such as card business or international banking networks, U.S. companies realized that they had considerable difficulties getting into foreign markets. These problems applied in similar ways to the American International Group (AIG), American Express, and Citibank, which started working together and eventually contacted the U.S. government to talk about these issues.[38] The U.S. government and the United States Trade Representative (USTR) in particular were enthusiastic about the idea of broadening the GATT framework and started working towards a U.S. position on the topic.[39] AIG, American Express, and CitiCorp founded the United States Coalition of Service Industries (USCSI) in 1982 to continue lobbying on the issue. In addition, the leaders and government affairs representatives of these financial service companies started working with William E. Brock, USTR from 1981 to 1985, and later with Clayton K. Yeutter, USTR from 1985 to 1989. The companies invested considerable amounts of resources into pressing for this cause and proposed new forums of consultation with the U.S. government. James Robinson, CEO of American Express, started chairing a private sector advisory group to William Brock in the mid-1980s and later moved to take the chairmanship of the President's Advisory Committee on Trade. John Reed, CEO of CitiGroup, and Maurice Greenberg of AIG followed into the same or similar positions. Further consultative groups advised the U.S. Department of Commerce or worked to affect other policymakers and public opinion.

36. Arkell, "Lobbying for Market Access for Professional Services"; Sell, "Big Business."
37. Quoted in Wesselius, "Behind GATS 2000."
38. Freeman, "A Pioneer's View of Financial Services Negotiations in the GATT and in the World Trade Organization."
39. See Feketekuty, *International Trade in Services.*

The coalition of multinational companies and U.S. government officials benefited from early discussion in the OECD and among economists and contributed to redefining the stakes in terms of trade, which helped to make demands more pressing both internally and externally.[40] Even though the coalition of U.S. firms was originally only from the financial sector and parts of the professional services sector, their ambition was from very early on to achieve a more global agreement on services. Financial services, consulting, advertising, data processing, telecommunications, and transport were all relevant services to their international operations, so they lobbied both for the benefit of their own service expansion and as user companies of other services. In a variety of multinational business associations, American firms urged their foreign counterparts to take up the cause. The companies most involved in the negotiations even met with representatives of foreign governments, making service trade one of the rare examples of "trilateral diplomacy" between businesses and governments.[41]

It is difficult to evaluate the precise impact of these activities, but they certainly contributed to the diffusion of ideas on service exchanges and helped to unify the position of American business on the issue. Large companies from all sectors of the economy started conceiving themselves as user companies of services. For Drake and Nicolaïdis "new ideas helped them to see the potential of networks and information systems and encouraged them to change positions with respect to global markets and government regulation."[42] In 1981, the International Chamber of Commerce (ICC) endorsed GATT negotiations on services. The United States Council for International Business (USCIB), an affiliate of the ICC, soon became an important forum for transsectoral lobbying and consulting on international service trade.

The importance of business lobbying in the case of services should not be underestimated, but its success was closely linked to the fact that it corresponded to the interests of the governments and nonbusiness policy experts working on these issues. With the backing of its industry, the U.S. government defended the strongest proposal for a service agreement during the Uruguay Round and was undoubtedly well equipped with information and expert knowledge on its service economy. Indeed, representatives of "CitiCorp, Goldman Sachs, Merrill Lynch and the insurance companies—particularly the American Insurance Group and Aetna—es-

---

40. Drake and Nicolaïdis, "Ideas, Interests, and Institutionalization," 46.

41. Interview with a U.S. business representative on 8 April 2003 in Washington, D.C. On "trilateral diplomacy," see Stopford and Strange, *Rival States, Rival Firms.*

42. Drake and Nicolaïdis, "Ideas, Interests, and Institutionalization," 49.

tablished command posts" near the WTO headquarters and conferred with American negotiators throughout the financial service talks.[43] The European negotiators soon saw the benefits of the close cooperation with business experts, but those active on service trade issues were almost exclusively American. Harry Freeman of American Express confirms:

> At the close of the Uruguay Round, we lobbied and lobbied. We had about 400 people from the U.S. private sector. There were perhaps four Canadians and nobody from any other private sector.[44]

EU Trade Commissioner Sir Leon Brittan regretted the lack of support from European business organizations throughout the Uruguay Round and between 1995 and 1999 started creating a series of associations that were meant to encourage the political participation of firms throughout Europe. The most important of these groups was the Transatlantic Business Dialogue (TABD), a forum for American and European firms and policymakers.[45] To break the deadlock in the sectoral negotiations on financial services in the WTO, the U.S. government and the EU Commission furthermore agreed to found a similar group for financial services only. They invited Ken Whipple, then president of Ford Financial Services, and Andrew Buxton, then chairman of Barclays Bank, to form a high-level transatlantic business forum, the Financial Leaders' Group, of which the Coalition of Service Industries runs the secretariat.

The European Commission furthermore tried to establish regular contact with business representatives from different service industries. During the sectoral negotiations of the GATS in the 1990s, representatives from the Commission's Directorate-General for Trade (DG Trade) created an informal service network that allowed the Commission to get timely feedback from business on different issues and proposals.[46] The network was later formalized during the preparation for the GATS 2000 negotiation at Brittan's initiative. The European Service Network was launched on 26 January 1999 and in October renamed the European Service Forum (ESF). In its first meeting, Brittan emphasized the role he saw for the association:

43. Andrews, "Agreement to Open up World Financial Markets is Reached."
44. Quoted in Wesselius, "Behind GATS 2000."
45. Cowles, "The Transatlantic Business Dialogue and Domestic Business-Government Relations."
46. Interview with a representative from the European Commission's DG Trade on 16 February 2007.

I am in your hands to listen to what are your objectives, your priorities for liberalization either on a sectoral, geographical or . . . regulatory environment. . . . I count on your support and input, . . . so that we can refine our strategy and set out clear, priority negotiating objectives which will make a difference in the international expansion of business.[47]

The relationship between the European Commission's DG Trade and the ESF is thus unusually tight. Nonetheless, the ESF is a weaker and less active organization than its American counterpart. Like the TABD, the ESF suffers from the lack of active participation by European CEOs, who do not treat public relations as a part of their daily work to the same degree that American CEOs do.[48] As Shaffer underlines, trade policy lobbying in the European Union is much less aggressive than in the United States and depends heavily on government initiatives:

While the U.S. Trade Representative responded to onslaughts of private sector lobbying reinforced by congressional phone calls and committee grillings, the Commission had to contact firms to contact it.[49]

In service trade as on other trade issues, the European Commission has made a concerted effort to integrate firms and other private actors into the trade policymaking process, a curious phenomenon of "reverse lobbying."[50]

In sum, the issue of service trade is a policy area that business actors, above all from the United States, have helped to put on the political agenda and that they have influenced throughout the negotiations. Despite the considerable amount of time and money that these firms invested in the course of their lobbying, business-government relations in this area display several characteristics that distinguish them from typical pressure lobbying. First, they are marked by an unusual longevity: beginning in the late 1970s, business involvement lasted until the conclusion of the GATS agreement in 1994. For companies such a time horizon is extremely uncommon. Second, business actors sought to avoid competition among themselves and instead formed coalitions to present a united front on the issue. For financial service firms, this implied enlarging the issue beyond the narrow objective of extending their international card business to

---

47. Brittan, "European Service Leaders' Group."
48. Interview with an EU business representative on 13 November 2002 in Brussels.
49. Shaffer, *Defending Interests*, 70.
50. See Elsig, *The EU's Common Commercial Policy;* Van den Hoven, "Interest Group Influence on Trade Policy in a Multilevel Polity"; Shaffer, *Defending Interests.*

pushing for a new trading regime on services. Third, the U.S.-EU comparison shows how much governments depended on and solicited business actors to negotiate on an equal footing with their trading partners. The goal of government representatives is much less the pursuit of financial benefits than the ambition to negotiate the best possible trade regime for their national firms in order to secure them a share of the world market for services, as suggested by Stopford and Strange.[51]

The Case Studies

Unfortunately, it is difficult to say anything general about corporate trade policy preferences by simply looking at the lobbying of U.S. financial companies on service trade. The policy stances of American firms seem to have arisen in very specific political contexts, where firms saw an opportunity to influence the policies structuring their international operations to their advantage. We cannot say for sure whether a company like American Express correctly anticipated the payoffs of international liberalization and only invested the necessary amount of resources to reap these benefits, or whether it applied political entrepreneurship to define "new social values" and gain access to key policymakers.[52] For a more systematic analysis of the trade preferences and policy stances of firms on questions of international service trade, it is necessary to compare cases that allow specifying the effects of the elements that have been identified in the theoretical discussion: identities, changing beliefs, and strategic contexts.

Comparing Telecommunications and Air Transport

The international liberalization of telecommunication services and air transport and the policy stances of firms in the United States and the European Union were chosen as case studies because firms' identities, their beliefs, and the strategic constraints varied between countries, within sectors, and over time. At the level of identity, a number of service providers in telecommunications and air transport were initially public, sometimes even state-owned companies, which only later turned into competitive

---

51. Stopford and Strange, *Rival States, Rival Firms.*
52. Yoffie and Bergenstein suggest that American Express built "political capital" by "developing an issue which had broad political appeal and fit into the agendas of key politicians," even though the significance of the issue for American Express's business operations was not certain. Yoffie and Bergenstein, "Creating Political Advantage," 127.

firms. Beliefs were changing, because firms in each sector had to stop reasoning in terms of interconnection or strict reciprocity and start thinking about their international operations in terms of trade and foreign market access. Strategically, firms in Europe that had previously maintained privileged relationships with their home governments had to adapt to the peculiar multilevel system of the European Union.

Besides these sources of variation, the country and sector studies juxtapose broadly similar cases.[53] Both the United States and the European Union are important trading partners: by engaging in political activities with their governments, firms can hope to actually affect policy outcomes. Furthermore, we find a small number of large and important firms in each sector—United Airlines, AT&T, British Airways, France Télécom, Lufthansa, MCI, and Verizon, to name just a few—which we can all expect to have an opinion on international affairs and to have the resources to act on their preferences.

Concerning the dependent variable, policy stances, the cases also display variety. The liberalization of international telecommunications services was negotiated multilaterally in the years following the Uruguay Round, from May 1994 through February 1997. International air transport was almost completely excluded from the coverage of the GATS, but evolved independently in the 1990s. A first step in the liberalization of the international architecture was the U.S. policy of open sky agreements in the early to mid-1990s and later the European-led attempt to negotiate a liberal transatlantic aviation area. U.S.-EU negotiations on this issue began in 2003 and produced a first agreement in 2007. Faced with these different policy contexts, the stances of firms were quite different between the two sectors. In both case studies, it is nonetheless possible to locate the observed policy stances on a scale going from protectionism to support of liberalization.

In almost all cases, policy demands evolved over time as table 3.3 highlights. Initially, European and American network operators and airlines were quite reserved about liberalization. As the WTO telecom negotiations and the U.S. policy of open skies advanced, however, firms turned supportive of these projects. European airlines even drew up a new plan for more comprehensive liberalization in the late 1990s.

The objective of the following two chapters is to explain where these pol-

---

53. For further discussion, see Warren and Findlay, "Competition Policy and International Trade in Air Transport and Telecommunications Services"; Larouche, "Relevant Market Definition in Network Industries."

Table 3.3. Observed trade policy stances

	Protectionist ⟵		Liberal ⟶
U.S. telecom firms			Supportive of pro-competitive regulation
RBOCs	(1) Restricted market access	(2) Supportive of pro-competitive regulation	
EU telecom	(1) Inter-firm trade; subsidies	(2) Supportive of pro-competitive regulation	
U.S. airlines	(1) Subsidies; restrictions on foreign airlines	(2) Open skies	
EU airlines	(1) Subsidies; restrictions on foreign airlines	(2) Open skies	(3) Open aviation area

icy stances came from. The time period considered therefore starts in the years preceding the international negotiations—in telecommunications, the late 1880s, and in aviation, the early 1990s. In the case of telecommunications, the period ends with the conclusion of the 1997 agreement; in international air transport with the conclusion of the transatlantic open sky agreement in 2007.

The Economic Context

Before turning to the case studies, let us consider the material context in which firms in both sectors have to act in order to clarify the alternative hypotheses one might make from a materialist standpoint. How do material conditions differ between the two sectors and among firms?

For the sector comparison, we are interested in the specificity of the capital assets: To what degree is capital a mobile factor in telecommunications and air transport? Economists commonly distinguish between interregional capital mobility and interindustry mobility.[54] Air transport services are characterized by a higher degree of interregional mobility than telecommunication services. Planes can be moved at a much lower cost than telecommunications equipment: while airlines can shift the pattern

---

54. Interregional mobility can be studied by looking at differences in returns earned by similar types of assets held in different national markets. A proxy for interindustry mobility can be the stock market return to capital. See Grossman and Levinsohn, "Import Competition and the Stock Market Return to Capital"; Frankel, "Measuring International Capital Mobility." Hiscox discusses the different measurements in the economic literature and applies it to the study of trade policy. Hiscox, *International Trade and Political Conflict*, chap. 2.

of their hub-and-spokes systems or develop multihub services in the event of liberalization, telecommunication networks cannot be moved geographically. However, they can be rented out to other users, which brings us to interindustry mobility. In essence, the question here is how costly it would be for a firm to redeploy its assets in a different sector of activity.[55] In this respect, telecommunication assets are in many ways not very different from air transport assets. All infrastructure services have high asset specificity: capital investment concentrates on sector-specific technologies, sunk costs are high, and/or employees receive special training that enables them to fulfill the particular requirements of their jobs. Redeploying assets without high costs is possible only in related services, such as other forms of communication or cargo transport. Considering both interregional and interindustry mobility, it thus seems accurate to say that telecommunication services are marked by a lower degree of capital mobility than air transport, even though the latter is mainly due to interregional mobility.

With respect to firm differences, we need to know how important international operations are for individual firms. A sensible measure for this is the percentage of revenue coming from international operations. Foreign direct investment and international production-sharing differentials between firms are equally important. Since information for consecutive years is difficult to obtain, the tables 3.4 and 3.5 concentrate on the years 1997 for telecom companies and 2002 for air transport.

As one would expect, international as a percentage of total revenue in telecommunications is highest for large American service providers and the operators of small European countries. Foreign investment and joint ventures, in turn, are important for operators from large European countries, competitive U.S. service providers and to a lesser degree the U.S. RBOCs. Overall, international revenue constitutes a relatively small portion of revenue, especially when one compares it to air transport.

International operations constitute a much bigger part of total revenue for airlines. In the European cases, international operations do not include European transborder traffic, but they still generate almost 63 percent of revenue in the case of KLM. For most large U.S. carriers, international traffic represents around 30 percent of their total revenue. All international carriers maintain alliances today, but some started earlier than others and several carriers have not sought to obtain antitrust immunity for their partnerships.

55. Williamson, "Comparative Economic Organization," 281.

Table 3.4. International orientation of telecom companies, 1997

Company	Home market position	Joint ventures and foreign investment[a]	Total telecom revenue (US $ million)	International telephone revenue (US $ million)	International as % of total revenue
MCI (US)	competitor	JV / + +	19,653	4,243	21
AT&T (US)	competitor	JV / + +	51,319	8,351	16
KPN (NL)	incumbent	JV / +	7,671	1,037	13
PTA (A)	incumbent	n/a	3,733[b]	492	13
Belgacom (B)	incumbent	n/a	4,513[b]	547	12
Sprint (US)	competitor	JV/+ +	14,874	1,478	9
British Telecom (UK)	incumbent	JV/+ +	26,277	2,609	9
France Télécom (F)	incumbent	JV/+ +	26,174	2,110	8
Deutsche Telekom(D)	incumbent	JV/+	37,694	2,734	7
Worldcom (US)	competitor	n/a	7,790	500	6
Telecom Italia (I)	incumbent	n/a	24,204	1,412	5
Telefónica (E)	incumbent	+ +	15,577	795	5
Bell Atlantic (US)	incumbent	+ +	30,194	0	0
SBC (US)	incumbent	+	24,856	0	0
GTE (US)	incumbent	n/a	23,260	0	0
Bell South (US)	incumbent	+ +	20,561	0	0
Ameritech (US)	incumbent	+ +	15,998	0	0
US West (US)	incumbent	+ +	15,235	0	0
Cable& Wireless (UK)	competitor	+ +	8,940	n/a	n/a
Telia (S)	incumbent	JV	4,694[b]	n/a	n/a

Source: Assembled by the author based on the following publications: ITU, "Top 20 Telecommunication Operators," (1997), http://www.itu.int/ITU-D/ict/statistics/; WTO, "Data on Telecommunication Markets covered by the WTO Negotiations on Basic Telecommunications" (1997), http://www.wto.org/english/news_e/pres97_e/ data3 .htm; FCC, "Report on International Telecommunications Markets, 2000 Update" (Washington, DC: International Bureau of the Federal Communications Commission, 2001). Foreign investment information is taken from Crandall, "Telecom Mergers and Joint Ventures in an Era of Liberalization."

[a]JV indicates major joint ventures, + indicates a case of foreign investment, + + indicates several.
[b]Estimate based on country data; n/a indicates that data was not available.

According to the materialist perspective, firms with the highest percentage of international revenue are most likely to press for reciprocal market access. In the case of telecommunications, these should be AT&T, MCI, KPN, PTA, Belgacom, and maybe also Sprint, British Telecom, and France Télécom. In air transport, KLM, British Airways, Air France, TAP, Lufthansa and United should be most interested in reforming the international architecture to facilitate operations. If one considers alliances and foreign investment, the pro-liberalization lobby in telecommunications might center more on competitive U.S. providers and large European operators; in air transport, it might include carriers such as Northwest, with otherwise average international operations.

Table 3.5. International orientation of airlines, 2002

Carrier	International alliances[a]	Operating revenue (US $ million)	International[b] as % of total revenue
KLM (NL)	EA, at, eq	7,004	62.9
British Airways (UK)	EA, at, eq	12,166	61.5
Air France (F)	LA, at	13,702	53.8[c]
TAP (P)	LA, at	1,524	51.1
Lufthansa (D)	EA, at	18,057	49.0[c]
United (US)	EA, at	14,286	34.8[c, d]
Continental (US)	EA	8,402	33.7
Iberia (E)	EA	4,925	32.6[c]
Northwest (US)	EA, at, eq	9,489	30.1[c]
American (US)	EA, at	17,403	29.0
Delta (US)	EA, at	13,305	21.3[c, d]
SAS (DK, S, N)	EA, at	7,429	14.3[e]
US Airways (US)	EA, eq	6,977	13.1
Alitalia (I)	EA, at	4,868	7.9[f]

Sources: International alliances: based on Young, *Extending European Cooperation,* 116. International revenue: assembled by the author from Annual 10 K Report of US carriers; Annual Reports of EU carriers; AIW (2002) World Airline Report, available at www.atwonline.com/stats_traffic.cfm.

[a]EA denotes early alliances (starting in the mid-1990s), LA late alliances; at indicates that the alliance partners have sought antitrust immunity from the US government; eq denotes an equity stake.

[b]U.S. carriers: nondomestic revenue. European carriers: revenue from outside the European Aviation Area.

[c]Percentage refers to passenger operating revenue only.

[d]Canada and Mexico not counted as international service.

[e]Percentage refers to intercontinental flights only. The remaining 78% includes domestic, inter-Scandinavian, and European flights.

[f]Percentage refers to passengers carried on intercontinental routes. Alitalia carried 54.4% of its passengers on purely domestic routes and 37.7 on European or Mediterranean routes.

However, it is difficult to determine just from looking at these figures where one would expect to draw the cutoff line between supporters and opponents of liberalization. In particular, international activities in telecommunications seem in general low. A service provider like Sprint derives only 9 percent of revenue from international operations: hardly a figure that leads us to expect a great interest in this sector of activity. The low international involvement of telecom companies becomes even more striking when we compare it with air transport. Almost all airlines have a higher percentage of international revenue than telecom providers. Comparing international orientation between sectors might even lead us to predict that telecom companies as a whole should be opposed to liberalization, while airlines will tend to favor it. This is all the more true if one combines the data on individual firms with the information we have about capital mobility in each sector.

When considering the actual lobbying observed, it turns out that the sectoral predictions do not hold, while the relative engagement of firms within each sector corresponds roughly to the ranking presented in tables 3.4 and 3.5. Firms that have engaged most explicitly in support of further liberalization—companies such as AT&T, MCI, Sprint, France Télécom, Deutsche Telekom, KLM, British Airways, Air France, and Lufthansa—have comparably large international activities, at least with respect to other firms in their sector. Conversely, those that have been conspicuously absent from the liberalization discussion—Bell South, SBC, Ameritech, SAS, US Airways and Alitalia, for example—have comparably small international activities. For the relative degree of support for liberalization, the degree of international orientation is thus a helpful first indicator of the preferences firms will have with respect to foreign opportunities and home market protection. However, the firm data do not seem to give an indication of the threshold at which firms start to lobby in support of liberalization. One could ask why Sprint was among the early supporters of a WTO agreement, even though its international activities are closer to those of the major European network operators rather than MCI or AT&T. And why did NYNEX, later as Bell Atlantic, get involved more actively than other Regional Bells, even though some of them also had foreign investments? Moreover, it is hard to see why international air transport as a whole is more conservative about international trade than telecommunications. In telecommunications, a tenth of revenue from international operations seem to suffice to make a firm interested in foreign trade, while 33 percent of international operations is seemingly insufficient for U.S. airlines.

Conclusion

When one starts to analyze the relative degree of involvement in support of liberalization across cases, one quickly starts to see fault lines between countries and sectors that cannot be explained by the economic context alone. The argument pursued here is that sectoral differences and country differences matter independent of the economic setting, because they affect the micro-foundations of firms' trade preferences. Information about material differences is therefore helpful only once we have sufficient information about these micro-foundations or once we know that these are stable. In other words, the ways in which firms react to economic incentives are embedded in a larger sociopolitical context. The following empirical chapters survey this context by concentrating on the different components of preference translation identified in the preceding chapter.

To a certain degree, the argument of this book crystallizes the difference between predicting and understanding cases. Scholars interested in large-scale comparison might argue that the cases I present are only of marginal importance. What I say might be theoretically true, but empirically trivial. In this chapter, I have sought to argue that what we find in the case studies is likely to apply to all areas where the stakes are regulatory reform rather than pure market opening. It is up to the judgment of the reader whether these domains constitute an important or a marginal area of current trade negotiations. However, the increasing discussion of standards in trade negotiations—whether product, labor, or environmental—leads me to believe that one needs to move beyond the logic of tariff negotiations in the analysis of trade policy issues.

4

Basic Telecommunication Services

Telecommunication services were one of the first areas in which sectoral negotiations were conducted after the signing of the Marrakech agreement in 1994. During the Uruguay Round, telecommunication had been a central but heavily disputed element of service talks. Basic telecommunication services—all end-to-end transmissions such as voice telephone service, telex, telegraph, and facsimile service—were at the heart of the contentions. Countries committed to the liberalizing of so-called value-added services, which enhance the form of the customer's information.[1] On all other issues, they finally agreed to disagree and provided for further negotiation on a sectoral basis after the conclusion of the round. Only a month after the signing of the Marrakech agreement, separate negotiations began on basic telecommunication services under the auspices of a group called the Negotiating Group on Basic Telecommunication Services (NGBT). The deadline for the negotiations was 30 April 1996, later extended to 15 February 1997.

When sectoral negotiations started, many network operators did not pay attention to these multilateral negotiations. The companies most actively following the talks were competitive American service providers such as AT&T, MCI, and Sprint. NYNEX, an RBOC, eventually joined the service

---

1. Examples of value-added services are voice mail, e-mail exchanges or on-line data processing. Further information on basic and value-added telecommunication services can be found on the WTO website: www.wto.org.

providers in Geneva. European network operators, however, were almost entirely absent in the first round of the sectoral talks. This changed when the negotiations entered into their second round after the extension of the deadline in 1996. From this point on, many European network operators such as British Telecom, France Télécom, Deutsche Telekom, and Telefónica actively engaged in the talks and ended up supporting multilateral liberalization. What explains this surprisingly unanimous position of American and European telecom companies? Why did even companies that had traditionally insisted on protecting their home markets turn to supporting multilateral liberalization?

The most important determinants of these business stances were the regulatory and political arrangements within which these firms had to act. The relationships telecom companies maintained with their governments, users, and competitors did not merely structure the strategic setting by providing incentives for or against liberalization. They also shaped the beliefs firms had about their international operations and help to explain why companies identified themselves as public service providers, incumbent operators, or competitive firms. Careful attention to the important changes in the regulatory framework governing telecommunications in each country is thus necessary to understanding how firms interpreted economic opportunities. After an introduction to the history and the issues of the telecom revolution in the 1980s and 1990s, this chapter shows how regulatory changes and political relations affected firm identities, beliefs, and strategic environments.

The Telecom Revolution

The Old International System

Due to the high capital intensity of the sector, the provision of telecommunication service was long perceived as a "natural" monopoly.[2] Ensuring that the monopolist could guarantee universal access without abusing its market power led to the regulation of the sector, either through direct government control or through regulatory agencies. In the United States, telecommunication provision was traditionally in the hands of the private monopoly of the American Telephone and Telegraph Company (AT&T) founded in 1877. In 1934, the U.S. government established the Federal

---

2. For the economic justifications of national monopolies and their counterarguments, see Welfens and Yarrow, *Telecommunications and Energy in Transforming Economies*.

Communications Commission (FCC) as an independent agency responsible for the regulation of interstate and international communication directly reporting to Congress.

In most European countries, telecommunication provision was not just under tight state control, it was most often provided through a public monopoly. State-owned companies were in charge of both networks and services, even though specific national solutions varied. In France and Germany, the administrative units responsible for telecommunication and postal services (PTTs) were part of the civil service and operated under ministerial control. In Britain, the Post Office was a government department until 1969 when it became a public corporation. Italy, by contrast, had several public network operators. PTT ministries combined the function of national regulators, policymakers, and suppliers of networks and services, so there was no need for an independent regulator like the FCC in the United States.[3]

The logic of the international regime governing telecommunication service exchanges arose from the ways the sector was structured domestically. The traditional framework perfectly suited the monopolistic regimes which provided telecom services and products in the majority of industrialized countries.[4] Therefore, the international exchange of telecom services in this tradition meant finding a way of interconnecting and pricing phone calls that went from country A to country B. Cooperation was necessary, because other forms of market access were not possible under monopoly provision.[5] The joint supply of services has traditionally taken the form of switched services. In switched services, a telephone call is billed in the home country A, even though a foreign operator agrees to transmit the phone call through its network in country B. This transaction results in a settlement liability of carrier A, who needs to pay the termination cost to carrier B. The amount of this cost is fixed in terms of an accounting rate in a bilateral agreement between the two carriers. The actual settlement rate, payable by the carrier with most outgoing minutes, is a function of the accounting rate multiplied by the number of net outbound minutes.

---

3. For further information, see Noam, *Telecommunications in Europe;* Schneider, *Staat und technische Kommunikation;* Thatcher, *The Politics of Telecommunications.*

4. Cowhey, "Telecommunications."

5. Henry Ergas calls the traditional international framework the "cooperative model," since telephone services depended on the cooperation between national providers at three levels: in the joint supply of facilities used for international service, the joint provision of services, and the setting of technical standards and operating procedures. Ergas, "International Trade in Services."

Hence, the carrier sending more calls than it receives incurs a settlement liability on the volume of net traffic. This accounting rate system was a central feature of the traditional international architecture. Moreover, under public monopoly service, it was an important source of revenue for countries with few outgoing international phone calls.

In order for these switched services to be compatible, a more general coordination was needed on technical standards and operating procedures, governed by one of the oldest existing international organizations, the International Telecommunication Union (ITU). Founded in Paris in 1865 as the International Telegraph Union, the organization's mission has been since the beginning to ensure cross-border telecommunication by setting standards on equipment, adopting uniform operating instructions, and laying down common international tariffs and accounting rules. In its early years, the ITU was comprised of PTT administrations only, and nationalization or complete state control over telegraphy was always an unwritten prerequisite for membership.[6] In the absence of a PTT administration and in defiance of international obligations, the United States refused to join the ITU until 1932, the date of the renaming and restructuring of the organization. Under an agreement of the newly created United Nations, the ITU became a UN specialized agency in 1947, with headquarters in Geneva, bringing together national administrators and private sector representatives. Despite its membership, the United States was always somewhat mistrustful of the international regime governed by the ITU, because it was a logical extension of the monopoly provision of domestic services and thus distinctly European.[7] Still, the international order that the PTTs designed remained stable for over a century.

Domestic Deregulation and Pressures for Change

Starting in the 1960s and 1970s, the accumulation of technological innovations triggered a worldwide paradigm shift that put into question the idea of a natural monopoly and led to a transition toward competition-oriented domestic markets.[8] In the United States, MCI, originally a company concentrating on two-way radios for truckers, challenged AT&T's rule and

---

6. Codding, *The International Telecommunication Union,* 42.

7. Cowhey and Aronson, *Managing the World Economy,* 166; Drake, "The Rise and Decline of the International Telecommunications Regime."

8. A growing literature exists on this paradigm shift and the regulatory reforms in different countries. See for example, Vogel, *Freer Markets, More Rules;* Thatcher, *The Politics of Telecommunications;* Schneider, *Die Transformation der Telekommunikation.*

won an antitrust case in 1982. On 1 January 1984, AT&T's Bell System had to divide into seven regional holding companies, the so-called "Baby Bells" (RBOCs): Ameritech, US West, NYNEX, Pacific Telsis, Southwestern Bell, Bell South, and Bell Atlantic. AT&T remained in charge of long-distance calls, an area that was now open to new market entrants.[9] Local communication continued to be under monopoly provision until the Federal Telecom Act (TA96), which was approved by Congress in 1996 and signed into law in 1999.

In Europe, technological and economic changes in the 1970s led to little more than discussion, with the notable exception of Great Britain. The new Conservative government first separated telecommunication from postal services and created British Telecom in 1981. In 1984, British Telecom was privatized and a semi-independent regulator was established. The Scandinavian countries were also an exception to the tight state-owned monopoly models in the rest of continental Europe. The Danish system, for example, had always resembled the U.S. system after the divestiture of AT&T and was liberalized even further in 1990.[10] In all other European countries, however, there was no real momentum for domestic reform, despite growing transnational pressures.

In the 1980s, the European Community started working on the issues, as it was the desire of the European Commission to overcome the disadvantages of fragmentation in the European market. Inspired by the experience of the United States and encouraged by several member states which also followed a more liberal approach, the Commission used its competition powers under Article 86.3 (formerly Article 90.3) of the Treaty on European Union to force liberalization of telecommunications equipment and later services and networks. The first major step in this process was the publication of the "Green Paper on the Development of the Common Market for Telecommunication Services and Equipment" in 1987. Several member states attempted to challenge the Commission's competence in this area, but in 1992 the European Court of Justice (ECJ) upheld the Commission's decisions regarding both equipment and services. This paved the way for proposals involving telephone services in 1993 and infrastructures in 1994, in the form of both liberalization directives and harmonization of

9. Cf. Evans, *Breaking Up Bell;* Faulhaber, *Telecommunications in Turmoil;* Cohen, *The Politics of Telecommunications Regulation.*

10. Sweden introduced competition to the national company Televerket before it entered the European Union in 1995. Finland never had a national monopoly, but instead almost fifty companies competed with the national monopoly. Noam, *Telecommunications in Europe;* Smith, "Re-Regulation and Integration."

standards for interconnection, licenses, and universal service. In 1996, the Council adopted the "Green Paper on the Liberalization of Telecommunications Infrastructure and Cable Television Networks," which provided the basis for full liberalization of the infrastructure by 1 January 1998.[11]

The liberalization design addressed several dimensions. A first step consisted of the separation of regulatory and operational functions in the former telecommunication administrations and the opening up of networks to competition. In addition, EU legislation required the establishment of an independent regulator at the national level, in order to ensure fair competition practices and transparent regulation, especially with regard to interconnection agreements.[12]

Domestic deregulation, in turn, put pressure on the international regime governing telecommunications. Based on reciprocal exchanges, the international accounting rate system disadvantaged countries that had chosen to deregulate their domestic markets, because it created an important bias against competitive pricing. The United States, for instance, experienced an annual balance-of-payments deficit on telecommunications services approaching $3 billion by the early 1990s. Starting in 1986, the United States fought a six-year battle in the ITU to reform the accounting rate system and to make it cost-oriented, a requirement that implied a fundamental paradigm shift in the traditional regime.[13] In March 1992, the United States obtained an ITU agreement that introduced cost-orientation into the accounting rate system and set up a procedure for its application and oversight. Still, the relative decline of accounting rates was not sufficient in the eyes of the FCC and U.S. carriers and the payments deficit continued to grow. By the mid-1990s, almost all of the most important policy actors in the United States had become interested in more comprehensive reforms.[14]

Simultaneously, large companies started to consider telecommunication

11. European telecom policy has been the subject of many studies, which still disagree about the most important motors for change. See Sandholtz, "The Emergence of a Supranational Telecommunications Regime"; Schmidt, "Commission Activism"; Thatcher, "The Commission and National Governments as Partners"; Holmes and Young, "Liberalizing and Reregulating Telecommunications in Europe."

12. The EU later unified and simplified regulation of all types of electronic communication through a telecom package in 2001.

13. For a discussion of the growing U.S. discontent with the old accounting rate system, see Alleman, Pappoport, and Stanley, "Alternative Settlement Procedures in International Telecommunication Service"; Ergas and Paterson, "International Telecommunications Settlement Arrangements."

14. See Cowhey, "Telecommunications."

prices as an obstacle to their international commercial activities and created user groups pressuring for more competition in the international market. Parallel to the service trade lobbying within the USCSI and USCIB, user companies formed the International Telecommunications Users Group in Brussels in 1974 which worked closely with the European Institutions and the ITU to press their cause. In spite of opposition, user demands gained legitimacy through the OECD's Special Session on "Changing Market Structures in Telecommunications" in 1982, and later through follow-up sessions in 1985 and 1990. By the late 1980s, a reform of the international telecommunication regime was supported by a coalition of user groups, business organizations, and international organizations. Frustrated with past attempts to reform the ITU's accounting rate system, the U.S. government embraced these positions and was joined by the European Commission, which felt that a reform of the international architecture would help to consolidate its internal liberalization process. The parallel negotiation of a service agreement in the Uruguay Round made the GATT the most promising forum for reforming the international telecommunications regime.

Tackling International Reform through the GATS

During the 1980s, the USTR had established a close working relationship with the financial service companies represented in the USCSI. In the elaboration of a common understanding of service exchanges as trade, the coalition of U.S. firms and the USTR proposed that the joint provision of telecommunication services in fact constituted trade as well.[15] For the European Commission, a trade solution was especially appealing. After all, it was the Commission that negotiated EU trade policy within the GATT framework and later within the WTO. In the ITU, by contrast, the EU member states were represented individually, whereas the Commission merely had observer status. Governing international telecommunication service provision through a trade regime was thus all the more attractive. As a consequence, the Commission pursued a double strategy toward the liberalization of telecommunication services throughout the 1990s: negotiating internal liberalization with the member states, it seized the opportunity of WTO negotiations to tie international to European liberalization.[16]

---

15. For further information, see Aronson and Cowhey, *When Countries Talk;* Feketekuty, *International Trade in Services.*

16. Holmes and Young, "Liberalizing and Reregulating Telecommunications," 23–38; Young, *Extending European Cooperation.*

Although the European Commission clearly favored a trade agreement on telecommunications, it did not have exclusive competence on this policy issue.[17] During the Uruguay Round, member states governments and the Commission could not decide on the competence distribution regarding international service negotiation. The Commission conceived of agriculture and services as a package that should be negotiated as a whole, while the member states insisted that the new issues of services, intellectual property rights, and investment required ratification by themselves. Failing to find a political solution, the Commission referred the question to the European Court of Justice, which ruled against an expansion of Community competences.[18] The WTO negotiations on basic telecommunications were thus under mixed competences between the Commission and the member states.[19]

During the early 1990s, negotiations advanced in parallel on the framework text for the GATS itself, annexes for a number of service sectors, and national schedules on specific commitments. Telecommunications, it was agreed, should be treated in a separate annex, because of the particular problems it presented. Despite its desire for a comprehensive GATS agreement, the United States had the strongest view on telecommunications. In particular, it did not want to undertake specific telecommunication commitments that it felt would not be matched by countries with more rigid public monopoly provision. However, the annex did not aim at excluding telecommunications altogether. Rather, the concern was to reach an agreement allowing reasonable and nondiscriminatory access to public networks and services. The special annex drafted in the autumn of 1991 set the conditions under which participants would allow services suppliers of other countries to connect to or use the networks of national public telecommunication systems. After a general standstill of Uruguay Round discussions in 1992, the major players, commonly referred to as the Quad group (the United States, the European Communities, Canada, and Japan), helped to relaunch both the Uruguay Round and the service talks in Tokyo in July 1993. The Tokyo agreement was somewhat vague on ser-

17. Meunier, "EU Trade Policy"; Woolcock, "European Trade Policy," 377; Meunier, *Trading Voices*.

18. European Court of Justice, "Competence of the Community to conclude international agreements concerning services and intellectual property," Opinion 1/1994 of 15 November (Brussels, 2004). See also Woolcock, "European Trade Policy," 377.

19. This mixed competence solution lasted throughout the basic telecom negotiations in the WTO. A new solution for international service trade negotiations was only introduced in the Treaty of Amsterdam, signed in October 1997, which provided that member states could extend exclusive EU competence to the Commission by unanimous vote.

vices, but fixed in principle that negotiations on basic telecommunications should continue in sectoral negotiations after the conclusion of the Uruguay Round.

Participation in the subsequent sectoral negotiations was voluntary. Like earlier discussions, the NGBT talks were dominated by developed countries interested in advancing on the concrete issues of telecommunication service liberalization. Most importantly, the participants worked on producing a so-called "Reference Paper" that contained specific indications concerning the regulatory framework that was to guide national liberalization.[20] However, the enthusiasm of the leading countries was not shared by all other participants.[21] By April 1996, thirty-four offers from forty-eight governments were on the table. Yet there was a general sense, particularly in the United States, that these offers were insufficient. The United States feared that it would open its market without getting significant market access in return. Moreover, in the final phase of negotiations, the issue of satellite services disturbed the discussion: To what extent did the offers cover these services? By 30 April, the negotiations threatened to fail.

Unable to reach the scheduled conclusion, Renato Ruggiero, at the time WTO director general, suggested preserving the proposals in the "Fourth Protocol to the General Agreement on Trade in Services." Countries should be given a chance to improve their offers, and 15 February 1997 was established as a new deadline. The negotiating group was renamed the Group on Basic Telecommunications (GBT). This second round became the most important period of negotiations. Difficult issues continued to lead to lively discussions: in particular, disputes revolved around satellite service, the "critical mass" of offers to aim for, anticompetitive practices, international accounting, and audiovisual services. Gradually, however, technical and political solutions began to emerge. The United States unilaterally proposed a new policy toward international settlement rates in December 1996, helping to deflate much of its own fears of asymmetric benefits.[22] There was agreement that schedules should be technology-

20. The Reference Paper can be consulted at the WTO's website at www.wto.org/english/tratop_e/serv_e/telecom_e/tel23_e.htm. A detailed explanation of the elements of the Basic Telecommunications Agreement and the Reference Paper in particular can be found in Tuthill, "The GATS and New Rules for Regulators." For the negotiating history of the Reference Paper, see Sherman, "'Wildly Enthusiastic' about the First Multilateral Agreement on Trade in Telecommunications Services."

21. For a detailed discussion of the reservations held by developing countries, see Narlikar, *International Trade and Developing Countries*, chap. 2–6.

22. For further information, see Cowhey, "FCC Benchmarks and the Reform of the International Telecommunications Market"; Cowhey and Richards, "Dialing for Dollars," 165.

neutral (i.e. cover all transmission from wire to satellite), and the overall acceptance of the Reference Paper helped to calm concerns about anti-competitive practices.

In early 1997, it became clear that an agreement would be achieved by the scheduled deadline. The Basic Telecommunications Agreement was finally adopted on 15 February 1997 and entered into force on 5 February 1998. Sixty-nine countries submitted schedules, which entered into force on the same date as an integral part of the GATS schedules of services commitments already in force since 1994. Sixty-three of these countries had furthermore made specific commitments on regulatory disciplines, the great majority by accepting the whole of the Reference Paper or adding only slight modifications. Providing the framework for global liberalization of the sector, the Basic Telecommunications Agreement is considered a landmark agreement in the eyes of many observers, potentially even a "trillion dollar deal."[23]

How did the firms affected by these changes experience the telecom revolution? When did they engage in political activities and what explains their policy demands? By means of interview data, the following section will show that regulatory changes and political relations shaped the definition of firms' political interests (1) by encouraging former monopolies or incumbent providers to conceive of themselves as competitive players; (2) by framing international activities as trade rather than the joint provision of services; and (3) by conditioning strategic interactions and feasible political alliances.

Changing Identities: From National Champions to Global Players

The most basic transformation shaping the policy demands of telecom companies was the changing nature of these actors. The only telecom companies that were competitive service providers from the beginning of the talks were AT&T, MCI, Sprint, the mobile company Motorola, and the satellite provider ComSat. A study of European and American network operators reveals how the transition towards competitiveness was reflected in the evolution of their policy stances. Variation between companies depended on the degree to which they embraced their new corporate identity or insisted on their incumbent status.

23. Petrazzini, *Global Telecom Talks*. For a more skeptical view, see Drake and Noam, "The WTO Deal on Basic Telecommunications."

European Operators

In European countries, the line between the government and the tele-communication operator was often thin. A U.S. lobbyist remembers: "within Washington, the person from Deutsche Telekom was for a long time an attaché at the German embassy."[24] However, traditions had changed by the time telecom services were negotiated in Geneva. British Telecom had been privatized since 1981. Even for other countries, the nature of government-operator contacts transformed rapidly in the mid-1990s. As an official from the WTO secretariat put it, "Deutsche Telekom and France Télécom looked very similar to AT&T" by 1996. When dealing with one of the European operators, many observers began to feel "that this was a company."[25]

However, the former public service status of these companies often explains why there was a greater exposure to political issues within the management of the providers. France Télécom, for example, was one of the very early companies following the developments in Geneva. The director of international relations of France Télécom had previously worked for the European Commission and followed trade issues on telecommunications, while the manager of governmental affairs who put him in charge of the GATS dossier had been exposed to the trade agenda while working in the cabinet of former French Prime Minister Edith Cresson.[26] If such personal trajectories can explain some initial political awareness and trade expertise, there is little evidence that ties between business and government representatives were particularly close in Europe during the basic telecom negotiations, especially since careers at the intersection of the public and the private sector are also common in Washington. Nonetheless, policy stances of European operators in the late 1980s were almost impossible to separate from government stances.

This slowly changed in the 1990s, when operators started distancing themselves from governmental policy objectives. An important empowerment of European operators happened in the context of the European liberalization project. Most notably, the European Commission assembled a top-level group around Commissioner Martin Bangemann in the context of the Telecom Review between 1992 and 1993. For the first time, the telecommunication operators in this group were represented not by their government affairs personnel, but directly by the heads of the companies. A high-ranking Commission official explains, "essentially, we let the operators decide and they then started driving the process through their political connections."[27] In the eyes of many observers, the group was crucial for advancing on European liberalization. The result of this consultation process, known as the Bangemann Report, was submitted to the European Council in Corfu in 1994 as the opinion of European operators and underlined the need to speed up the process of liberalization.[28]

The transition from public companies embedded in national regulatory transitions to competitive European telecom firms was particularly visible at the European level and was manifested in the lobbying stances of the European Telecommunication Network Operators' Association (ETNO). ETNO was founded in 1992 in response to the internal liberalization efforts of the Commission. However, initial activities were difficult. European network operators had been exposed to different regulatory traditions and the majority of them were suspicious of anything threatening their home market control. Despite the formation of ETNO, operators could not agree on a common approach to market opening. "1992 was too early," explains one of the founding fathers.

> The divergence between the European operators was too great. There was no ideational base for a good cooperative effort to develop common viewpoints and goals.[29]

As a consequence, "ETNO was more protective in its approach in the beginning."[30] Despite the activities of some liberal-minded operators, the EU telecom lobby as a whole was quite protectionist in the early 1990s.

Once operators and regulators had been separated, several of the large operators started realizing that the existing close government tutelage was disadvantageous to their new and ambitious commercial strategies. A government-owned company, for example, cannot establish operations abroad in most countries.

---

27. Interview with a Commission representative in Brussels, 10 September 2003.
28. Consultation later included user companies and other telecommunication companies as well. The consultation process is summarized in European Commission, *European Governance.*
29. Interview in Brussels, 3 September 2003.
30. Interview in Brussels, 14 February 2003.

Organizations like France Télécom started pursuing the self-interest of commercial autonomy. In exchange, they were ready to give up their monopoly over service provision. Of course, at the time, they did not know what that would actually mean. In 1993, we made the compromise to open up the monopoly in 1998 only. And everybody thought, "five years is a long time."[31]

Fundamentally, most European operators were torn between the desire to develop their commercial autonomy and the desire to receive privileged treatment. Even American observers confirm: "Everybody is in favor of national treatment."[32] However, privileged national treatment is not always politically feasible, as telecom companies learned in the 1990s.

The reorientation of these operators toward the pursuit of commercial autonomy was facilitated by the boom in the telecommunication industry at the time. Against the background of growth and expansion of the industry, "every company wanted to become a European or a global leader in a certain number of segments," a business representative emphasized.[33]

It happened during the time of the internet bubble. New markets were potential jackpots. All analysts were advising to go into it. Billions were invested in nothing.[34]

Technological change and the growth potential of the industry at the time provided important incentives for European operators to assume their new roles as competitive players in the future European and global markets.

Regional Bells

For the Regional Bells in the United States, a similar transformation happened in the context of the Federal Telecom Act in the mid-1990s. Even though the divestiture of AT&T is often cited as the event that ended monopoly service in the United States, it had only applied to the long-distance market. The Telecom Act of 1996 (TA96), by contrast, removed regulatory barriers between the provision of local and long-distance telephone service, and between cable television and telephone service. In Washington D.C., there was a sense that the new law "was the [telecom] industry equiv-

---

31. Interview with a Commission representative in Brussels, 10 September 2003.
32. Interview with a business representative in Washington, D.C., 8 April 2003.
33. Interview with a European network operator, 3 July 2003.
34. Interview with a business representative in Brussels, 13 November 2002.

alent of the Berlin Wall being broken down."[35] For the Regional Bells and
for the basic telecom negotiations in Geneva, TA96 had two effects: first, it
accelerated the internationalization strategies of the Regional Bells; second, it provided a framework through which RBOCs were willing to consider international liberalization while still preserving their incumbent
interests. Let us consider these two points in turn.

The WTO negotiations on basic telecommunications and the domestic
telecom reform in the United States together created an atmosphere
where Regional Bell operators started anticipating a new regulatory context and preparing international commercial strategies. As Robert Crandall points out, the U.S. telephone companies were among the most
aggressive of those investing in foreign operations in the 1990s.[36] The
Regional Bells, in particular, started major foreign investments in New
Zealand, Australia, Mexico, Chile, and Eastern Europe. Unlike U.S. long-
distance carriers, the Regional Bells did not worry about being able to deliver end-to-end international phone calls through elaborate networks, but
rather about protecting and expanding their investments. "We were very
much getting into markets around the world, but we wanted to have clear
rules in those markets," explains a representative.[37]

One might assume that internationalization through foreign direct investment led the RBOCs to support market opening more generally. Yet
they mainly invested in incumbent telephone operators abroad, which
were in a similar position to that of the RBOCs in the United States. The
lack of competition in those countries tended to drive up margins for the
operators they had a share in. A WTO agreement, Cowhey and Richards
argue, was likely to expand the number of competitors in those markets
and reduce their profitability.[38] According to this calculation, the RBOCs
should simply have been opposed to the GBT negotiations.

However, this was not the case. Especially NYNEX, which had the most
extensive network of foreign investment, but also SBC (formerly Southwestern Bell) and Bell South, supported the WTO liberalization actively.[39]
Yet this does not mean that these companies enthusiastically abandoned
their monopoly rights.

35. Robert Mayer, senior manager of Deloitte Touche, quoted in *Washington Post,* 2 February 1996, p. A15.
36. Crandall, "Telecom Mergers and Joint Ventures in an Era of Liberalization," 112.
37. Interview in Washington, D.C., 25 June 2002.
38. Cowhey and Richards, "Deregulating and Liberalizing the North American Telecommunications Market," 104.
39. Interview in Washington, D.C., June 2003.

> The word comes down that there will be competition and you absolutely
> hate it. . . . When you get right down to it, the thought of competition is a
> scary thing. But with time, you get over it.[40]

Most importantly, reservations about liberalization got attached to the
ways in which liberalization was pursued. In this context, the domestic regulatory negotiations turned out to be crucial for explaining the international expectations of U.S. companies. In fact, the division between
Regional Bells and U.S. long-distance companies was copied from TA96
into the Reference Paper in the NGBT talks. On the domestic front, the
question was when and how to introduce competition into local markets.
The compromise in TA96 was to grant the RBOCs entry into the long-
distance market in return for opening their networks to local service competition. The bargain was bound by a "checklist" of interconnection obligations that aimed at reducing the incumbents' ability to drive potential
competitors out of the market. This domestic agreement provided the blueprint for the regulatory framework suggested by the Reference Paper.[41]

Moreover, the Reference Paper not only replicated some of the framework enshrined domestically in the TA96, it also brought the domestic division between network owners and competitors to the international front.
The central interest of the regional operators was to follow up on their often extensive foreign investment. "When we first started talking about the
Reference Paper, we were amazed," a former representative remembers,
adding "it seemed like a real lever."[42] United States incumbents agreed
with their competitors on the need for competitive safeguards, but they did
not agree on the scope of the Reference Paper and how it might be interpreted. A representative of USTR explains, "this was all the more the case
since the Reference Paper has implications for offensive market entry, but
also for the structure of the domestic market."[43] The central issue revolved
around the cost-orientation of settlement rates. How much did it actually
cost to transmit a phone call? The answer fundamentally depended on
whether you included or excluded the costs of building a network.

> AT&T believes that you shouldn't reimburse an operator for the costs as-
> sociated with building a network. But if nobody has an incentive to build a
> network, then they won't have any access to it.[44]

40. Interview with a business representative in Washington, D.C., 8 April 2003.
41. Hoekman and Kostecki, *Political Economy of the World Trading System*, 261.
42. Interview in Washington, D.C., 25 June 2002.
43. Interview in Washington, D.C., 27 June 2002.
44. Ibid.

Yet in the eyes of competitors, there was more to the position of the RBOCs than the protection of their previous investments. This is all the more evident when one considers the increasing internationalization of companies like NYNEX. As a competitor underlines,

> [They] send international long-distance calls, lease lines, and invest overseas. So [their policy preferences] should be the same as ours. But a lot of pro-competitive actions that we want the U.S. government to enforce, they don't want. Why is that? Because they have decided that you need to protect the incumbents in general, because it supports their views here in Washington. . . . In my view, they have made a fundamental company decision to protect their incumbent business and in order to do that, they decided to not go after incumbents overseas.[45]

The position of the U.S. Regional Bells was shaped by their desire to move into international markets, but also by their interests as incumbent operators in the domestic market in the United States. The challenge for a company like NYNEX was to be sufficiently open to liberalization to further its international objectives and to participate in the making of the new framework, while at the same time preventing alterations in the regulatory details that reinforced its domestic position. As for European network operators, the transformation of the regulatory context and consequent changes in the nature of these economic actors profoundly affected their policy stance on multilateral liberalization. Incumbent operators defended positions that were quite different from competitive service providers, despite comparable foreign direct investment and international activities that might benefit from a WTO agreement. Understanding the position of a company like NYNEX thus requires understanding the deep ambivalence that came from its double strategy of being both an incumbent and a global competitor in mid-1990s.

Cognitive Shifts: From Interconnection to Trade

Despite the companies' international operations, lobbying on multilateral telecom liberalization developed only slowly. Especially in the early 1990s, companies did not even feel that multilateral trade talks were relevant to their activities, because telecom exchanges had previously been organized in the form of interconnection agreements through the cooperative framework of the ITU. A major shift in the position of companies occurred when

---

45. Interview in Washington, D.C., 24 June 2002.

they started to reframe their international activities in terms of trade. Adapting to this logic, however, was not always easy, and only happened in response to pressure from users, competitors, and governments.

Learning Trade

The universe of trade policy was foreign to the technical governance of telecommunication services. Even in the beginning of the 1990s, halfway through the Uruguay Round where services were intensively negotiated, many companies were not well informed about GATT issues and international commerce in general. This was true even for competitive service providers in the United States. A large part of the U.S. government's effort went into "trying to inform them about why we thought this was a good idea."[46] For companies, the fundamental issue was simply to understand what was going on and whether this was important enough to invest their time and resources.

> So we actually went out and took some initiative to ask what this was about. I mean, we didn't even know what the GATT was until the early 1990s.[47]

The lack of knowledge was striking on both sides. Most trade representatives had never worked on telecommunications, and most telecom people had never worked on trade.

> We were extremely concerned about the negotiations, especially when we realized that some of the trade people did not know what a common carrier was.[48]

One or other aspect of the issues was new to each of the participants, whether governments or companies. Among U.S. companies that had chosen to follow the early developments, there was a sense that the ambitions of the trade agenda were ill-matched with the realities of telecom services. The abandonment of bilateral agreements and the ideas enshrined in the MFN principle seemed quite threatening.

> When we first read a draft version of the GATS, we felt that USTR could just trade off our entire business against another service or agriculture.[49]

46. Interview with a U.S. government representative, Washington, D.C., 20 June 2003.
47. Interview, 2 July 2003.
48. Ibid.
49. Ibid.

Yet even the most interested telecommunication companies only realized the implications of the Uruguay Round when it was close to being completed. Only AT&T, MCI, and Sprint followed developments already in the late phase of the Uruguay Round, as an observer confirms.

> They were following it pretty closely. I am not sure how well they followed it, but they certainly followed it closely . . . but without necessarily understanding all of the implications of what they were doing.[50]

The issues were highly technical legal ones, and remained obscure to most other telecommunication companies. Quite often, it was the trade representatives of the respective governments who tried to bring businesses into the process. A U.S. official explains with reference to telecom services, "we basically had to start at square one and explain trade terminology to them."[51] Similarly, the European Commission sought to work with business representatives in Europe, but initial contacts were rather frustrating. A Commission official remembers that business contacts were "remarkably uninterested in the whole process."[52] In the early 1990s, several of the European companies did not imagine the impact the WTO negotiations would have. Even though sector-specific negotiations had been going on since 1994, and despite the fact that value-added services had even been opened to competition by the end of the Uruguay Round, many companies affected by the changes were not engaged in the process. As a representative of a former European monopoly recalls,

> I have to admit, I only discovered the WTO at the margin. Initially, people considered the WTO to be something quite abstract: "value-added," "basic services" . . . ? In most countries, you didn't really have a realization that there was a new reality . . . that you couldn't do anything anymore without paying attention to the WTO.[53]

At the time, international telephony was discussed through negotiation of interconnection modalities in the ITU. For many providers, the WTO only entered the picture once it examined an issue traditionally dealt with by the ITU: accounting rates. Overall in Europe, companies started orga-

---

50. Interview with a Commission official, Brussels, 3 September 2003.
51. Interview, Washington, D.C., 18 June 2003.
52. Interview with a representative of the European Commission in Brussels, 3 September 2003.
53. Interview with a European business representative, 3 July 2003.

nizing only after the failure of negotiations in 1996, when the GBT talks started getting serious.

During the 1996–97 negotiations, companies got more used to the basic concepts of trade negotiations, but generally the procedures and terminology remained confusing. A U.S. company representative who participated very actively in Geneva explains:

> Nobody knew how to read a schedule of commitments. We even had people think that ". . . none . . . none . . . none" meant that "none" had market access.[54]

Naturally, companies did not have the opportunity to ask all the questions that were one their minds, especially if they were following a trade-related meeting in Geneva with an already tight schedule.

> We developed a sort of code to talk to one another while government representatives where in the room. We made sure we would start our phrases by saying "Just to review a little bit what has been said . . ." so that everybody understood what was going on.[55]

Despite these difficulties, most large European operators agree that from 1996 onward, "there was such an empowerment of the WTO that many companies discovered its importance."[56] The same is true for U.S. companies. Within only two to three years, the stakes had become clear and salient to almost everybody.

Jumping on a Moving Train

It is important to note, however, that the reframing of international telecommunication business in terms of trade was a collective process. Each participating company studied the behavior of other actors in order to best anticipate what the most useful behavior might be. For some companies, the rationale for supporting liberalization was ideological. It was tied to a larger reflection about competition and access, at least at a rhetorical level. A company representative explains,

> MCI would like to think that it created competition . . . in the world of telecommunication services. So the view was always: competition is good

---

54. "None" means the opposite: it answers questions about remaining market access restrictions. Interview with a U.S. business representative, Washington, D.C., 2 July 2003.
55. Ibid.
56. Interview with the representative of a European network provider, 3 July 2003.

and incumbents should be denied to prevent competitors from entry. That mantra has definitely carried over to [its] global vision of trade.[57]

Unlike the U.S. government and the FCC, U.S. carriers were not even sure about the monetary benefits of a WTO agreement. It is true that under the accounting rate system, the net settlement payments U.S. carriers made to other countries continued to rise to $5.4 billion in 1995 and to $6 billion in 1996. However, the costs of these payments were born by the telephone users, not the companies. In fact, the biggest profits for U.S. carriers still came from providing international telephone services under the traditional framework, in spite of the U.S. deficit.

> Thus, a [company like] AT&T wanted to expand globally if it could win effective competitive opportunities in the domestic market of foreign countries, but it was not sure that it had an interest in changing the basic rules for providing international telephone services between countries.[58]

What then explains the broad support of the telecom companies for the WTO liberalization project? To some degree, their mobilization has to be understood as an attempt to jump on a train that had visibly started moving. User groups and financial service companies working through the USCSI had advanced the issue of service trade liberalization to a point where telecom companies started perceiving it as inevitable. A member of the service lobby remembers that other companies joined despite the fact that they were not sure about the benefits of free service trade.

> A lot of companies were skeptical. They were wondering what we were doing, thinking that there were some ulterior motives behind our plans. . . . But they joined us because they wanted to take part in a process they were afraid of at least to control where it was going.[59]

A similar development happened in the USCIB, which turned out to be very important for lobbying efforts on sectoral telecommunication talks in the WTO. As negotiations progressed, RBOCs got increasingly involved.

> Our telecoms committee was driven by the business user community. . . . As we became successful, the incumbents realized that they had a stake, so they began to emerge and they all joined us, because we were seen as the organization that drove telecom liberalization.[60]

57. Interview with a U.S. business representative in Washington, D.C., June 2003.
58. Cowhey and Richards, "Dialing for Dollars," 156.
59. Interview with a member of the association in Washington, D.C., 8 April 2003.
60. Interview with a U.S. business representative, New York, 2 April 2003.

Embracing trade as the new frame of reference happened because telecom companies realized that if they were not prepared to participate in the reshaping of their regulatory framework, the world would move on without them. Similar anticipative behavior might even explain why internationalization became a major theme for telecom companies in both the United States and Europe through the 1990s. Even though "they did not earn their largest profit margins by executing global strategies, . . . big phone companies believed that user needs would force them to go global."[61] In essence, the real driving forces behind liberalization were governments and user firms. Telecom companies eventually ended up supporting the new design with the same enthusiasm, essentially because they felt that they needed to seize these new opportunities in order to gain a competitive advantage in the future global market.[62] The reframing of international telecom operations as trade and no longer as interconnection and the joint provision of services had happened as a result of business-government and business-business interactions.

Strategic Differences: National and Multilevel Games

Nonetheless, the ways in which telecom companies pursued their policy preferences were quite different in the United States and the European Union. To begin with, the aggregation of individual firm positions was more complex in the European Union. While U.S. companies could lobby their government directly and insist on the need for reciprocal market access, EU companies would have had to operate through a European association in order to work effectively with the European Commission. Expressing an opinion which diverged from the collective stance of the relevant association, however, was difficult for an individual firm. Instead, such differences were pursued not as "industry interests" but as "national interests" between member states and the European Commission. In order to overcome these disputes, the European Commission therefore tied the negotiations over internal liberalization to the WTO negotiations. Once European Union—wide liberalization was put into place, this strategy made it politically infeasible for European operators to lobby for national protection. Companies who wanted to continue participating in the

---

61. Cowhey and Richards, "Dialing for Dollars," 156.

62. U.S. industry representatives actually greeted the negotiating team at a briefing session two days before the conclusion with signs reading "Wildly Enthusiastic." Sherman, "Wildly Enthusiastic."

WTO talks had to accept aggregating their preferences through the European association ETNO, which effectively meant embracing multilateral liberalization.

Lobbying by U.S. Firms for Immediate Concerns

Business-government relations have a long tradition in the United States, which makes it easy for companies to lobby for their immediate concerns. While the most active U.S. companies formed an industry group that followed the U.S. delegation to Geneva and gave regular feedback late in the Uruguay negotiations and between 1994 and 1997, there was no industry presence on the European side that directly followed the negotiations.[63] To some degree, the activities of individual U.S. firms are oriented by the concrete opportunities the U.S. government provides for their participation.

> If you are a significant American company, a lot of times the government might ask you to be part of the delegation. Then you are more likely to say yes, because they asked you to be there.[64]

Companies do not need to operate through trade associations to express their demands. In fact, beyond the activities of associations based on broad membership like the USCSI and the USCIB, the activities of more specific sectoral associations are negligible. To be sure, the activities of CompTel, the association of competitive telecom companies, are valuable to AT&T and MCI. Still, many feel that CompTel simply reflects these two companies' views behind the shield of an association name. Unlike Europe, where government representative consult mainly with associations, U.S. negotiators talk about "speaking with the companies."[65] These direct contacts enable firms to put their hesitations and fears about liberalization into very concrete policy stances. As a consequence, demands for reciprocity and pro-competitive safeguards have become intimately tied to the U.S. negotiation position.

According to U.S. service providers, their insistence on the need for reciprocity explains the U.S. position at the end of the Uruguay Round, most importantly the division between value-added and basic services:

> Our main concern was to try and get basic telecom services separated out of the Uruguay Round. We felt that there were no offers whatsoever com-

63. Interview with the chair of the U.S. industry group.
64. Interview with a U.S. network operator, Washington, D.C., 25 June 2003.
65. Interviews in Washington, D.C., 16 and 20 June 2003.

ing from abroad, and we were afraid of the consequences of opening our markets without getting anything in return. Most people don't remember anymore that the separation of basic telecoms from the advanced services happened because companies escalated the issue: we made the free rider problem a real urgency.[66]

Pressure by U.S. carriers late in the Uruguay Round was indeed intense.[67] When discussions stalled over basic services, the United States declared that it would not permit foreign firms equal rights in the United States if American firms did not have the same rights elsewhere. USTR started undertaking a series of bilateral and plurilateral negotiations, first with the United Kingdom and then with other countries, to find alternatives to a GATS agreement on basic telecommunications.

Seeing its negotiating position undermined, the European Community objected vehemently. More importantly, though, the United States also felt that bilateral solutions could not achieve as much as a comprehensive WTO agreement, because of the risk of "one-way bypassing."[68] Within the WTO, the risk of one-way bypassing remained, but it was possible to achieve a more global solution if all countries agreed to apply the same regime.

This rationale made it crucial for the United States to achieve a large number of commitments from other countries. In all government agencies, officials underline how much is at stake in a multilateral agreement based on MFN.

> You open your market to everybody who has signed the agreement, no matter how open their markets are. This lack of reciprocity leaves a large potential for free riders, so an essential component of the U.S.'s position throughout the negotiations was to achieve a critical mass of countries making serious commitments.[69]

The fear of a MFN regime with many free riders is particularly accentuated under the GATS, because countries have no obligation to open up anything they do not want. In other words, MFN has to be extended to all

---

66. Interview with a U.S. company representative, Washington, D.C., 2 July 2003.

67. Cowhey and Aronson, *Managing the World Economy,* 189.

68. This concept is based on the idea that the United States and Mexico, for instance, have an open market with low international settlement rates. Mexico, however, might then route South American calls to the United States through Mexico and collect the settlement payment from South American carriers for these calls. For a discussion, see Cowhey and Richards, "Deregulating and Liberalizing."

69. Interviews in Washington, D.C., 5 June, 18 June, 27 June, 2 July 2003.

parties, regardless of the content and timing of their market-opening schedules. While the GATT offers measures like antidumping to act against unfair competition, comparable tools available in theory under the GATS are very difficult to put into practice. American firms and the U.S. government alike confirmed that the idea of a "critical mass" of countries submitting acceptable schedules was their main concern through the negotiations. Moreover, the constitutional separation between the administration, which negotiated, and Congress, which had to authorize and ratify the agreement, underlined the need for this "critical mass." USTR needed a "big deal" to assure congressional backing, since a small deal would not protect it against the entrenched congressional skeptics who are always opposed to opening local markets to foreign competitors.[70]

With the deadline approaching in April, the feeling predominated that such a mass had not been achieved. Yet the U.S. government was divided over the best possible position. While many cautioned against an insufficient agreement, USTR, like all other international negotiators, also had the self-interest of achieving a successful conclusion. The straw that broke the camel's back then turned out to be the previously somewhat neglected issue of satellite transmission, again brought forward by U.S. industry.

> One has to understand that satellites only came to these negotiations relatively late. Before, it had been more traditional telecom companies. When they looked at the offer at that time, they could not find the word "satellite" anywhere. It is true that the framework was to be independent of the technology used, but the word "wireless" appeared very often.[71]

Once U.S. satellite companies started investigating the issue, they became very concerned about the implications of a basic telecom agreement for their international telephony. Like the other international providers, they were worried that their markets would be opened through the U.S. offer, while other countries could then argue that they had never made a commitment on satellite transmission specifically. In an effort to clarify the issue and the wording of the national schedules, the U.S. satellite industry organized a series of meetings, not only with its own delegation, but even with the WTO Secretariat in Geneva, which was probably "the first time ever such a meeting took place."[72]

70. Petrazzini, *Global Telecom Talks,* 13; Cowhey and Richards, "Dialing for Dollars," 158.
71. Interview with a U.S. company representative, Washington, D.C., 2 July 2003.
72. Ibid.

These new concerns contributed to the 1996 deadlock. The United States was discontented with the offer from the other Quad countries, but above all with the absence of commitments from developing Asian economies such as Indonesia and Malaysia. In reaction to what it deemed an insufficient number of commitments, the United States withdrew its satellite offer. The deal collapsed.

The United States asserted that the failure was due to the limited EU and Asian offers. Represented by its head negotiator Sir Leon Brittan, the European Union argued that the United States had walked away from the deal because of narrow domestic political interests. To them, it seemed as if U.S. satellite service firms such as Motorola or Odyssey had calculated that they would be better off without a deal, handicapping foreign companies such as the British ICO Global Communications.[73] Indeed, five major U.S. satellite companies wrote to the FCC in late April urging the United States to withdraw its offer.[74] The failure of the talks in April 1996 is therefore referred to as the satellite issue, or even the Motorola issue, much to the dislike of the company in question. An observer tells the following anecdote.

> On a flight from Geneva back to the U.S. after the negotiations blew up, the government affairs representative of Motorola sat next to the representative of AT&T. She told him that the company board was very upset with the outcome of negotiations, because the newspaper presented the clash to be Motorola's fault. As a consequence of such negative newspaper attention, she almost got fired.[75]

However, reducing the U.S. withdrawal of its offer to the satellite issue alone is somewhat oversimplified. The United States argued that it had followed a broader reasoning: companies in countries with high barriers might buy a piece of other global satellite systems, without simultaneously opening their own markets. Only about ten participants had guaranteed U.S. access to their own satellite markets.[76] Again, the issue was one of reciprocity and a critical mass, and the satellite companies had not been the only ones to pressure the U.S. government to refuse an agreement. AT&T

73. Cf. Petrazzini, *Global Telecom Talks*, 7.

74. Frances Williams and Guy de Jonquières, "WTO Telecom Talks Stall over Satellites," *Financial Times*, 27 April 1996, p. 2.

75. Interview with an observer, 25 October 2002.

76. Frances Williams, "U.S. Keeps Rest of World Hanging on Line," *Financial Times*, 2 May 1996, p. 2.

had also argued in late April that it might be advisable to downgrade the U.S. offer unless the talks yielded improved market access abroad, notably by refusing to guarantee foreign competitors the right to operate international services from the United States. AT&T confirmed that it was in favor of an accord, "but it would rather have no agreement at all than a mediocre agreement."[77] In the European Union's view, the pressure on the U.S. delegation from its companies was considerable. "They are playing hardball and I am not sure they will be able to compromise," commented an EU Commission official a few days before the deadline.[78]

To all observers, the failure in April 1996 can be traced back to the policy demands of U.S. industry. The direct contacts between business representatives and the U.S. negotiating team are thus crucial in explaining the evolution of the U.S. position during the negotiations. Domestic interests and company lobbying mattered. What is noteworthy about this apparently trivial observation is that the situation was considerably different on the European side.

Multilevel Games in the European Union

In the European Union, firms lobbying on WTO trade negotiations are faced with a challenging multilevel system of decision-making. On the governmental side, telecom companies have influential ties with their national governments, which decide on the negotiation mandate and ratify agreements; but they also need to interact with the European Commission, which negotiates for the member states in Geneva. On the associational side, this means that they can pursue some of their interests nationally, but they also have to aggregate their preferences into a common European stance, if they want to work closely with the European Commission through a European association. As a result of this aggregation process and the difficult requirements of the multilevel policy process, firms adapt their preferences considerably to the position of the governmental negotiator, not the other way around as in the United States.

Concerning the evolution of the policy demands of European operators, the multilevel structure has two effects. First, the aggregation work done by the European association ETNO implies a reorientation towards pan-European policy stances. Second, the competence struggle between the

---

77. Quoted in Guy de Jonquières, "WTO Needs Telecom Deals for Its Credibility: U.S. Has Thrown Down the Gauntlet," *Financial Times,* 18 March 1996.

78. Quoted in Frances Williams, "U.S. Balks at Signing Global Deal on Telecoms: EU Warns Satellite Service Plan Could Break Up Talks," *Financial Times,* 29 April 1996, p. 1.

European Commission and the member states led the Commission to tie internal liberalization to WTO liberalization. This strategy makes protectionist trade policy demands politically infeasible.

Let us begin by considering the aggregation of preferences across the European Union. While the U.S. administration works predominantly with individual firms, the European Commission, for its part, rarely contacts individual businesses. Consultation happens "first and foremost with the associations."[79] EU telecom companies agree that associations, ESF and ETNO, are the most important means of voicing their concerns about GATS-related issues.[80] During the GBT talks, ETNO was the only telecom company representation that closely followed the negotiations, despite the fact that it represented traditionally public network operators. However, activities on WTO-related issues only started in the mid-1990s. After some initial position papers, a working group on WTO affairs was established within ETNO and closely followed the GBT talks during its final phase from about 1995 to 1997. The most active members were those operators that already had experience with liberalization or that simply were large enough to be interested in foreign market access: British Telecom, France Télécom, Deutsche Telekom, Telia, and Telefónica.

Smaller operators followed and supported the working group's activities, but in some cases for convenience only. Mobilizing the resources to lobby individually was often not considered worth the effort, all the more since ETNO was seemingly doing a good job. As the representative of a smaller European operator explains, "I don't really work on WTO affairs; I only participate in the working group of ETNO. We just try to follow what is going on." When asked if the operator was for or against liberalization at the time, he explained that they did not have a position: "Even in 1996, the WTO was not an important issue for us."[81] Other smaller operators stress that the WTO in and of itself was not of real importance to them in the 1990s, but that they nonetheless chose to participate in ETNO's working group.[82] It is thus no surprise that a member of ETNO describes the working group as a night train: "there was a locomotive, some service cars, and many sleeping cars."[83]

Coordinating their political activities through ETNO did not mean that

79. Interview in Brussels, 21 October 2002.
80. Pointed out by all EU companies interviewed.
81. Telephone interview, 22 October 2003.
82. E-mail exchange with a company representative, 28 October 2003.
83. Interview in Brussels, 3 September 2003.

European companies were not interested in or even opposed to the GBT talks. On the contrary, as the representative of an operator that had started to invest heavily abroad in the 1990s explained,

> In a way, the WTO was a very welcome way to seize this opportunity more fully. But the main initiative was the investment, not the political representation. Of course, you always have to do a little bit of everything. In business, I think you first try to open up new markets and then you start thinking about politics. For us, the WTO was an opportunity to ensure that what we have put in place would continue in an adequate political framework. Once you get into the market, you start worrying about the conditions.[84]

The political engagement of these companies through ETNO was also a reaction to solicitation by the European Commission, which was looking for company support but initially got feedback only from American firms:

> At the time, we were in regular contact with U.S. companies who were seeking out our views on trade talks. So we figured out what the interests of U.S. companies were and extrapolated from there.[85]

Frustrated by the lack of mobilization on the part of European companies, the Commission actively promoted the work of EU associations on the WTO talks. In the beginning, European operators did not really understand why they should work closely with the Commission, since they already had good contacts with national governments. Eventually, they simply followed both avenues.

> We had so many conversations with the Commission and national governments. At the time, it wasn't very clear who was responsible for the issue.[86]

As a matter of fact, the shared competency between the European Commission and the member states was quite a challenge for the governments as well and was reflected in the size of the EU delegation. Apart from five to six representatives of the Commission, there were at least two representatives of each member state: the delegation quickly grew to about forty people. Despite an agreed code of conduct, the competence division often led to confusion.

84. E-mail exchange with a business representative, 28 October 2003.
85. Interview with a representative from the European Commission in Brussels, 3 September 2003.
86. Interview with a business representative in Brussels, 3 September 2003.

We didn't know very well what was within Community competence and what was within the competence of the member states. When the meetings were well prepared, there was no problem. But when the objective was not clear or when the Commission went beyond its mandate, it became much more complicated. In the same meeting, you would have first the EU and then the member states speak up, and they did not say the same thing. This was not the general rule, but it happened.[87]

Members of the U.S. delegation confirm this impression:

We were constantly observing that. Before every meeting, the EU delegation met in the morning in order to try a hammer out a position. If they weren't successful, the meeting we had with them afterwards would be like treading water.[88]

Agreement among European member states was a necessary prerequisite for coherent international negotiations. Although the European Commission did not pressure its member states into a particular set of concessions, much of the elaboration of how basic telecom service provision should be understood happened within these forums.[89]

Despite the agreement on the overall objectives of negotiations, the most important challenge for the European delegation was to coordinate policy preferences between the member governments and the European Commission. Negotiations in the WTO were critical for both the Commission and the member governments, especially because the internal process was still underway. Early in the process of WTO negotiations, there was therefore a clear understanding that "external negotiations cannot proceed faster than the internal process."[90] The EU negotiation position in the WTO telecom talks was thus based on a two-tiered consensus, as Holmes and Young note: "The external negotiation position would be based on the agreed internal framework, and the internal framework had been agreed unanimously."[91] During the entire period of the NGBT and the GBT negotiations, services remained under shared competence, so

---

87. Interview with a government representative of an EU member state, 9 December 2002
88. Interviews, 19 February 2003 in Brussels and 5 June and 18 June 2003 in Washington, D.C.; interview, 18 June 2003 (quoted).
89. Niemann, "Between Communicative Action and Strategic Action"
90. European Commission, "Report by the Commission on the GATS Negotiations on 'Basic' Telecommunications," Commission DG XIII A 6, 16 November (Brussels, 1994); European Council, "Council Resolution of 18 September 1995 on the Implementation of the Future Regulatory Framework for Telecommunications," 95/C 258/01, *Official Journal of the European Communities*, 3 October (Brussels, 1995).
91. Holmes and Young, "Liberalizing and Reregulating Telecommunications," 139.

that offers and statements were authored jointly by the European Commission and the member states.

The initial EU offer presented to the NGBT in October 1995 reflected this division.[92] It was based on the agreed internal framework and illustrated the willingness of the EU member countries to bind their internal liberalization to the regime of the GATS. The central objective was securing "effective and comparable" market access in third countries, but the markets of Quad countries were a priority, in particular national ownership restrictions in the United States.[93] Yet beyond these overarching principles, the EU offer looked like a list of the individual countries' offers. Because of the divergent situations in EU member states, the countries that had been granted an extended deadline for internal liberalization (Ireland, Spain, Portugal, and Greece) demanded exceptions for national ownership restrictions and transition periods. On behalf of the French and Belgian governments, the offer furthermore specified that audiovisual services were not included in "basic telecommunication services." Austria, Denmark, Finland, Germany, the Netherlands, Sweden, and the United Kingdom made no reservations. The Italian government was the only EU country not to seek to exempt the ownership restrictions it had in place.

The divergent standpoints of the European Commission and some of its member states contributed to the deadlock of April 1996. Part of the U.S. discontent was directed at the EU offers in particular. The United States had submitted an improved offer in February 1996 and considered that the European Union should do likewise. Internally, the Commission sought to convince the Belgian, French, Italian, Portuguese, and Spanish governments to withdraw their foreign ownership restrictions; the Spanish government to accelerate liberalization; and the Belgian government to abandon certain requirements for granting radio licenses.[94] These countries refused, accusing the Commission of wanting to give ground before it was sure of receiving anything in return—the opposite of the U.S. strategy, which had made it clear that its offer was conditional. Other WTO members tried to schedule improved offers by the proposed deadline, with limited success. By 30 April 1996, the European Union could do nothing but restate its original offer.

In the second round of talks from 1996 to 1997, the Commission relied

92. European Commission and the Member States, "Draft Offer on Basic Telecommunications," S/NGBT/W/12/Add. 100, 16 October (Brussels, 1995).

93. Bronckers and Larouche, "Telecommunication Services and the World Trade Organisation."

94. Holmes and Young, "Liberalizing and Reregulating Telecommunications."

on its role in merger policy and its oversight of the implementation of national transition deadlines. When Telefónica tried to join the Dutch-Swedish-Alliance Unisource, the Commission agreed on condition that Spain drop its foreign ownership restrictions and accept a transition period for full liberalization of only eleven months.[95] It was able to exert similar pressures on Germany and France in the context of the Global One Alliance,[96] which it used to stress that liberalization—both internally and externally—was to the advantage of telecom providers, which could seize these historic new opportunities.

> In that sense, France has been liberalized in order to promote France Télécom and not the other way around. The same was true for Germany. Liberalization did not happen due to an abstract belief.[97]

The Commission also used its power to approve specific durations of transition periods for internal liberalization, granted in March 1996, to work toward improved WTO offers from countries that had previously requested exceptions. Furthermore, the Commission persuaded Belgium to reformulate its reservations about the public ownership of Belgacom as a general statement that public ownership did not constitute a market access barrier.[98] The new EU offer was put on the table on 12 November 1996 and, together with the U.S. offer, reinvigorated the negotiations.

The evolution of the EU delegation's position clearly depended to a much larger degree on the coordination of the two EU levels of governance than on lobbying by European telecom operators. This becomes all the more evident when one considers the European stance toward the Reference Paper. An important point of contention between incumbents and competitors in the United States, the Reference Paper did not inspire nearly so much discussion among European operators. This is surprising, since European officials stress that European companies "were initially very much opposed to the Reference Paper," adding "they did not want pro-competitive regulation."[99] Still, it was again the European Commission and the member states, not the companies, that mildly confronted each other over the drafting of the document.

95. European Commission, Competition Ruling IP/96/1231, 20 December (Brussels, 1996).

96. Borrmann, "Corporate Strategies in the Telecommunciations Sector in an Environment of Continuing Liberalization."

97. Interview with a Commission official in Brussels, 10 September 2003.

98. Holmes and Young, "Liberalizing and Reregulating Telecommunications."

99. Interviews with negotiators from the EU delegation, Paris, 15 February 2007.

"By the time the member states got introduced to the Reference Paper," remembers a member state representative, "it had already been under discussion for three or four months."[100] In fact, the European Commission and Japan had begun to work informally with the United States on the drafting of the Reference Paper, but none of the countries wanted to flag this as its initiative.[101] The first time the Commission's delegation introduced the draft to the member states it was therefore done in a somewhat unusual way, as a member state official recalls.

> We weren't even told that it was being discussed. The Commission negotiator, Karl-Friedrich Falkenberg, suddenly brought it to a meeting and said "Oh, look what I found just lying around on a street corner."[102]

Despite these initial frictions, the European Communities quite liked the Reference Paper, because it was a way of securing an agreement on the European Union's type of regulatory vision at the multilateral level. A representative of a European network operator who was involved at the time states that the Reference Paper had not been modified significantly by EU industry.

> The Commission quickly realized that it wanted to give an official format to the framework that allowed for European liberalization. So it needed to preserve the coherence of this framework at the time the rules were debated globally.[103]

The defense of the framework of the EU directive on interconnection was a preoccupation of the European Commission, all the more since European industry became slowly more comfortable with the Reference Paper or at least did not exert pressure against it.

Should we conclude from this that European companies were altogether absent from the WTO negotiations? No, but their mobilization crucially depended on the development of internal liberalization. The Commission strategy of tying the two projects together thus had a lasting effect on the policy demands expressed by European firms. Most immediately, the conjunction of dates was central. In 1993 and 1994, the Council unanimously adopted two resolutions establishing the liberalization framework and set-

---

100. Interview, 4 October 2003.
101. Interview with representatives from the European Commission in Paris, 15 February 2007.
102. Interview with an official from an EU member state, 4 October 2003.
103. Interview, 3 July 2004.

ting a deadline of 1 January 1998, with longer transition periods for Greece, Portugal, Spain, and Ireland.[104] A member of the WTO working group of ETNO affirms:

> The date: 1 January 1998! That's when we knew liberalization would really happen. When we knew what would come, it became possible to promote a common platform concerning our goals for the international liberalization of telecommunications.[105]

Late in the GBT negotiations, large European operators were especially enthusiastic about WTO talks, but all national operators supported the EU negotiating position. They were confident in their own markets and they wanted to expand. With the announcement of the 1998 date for European Union—wide network liberalization, ETNO started communicating its common views on WTO affairs to the European Commission, which was very responsive. A member of ETNO remembers:

> We had a good working relationship with the Commission, because there was no opposition on this issue. The Commission works for Europe, and we work for Europe. Our objectives are the same. This is not always the case in commercial issues, where there may be conflicts between small and large businesses and the Commission becomes the judge. But on trade with third countries, there is no conflict.[106]

During the GBT negotiations, European operators engaged actively in support of WTO talks, led by the WTO working group of ETNO. In any case, explain most operators, protectionism was not politically feasible anymore.

> Of course, an operator wants to defend his home turf. But the [network operators] could not have spoken out against liberalization. It rather comes up through details, like the provision of lines or the exaggeration of technical difficulties in the opening of networks. These issues did not come up during the theoretical discussion, though.[107]

104. Council of the European Union, "Resolution of 22 July 1993 on the Review of the Situation in the Telecommunications Sector and the Need for Further Development in that Market," 93/C 213/01 (Brussels, 1993); Council of the European Union, "Resolution of 22 December 1994 on the Principles and Timetable for the Liberalization of Telecommunications Infrastructures," 94/C 379/03 (Brussels, 1994).

105. Interview in Brussels, 3 September 2003.

106. Ibid.

107. Interview with the representative of a European operator, 6 August 2003.

The principle of liberalization had become an accepted maxim, and opposition had to be framed in new terms. The representative of a European operator explains, "the question was always: What does liberalization mean?"[108] As in the United States, the issue was no longer the "if," but the "how" of liberalization. A representative of a somewhat reserved member states confirms this: "in 1996, at the time it seemed like the negotiation would fail, the European Union was ready to go ahead even without the United States."[109] Within a very short period of time, EU telecommunication companies had embraced the project of multilateral market opening through a basic telecom agreement. All observers agree that on the principles of telecom service liberalization, there was a sense of "European unity" and a general enthusiasm. Support for liberalization by European telecom firms, however, was a direct consequence of the constraints of the multilevel trade policymaking procedure, which effectively precluded more nuanced or outright protectionist lobbying at the European level.

Summary

Looking at the lobbying of telecommunication companies during the WTO's basic telecom negotiations, we find a surprising picture. Very generally speaking, all relevant telecom companies supported liberalization through the WTO by late 1996, even if many had reservations about the details of the agreement. U.S. service providers tied their support to the obligation of reciprocity, and U.S. network operators had qualms about the conceptualization of cost-orientation integrated in the Reference Paper. European telecom companies were much less active than their American counterparts, but they nonetheless engaged in favor of an agreement through their European association ETNO once internal liberalization was underway.

The evolution of policy demands from national treatment to support for liberalization was due to the changing nature of telecom firms and to the new trade paradigm. Incumbent operators in both the European Union and the United States had to find ways to combine the stances that corresponded to their traditional privileges and the benefits of new international opportunities. Yet in the context of the telecom boom in the 1990s, even these operators decided to develop their international activities in or-

---

108. Ibid.
109. Interview, 9 December 2002.

der to compete on the global market. However, changing identities and new beliefs about trade did not come overnight. They were the result of considerable pressures from users, competitors, and governments. In Europe and in the local telecom market in the United States, companies resisted these pressures as long as they were able to maintain their protected regulatory arrangements in their domestic markets. Once the reform of domestic regulation became a certainty, network operators decided to embrace liberalization in order to be able to influence the details of the new international regime. As we will see in the following chapter, the story is surprisingly similar in international air transport: ideational changes were crucial for the reorientation of business lobbying, but cannot be understood without the pressures coming from regulatory changes and government initiatives.

5

International Air Transport

In contrast to telecommunication services, international air transport was explicitly excluded from the coverage of the GATS. However, the state-centered architecture of civil aviation came under increasing pressure from domestic and regional liberalization in a manner quite similar to the evolution of telecommunication services. While the United States pursues liberalization bilaterally, the European Union continues to press for a more comprehensive reform of international aviation. These two ambitions led to the conclusion of a liberalizing transatlantic agreement in 2007.

The positions of U.S. airlines concerning the liberalization of international air transport have been quite mixed over time. After initial reservations, the airlines grew very supportive of bilateral liberalization through open skies agreements, but have been very hesitant to engage in favor of more comprehensive transatlantic liberalization. European Union airlines, by contrast, have very actively lobbied for a revision of the international architecture and even designed a blueprint for an ambitious transatlantic aviation area that the European Union has pursued in negotiations with the United States in the early 2000s.

As in telecommunication services, the cognitive changes and strategic readjustment of airlines have been shaped profoundly by the regulatory changes of the 1990s. This chapter therefore begins with an introduction to the issues in the liberalization of international air transport and then discusses the changing nature of the airlines, the new trade paradigms, and the challenges of the respective strategic environments of American and European carriers.

The Changing Architecture of Civil Aviation

The Old Framework

Aviation has been an international business since its beginning. Because of the security implications of this border-crossing mode of transport, international regulation even preceded national and local regulation. The current architecture dates back to the Convention on International Civil Aviation, signed in Chicago on 7 December 1944.[1] The Chicago Convention established that access should be granted through bilateral agreements between governments.[2] It further set up a permanent organization, the International Civil Aviation Organization (ICAO), whose mission is to assure cooperation in and standardization of international aviation. In response to the creation of this intergovernmental forum, the airline industry organized itself in a separate forum, the International Air Transport Association (IATA), in 1945.

In 1946, the United States and the United Kingdom decided to meet bilaterally to resolve questions left unanswered by the Chicago Convention two years earlier. The resulting Bermuda agreement was the most decisive agreement for postwar international aviation. Most importantly, the Bermuda agreement designated IATA as the organization supposed to fix fare prices on UK-U.S. flights, subject to governmental approval. The postwar architecture of international aviation was thus a "regulatory triangle" composed of the intergovernmental ICAO, a bilateral regime for the exchange of commercial rights, and a multilateral price-fixing mechanism.[3]

In reference to its tight network of air service agreements, the regime is commonly referred to as the "bilateral system" of international aviation. Over two thousand bilateral agreements are currently registered with ICAO. Counting all written exchanges and additions, the number might even be as high as ten thousand.[4] The traffic rights negotiated between

---

1. The intergovernmental bargaining over the future framework of international aviation has been widely studied. See Gidwitz, *The Politics of International Air Transport;* Jönsson, *International Aviation and the Politics of Regime Change;* Sochor, *The Politics of International Aviation;* Milner, *Interests, Institutions, and Information;* Richards, "Towards a Positive Theory of International Institutions"; Richards, "Institutions for Flying."

2. Access rights negotiated bilaterally are labeled freedoms of the air.

3. Sochor, *Politics of International Aviation,* 15.

4. Interview in Brussels, 26 November 2002.

governments in the bilateral air service agreements cover a large number of details, including points to be served, routes to be operated, types of traffic to be carried, capacity, tariffs and tariff conditions, designation of airlines, as well as their ownership and control. This last item is one of the most important, because it traditionally requires an airline designated by a country to be effectively owned or controlled by its nationals.[5] In other words, the U.S. government can only designate U.S. carriers and the German government only German carriers. Within the bilateral framework, no airline can make seemingly simple business decisions common in other industries, such as increasing its flight offerings, targeting a new destination, soliciting foreign investment, or relocating its operating hub to a destination abroad.

At the national level, civil aviation developed under the strict oversight of governments. Like other areas of transport, aviation was considered a very sensitive domain, with implications for economic and regional development as well as national security. In the United States, the Civil Aeronautics Board (CAB), a federal agency created in 1938, controlled entry, exit, rates, route allocation, mergers, and subsidies of airlines in the domestic markets. The Federal Aviation Administration (FAA) was later created for the oversight of safety standards, but the CAB remained in place for economic regulation. Since air services were under the exclusive control of a governmental agency, even general competition policy—i.e. antitrust law—did not apply to the sector.

In most European countries, national control over the airlines was deeply rooted and many governments even owned their country's airline, the so-called "flag carriers."[6] Although the specific models varied, most European countries had established air transport as a heavily subsidized public service sector monopoly. Only the UK and the Netherlands had a somewhat less restrictive air transport policy. In particular, both followed a multi-airline policy, negotiating rights for more than just one airline on international routes. With a strong consumer lobby, the United Kingdom pioneered low-cost air travel in the 1960s and 1970s and was the only country in Europe to establish an independent regulatory authority for aviation in 1971.[7]

---

5. Effective ownership is defined in the United States as less than 25 percent foreign ownership, across the European Union as less than 49 percent.

6. Dienel and Lyth, *Flying the Flag;* Staniland, *Government Birds.*

7. Kassim, "Air Transport," 112.

Domestic Deregulation and Pressures for Change

As in telecommunication services, governmental control over air transport services came under attack, both as a result of domestic deregulation and because of the rigidities of the traditional international architecture. In the United States, criticism of the inefficiency of the system began to grow in the 1970s.[8] The Airline Deregulation Act of 1978 eventually provided for the phasing out of all of the CAB's activities by the end of 1984. Domestic deregulation led to radical reorganization of the American aviation industry.[9] Within fifteen years, the two most important international carriers, Pan American Airlines (Pan Am) und Trans World Airlines (TWA), had disappeared, selling their international routes to what became collectively known as the "Big Three": United, Delta, and American Airlines. Overall, the opening of the domestic market to new entrants increased the number of routes served and considerably lowered fares.

Eager to apply the new market orientation to its own aviation industry, the United Kingdom deregulated the sector in a similar manner under the Thatcher government in 1979. In the rest of Europe, the U.S. experience made little impression, even though European carriers were consistently operating at a loss. However, it did spark the interest of the European Commission, who wanted to apply the principles of a common market to intra-European aviation as well. The first two Commission memoranda on aviation in 1979 and 1984 received a frosty reception from most national governments and airlines alike. Only the United Kingdom and the Netherlands supported liberalization, and negotiated a bilateral agreement in 1984 which allowed any airline in either country to operate between the two without the need to seek further government approval.

With the two countries in favor of further liberalization, the Commission continued pursuing the idea of an EU-wide solution through a carrot-and-stick-approach. On the one hand, the Commission exploited an ECJ ruling, the *Nouvelles Frontières* decision, to act against national price fixing in the air transport sector by means of EU competition law.[10] On the other hand, positive incentives were necessary as well, as the firm opposition of

8. See, for example, Jordan, *Airline Regulation in America.*
9. Cf. Pickrell, "The Regulation and Deregulation of US Airlines"; Peterson and Glab, *Rapid Descent.*
10. The *Nouvelles Frontières* decision of 1986 annulled a French judgment against a number of private airlines and travel agencies operating in France, which had sold cheap, unapproved tickets. The ECJ ruled in favor of these agencies, arguing that the price-fixing mechanisms of the French Civil Aviation Code distorted competition within the European Community. See O'Reilly and Sweet, "The Liberalization and Reregulation of Air Transport."

Italy, Greece, Denmark, and Spain threatened to block a unanimous Council decision. The governments in favor of the proposal suggested a compromise that was brokered by the Commission: regional airports in the four countries were to be excluded during a first stage of liberalization, but further measures could not be retarded after the mid-1990. On the basis of this compromise, EU-wide agreement on the air transport package was reached in late 1987.[11]

The 1987 package began the transfer of EC authority over Community-wide air transport service trade and set off a gradual liberalization, followed by two further packages adopted in July 1990 and July 1992. By 1 April 1997, the internal air transport market among the seventeen states of the European Economic Area was completed. The third package, by far the most important, transformed national carriers into licensed "Community airlines."[12] It opened up all traffic rights to Community airlines and ended national restrictions on routes and fares.[13] Originally an international market, the European market resembled the U.S. market from 1997 on. The member states did, however, retain authority over external air service negotiations with governments that were not part of the European Economic Area.

Following domestic deregulation, both the United States and the European Union became interested in international reform as well, with the same time lag that had characterized internal liberalization. The U.S. policy objectives for international aviation emerged in the late 1970s, when fixed prices and flight obligations were increasingly seen as an impediment to growth and technological advance.[14] The important increase in the demand for international air travel was matched by the increased capacity of jet planes—but obstructed by restrictions imposed by the IATA price cartel: the high ticket prices fixed by IATA simply prevented airlines from filling their new planes.[15] The need to reduce ticket prices grew even greater when scheduled airlines encountered new competition from charter air-

---

11. See Kassim, "Air Transport"; Holmes and Francis McGowan, "The Changing Dynamic of EU-Industry Relations"; O'Reilly and Sweet, "Liberalization and Reregulation of Air Transport"; Staniland, *Government Birds*.

12. Mawson, "Air Transport Liberalization in the European Union."

13. Certain public service obligations and some control mechanisms remained in special instances.

14. Zacher and Sutton, *Governing Global Networks*, 82; Richards, "Positive Theory of International Institutions," 23; Richards, "Institutions for Flying," 1000.

15. In 1975, the unused capacity on the North Atlantic was equivalent to 15,000 empty Boeing 747 round trips, or more than 10 million unsold seats. Jönsson, *International Aviation*, 43.

lines that operated outside of the ICAO framework.[16] The deadweight loss imposed by the IATA price cartel became a heavy burden for international airlines during the fuel crisis of the 1970s, especially for those in competitive markets. Still, none of the airlines was willing to abandon operations or even just specific frequencies. Since the designation of frequencies by bilateral government negotiations was a fairly lengthy process, losing a route often threatened to have real effects on long-term shares in the international aviation market.

Motivated by the concerns of the industry and the consumer orientation that had led to domestic deregulation, the U.S. government set out to reduce the regulation of international aviation. A first step in a more market-oriented direction, the UK-U.S. bilateral "Bermuda II" agreement signed in July 1977, was quickly criticized as too protectionist, but it nonetheless broke with the traditional form of air service agreements.[17] Subsequent agreements were to be more comprehensive, above all the U.S.-Netherlands agreement signed in March 1978. Several European countries followed and negotiated more liberal agreements with the United States, which then continued with various agreements beyond Europe. Moreover, the United States attacked IATA's price-setting authority. In the late 1970s, the CAB questioned IATA's antitrust exception, which eventually led to the withdrawal of U.S. airlines from the pricing agreements and contributed to the eroding of the IATA price cartel.[18] In May 1982, the U.S. government signed a pan-European deal, which removed IATA from setting fares on North Atlantic routes.

From Open Skies to Transatlantic Liberalization

Despite these attempts to make the bilateral system less rigid, many of the fundamental elements of the international architecture remained in place. The efforts of airlines and the U.S. government to adapt their strategies to the constraints of the bilateral system therefore led to the interconnected development of strategic alliances and the U.S. policy of "open skies" in the 1990s. Previously, troubled U.S. carriers—Northwest Airlines and US Airways—had asked to be allowed financial support from foreign carriers.[19] Yet the early alliances between carriers such as Northwest and

---

16. Dutheil de la Rochère, *La politique des Etats-Unis en matière d'aviation civile;* Banks, *The Rise and Fall of Freddie Laker.*
17. Cf. Doganis, *Flying Off Course,* 57.
18. Jönsson, *International Aviation,* 127–51.
19. Tarry, "Globalization and the Prospect of Policy Convergence in Air Transport."

KLM Royal Dutch Airlines had to be granted antitrust immunity in order to be able to operate. The fact that cross-border alliances were tolerated by the U.S. government was part of its larger policy project. It started negotiating with foreign countries to liberalize bilateral agreements, and the granting of antitrust immunity for an alliance came at the price of opening the market of the airline's country.[20] Under an open skies agreement, airlines can operate more like normal businesses, without needing governmental negotiations if they want to change frequencies or capacities. The only restrictions that remain are (1) on the right to operate domestic services in the partner country, and (2) on foreign ownership: only Dutch and U.S. airlines can operate under the Dutch-American open skies agreement. Since early alliances were made in countries that had only one international airlines, the calculation worked out: what was good for KLM was good for the Netherlands, so the Dutch government considered the trade-off a fair one.

The first open skies agreement was signed between the United States and the Netherlands in September 1992. After a package of open skies agreements with smaller European countries, the next important step was an open skies agreement with Germany in 1996, with antitrust immunity being granted to an alliance between United Airlines and Lufthansa.[21] This created a domino effect: in early 2007 over one hundred open skies agreements had been signed, seventy-one of them involving the United States.[22]

The open skies policy of the U.S. government, in turn, motivated European airlines and the European Commission to think about more comprehensive liberalization alternatives. While European airlines benefited considerably from their alliances with U.S. airlines and from the new business opportunities under open skies agreements, European observers were critical of a perceived U.S. bias in these arrangements. The fragmentation of the European market was perceived to create an advantage for U.S. carriers.[23] While European carriers can only fly to the United States

20. See Yergin, Vietor, and Evans, *Fettered Flight*.

21. Bartkowski and Byerly, "Forty Years of U.S.-German Aviation Relations."

22. One of these is a multilateral open skies agreement. Two more open skies agreements exist for cargo services only. For further information see the website of the U.S. State Department: www.state.gov/e/eeb/rls/othr/2007/22281.htm.

23. Most importantly, foreign entities cannot own and control more than 25 percent of a U.S. carrier ("ownership and control") or establish a new carrier within the United States ("right of establishment"). A foreign carrier cannot provide domestic flights within the United States ("cabotage") or lease an aircraft with a crew to a U.S. company ("wet-leasing"). Lastly,

from their home countries, U.S. carriers can fly from any open skies country in the European Union to any U.S. point. United States carriers have also been ceded the right to fly from one open skies country to another, which is effectively a form of providing "domestic" flights ("cabotage") within the European market.[24] Most importantly, carriers within the European Union can only merge if the United States does not refuse to grant the same traffic rights to the new company. In the eyes of European observers, the bilateral liberalization championed by the U.S. government was a "divide and rule" strategy, as Sophie Meunier has stressed.[25]

But what alternatives existed to bilateral liberalization? Air transport has long seemed too sensitive for full liberalization under the GATS framework, which explicitly excluded hard aviation rights.[26] The large number of members made ICAO an equally unsuitable forum for the negotiation of ambitious deregulation.[27] Europeans therefore concentrated on a comprehensive transatlantic agreement. After some initial discussion within the European Union, the Association of European Airlines (AEA) proposed a plan for a so-called Transatlantic Common Aviation Area (TCAA) in 1995.[28] The European Commission enthusiastically supported the AEA project and made it its own policy objective for international aviation relations. However, the European Commission had almost no competency in external aviation relations. When an EU delegation went to Washington in December 1999 to propose the TCAA, the U.S. government therefore simply told the Europeans to come back when they had a comprehensive mandate for external relations.

Indeed, the European Commission had worked toward an external mandate both by trying to convince member states of the benefits to negotiate a common agreement and by calling upon the ECJ to decide on the com-

---

foreign carriers are excluded from a government program that assigns U.S. government personnel on flights operated by U.S. carriers ("Fly America").

24. While it is true that this right is little used by passenger airlines, it does facilitate cargo operations by U.S. airlines within Europe.

25. Meunier, *Trading Voices*, 150–54.

26. For further information, see Woll, "The Politics of Trade Preferences," 267–74. An overview of the GATS coverage of air transport can be found on the WTO's web site www.wto.org.

27. For theoretical debates about potential new frameworks, see, for example, Kasper, *Deregulation and Globalization;* Abeyratne, "Trade in Air Transport Services"; Hübner and Sauvé, "Liberalization Scenarios for International Air Transport."

28. Association of European Airlines, "EU External Aviation Relations," Policy Statement (Brussels, 1995); "Towards a Transatlantic Common Aviation Area," Policy Statement (Brussels, 1999).

petence question.[29] The first Commission proposal on external competences was refused by the Council of Ministers in 1993. In April 1995, the Commission raised the matter once more and gained a limited negotiation mandate under which it has been able to negotiate agreements with countries such as Norway, Sweden, and Switzerland. In December 1998, the European Commission then brought seven cases against the open skies agreements of its member states and a second batch later against agreements concluded after that date. In particular, the Commission argued, first, that the body of law applying to aviation had evolved so substantially that the Community should have exclusive competence over external aviation, and second, that elements of the bilateral agreements were already covered by Community legislation. Meanwhile, the Commission's Directorate-General for Energy and Transport (DG TREN) commissioned a study on the benefits of an open aviation area between the European Union and the United States from an American consultancy, the Brattle Group, to gather positive arguments for an EU-wide negotiation with the United States.

On 5 November 2002, the ECJ ruled largely in favor of the European Commission, but emphasized that the negotiation of traffic rights with third countries remained in the hands of the member states. The Commission was nonetheless able to exploit the ruling to give the question real urgency. In a first communication dated 19 November 2002 it called upon the member states to suspend the operations under the agreements in question.[30] The request was clearly too radical to be put into practice, but the European Commission sought to emphasize that it would have to be part of a new solution. The U.S. government did not necessarily see why this would be the case. If the nationality clauses of the open skies agreements would have to be changed to include the notion of Community carriers, then this would logically have to be negotiated between the member states and the U.S. government. Since the U.S. government was very open to reconsidering the nationality clauses, it proposed a meeting with its traditional negotiation partners in Paris in February 2003.

But the Commission was not willing to be sidelined. Without invitation, a representative from DG TREN appeared at the Paris meeting. His presence reminded the member states of the ECJ judgment, which stated that

29. See Woll, "The Road to External Representation."
30. European Commission, "Communication from the Commission on the Consequences of the Court judgment of 5 November 2002 for European Air Transport Policy," COM (2002) 649 final (Brussels, 2002), 15.

ownership and control were under Community competence, and made further negotiations impossible. Indeed, the ECJ ruling had left a real competence question for the future of air transport negotiations. While traffic right negotiations were outside of Community competence, several aspects of the agreements were within it. This paradox blocked member states from negotiating alone with the United States, but did not provide a legal base for the Commission entering into negotiations with that country. In a second communication on 26 February 2003 the Commission reiterated the need for a negotiation mandate, but modified its initially somewhat aggressive position by arguing that it was necessary to distinguish between the infringements on the Commission's competence involved in the existing negotiations and the need for a wider negotiating mandate for the Commission.[31] On 5 June 2003, the Council of Ministers finally granted an external negotiating mandate for talks with the United States. Furthermore, the Brattle Group issued its report on the project in late 2003, renaming it an "Open Aviation Area" to mark a break with the old TCAA.[32]

Immediately after the ECJ ruling in June, the Commission scheduled appointments with the U.S. government to negotiate a transatlantic aviation agreement between the two parties. While the EU negotiating team wanted to press for the European blueprint and insisted on the need for a removal of U.S. ownership restrictions, the U.S. team aimed for a U.S.-EU open skies agreement that would simply transform the nationality clause into a "European clause." In essence, Europeans preferred a scenario where both markets would be opened up to carriers from the trading partner, even for intra-European and U.S. domestic traffic. United States negotiators sought to agree on traffic rights for licensed European carriers and hoped to open up access to the previously restricted UK market, in particular Heathrow airport, but they were not willing to open up their own domestic market.

Starting in the fall of 2003, negotiations over a U.S.-EU open aviation area have led to a series of meetings in Brussels and Washington. After a prolonged standstill, the negotiating parties concluded a draft agreement in November 2005.[33] The draft was conditional on a proposal from the U.S. Department of Transportation to lift foreign ownership restrictions from

---

31. European Commission, "Communication from the Commission on Relations between the Community and Third Countries in the Field of Air Transport," COM (2003) 0094 final (Brussels, 2003).

32. Moselle et al., *The Economic Impact of an EU-US Open Aviation Area.*

33. "US-EU Negotiators Agree to Open Skies without Heathrow Carve-out," *Air Transport World Daily News,* 21 November 2005, www.atwonline.com.

25 percent to 49.9 percent of voting stock. Faced with heavy bipartisan opposition in Congress and union pressure, the U.S. Department of Transport eventually dropped the proposal in December 2006.[34] By 2007, it had become clear that statutory change of U.S. ownership law was beyond the control of the U.S. negotiators. The delegations therefore concluded an agreement on 2 March 2007 which did not require the United States to change foreign ownership rules. The deal allows American and European carriers to fly to destinations in Europe or the United States and then on to another country without returning home. European Union cargo carriers also have the right to establish a U.S. base and fly to any other country from there. Since this agreement opened up Heathrow airport to all airlines, the European Union insisted that the United States has four more years to make concessions on foreign ownership. A timeline for this second phase of liberalization is part of the U.S.-EU open skies agreement and European countries maintain the right to suspend their offers if they deem progress to be insufficient by mid-2010.[35] Despite an initial British unease with the unbalanced result, the twenty-seven transport ministers of the European Union unanimously accepted the U.S.-EU open skies agreement on 22 March 2007.[36] At the insistence of the United Kingdom, the deal will take effect with a five-month delay on 30 March 2008.[37]

During these moves to liberalize international air transport in the 1990s and 2000s, the policy demands of airlines on both sides of the Atlantic evolved considerably. As in telecommunications, regulatory reform profoundly changed the economic governance of airlines, especially in Europe, and thereby influenced their policy stances. Furthermore, for both U.S. and EU carriers, the reframing of international activities in terms of economies of scale—and not in terms of reciprocal access—was essential to supporting the open skies regime. At the strategic level, lobbying in the European Union affected the demands that airlines could voice, because airlines needed to shift their political activities to the supranational level. This severed the tight links between airlines and their national governments and obliged those carriers that sought to work closely with the European Commission to embrace liberalization.

34. "Open Skies Cloudy as DOT Withdraws Foreign Control Proposal," *Air Transport World Daily News*, 6 December 2006, www.atwonline.com.
35. "EU Says Has Lever over US on Opening Air Market," *New York Times*, 13 March 2007.
36. As mixed competence, the open skies agreement required unanimous approval. See also Tania Branigan, "Britain to Approve Open Skies Deal Despite Fears of American Advantage," *The Guardian*, 14 March 2007.
37. See "Open Skies Faces Bipartisan US Opposition," *Financial Times*, 15 March 2007.

Changing Identities in Europe:
From Flag Carriers to Competitive Airlines

Until the 1990s, most European flag carriers were difficult to separate from their governments.[38] Being organically connected with their national aviation administrations, they naturally accompanied their countries' negotiators in bilateral negotiations and assisted on all aviation policy matters. When there was only one international carrier, the government acted almost directly as a negotiating division for the flag carrier. Heavily subsidized, airlines were public service providers and profitability was not a real concern. Their main policy interest was to assure the stability of their operations, which translated into vocal demands for protection.

In particular, many European carriers were not keen on competition from the United States in the early 1990s. The flag carriers had maintained unprofitable operations and many felt threatened by the new U.S. international carriers to which Pan Am and TWA had sold considerable portions of their international routes. Germany and France in particular resented U.S. airline competition and complained about the capacity that these carriers were able to operate in the European market because of air traffic rights the U.S. government had been able to negotiate in their respective bilaterals.[39] Feeling strongly about the matter, the French government even denounced its bilateral with the United States in 1992 and Germany insisted on a capacity freeze by U.S. carriers.

European carriers incurred considerable losses in the early 1990s. Air France, for example, had a first-half loss of $680 million in 1993, and Sabena was close to bankruptcy. In order to prevent the disappearance of the flag carrier, the Belgian president of the European Union called an emergency meeting of transport ministers in September 1993 in order to devise measures to help the airlines. Sabena was backed by Air France in its call for state aid, and Aer Lingus, Iberia, TAP Portugal, and Olympic were all in worrying financial situations. This "protectionist lobby" called for a freezing of capacity and fares until 1996 and demanded an EU fund that would help with restructuring.[40] Protectionism was indeed the norm in European aviation and became quite visible when the European Commission published its first series of memoranda on internal liberalization.

38. Cf. Young, *Extending European Cooperation*, 112.
39. The complaints concerned the right by an airline from country A to carry passengers from country B to country C, the so-called fifth freedom right.
40. Dobson, *Flying in the Face of Competition*, 228.

At the time, the majority of the industry sought to obtain exemptions from competition rules and the Association of European Airlines' reaction to the Commission's proposals was at best "unresponsive."[41]

The granting of state aid to airlines was a difficult question for the European Union. Between 1991 and 1993, the Commission had approved state aid to Sabena, Air France, Air Lingus, Alitalia, Iberia, TAP, and Olympic, in some cases with the reservation that this would be "last chance" restructuring aid only.[42] British Airways chairman Sir Colin Marshall argued vigorously against conceding to the state aid demands: "as long as the European Commission continues to approve aid, there will be no sensible preparation to get Europe's airlines ready for world competition."[43]

Moreover, narrow protectionist demands were incompatible with the mission of EC aviation policy.[44] The European Commission saw the maintenance of national control as problematic now that it was successfully integrating intra-European aviation. In its assessment, "EC interests will be undermined if individual members try to safeguard their positions through bilaterals with the USA, which run contrary to the emerging common airline policy," simply because these agreements continued to lock in old standards.[45]

With these problems in mind, the Commission established a "Comité des Sages" in June 1993. Its mission was to look at structural problems afflicting European airlines and to consider to what extent the existing airline policy of the European Union needed to be reframed. The hearings before this committee and the airline lobbying of the Transport Minister Council in September of that year crystallized the opposing positions of several European flag carriers and the European Commission. While the ailing flag carriers stressed their need for state aid, airlines from countries with more liberal regulatory frameworks insisted on the need for reregulation. The Commission, in turn, was interested in further liberalization. DG TREN's aviation division insisted that the existing bilateral agreements were no longer compatible with EU integration. Nonetheless, the difficulties of European airlines were pressing and the recommendations of the committee eventually supported the idea of limited "last chance" financial

---

41. Holmes and McGowan, "Changing Dynamic of EU-Industry Relations," 173.
42. Cf. Young, *Extending European Cooperation*, 114.
43. Quoted in Dobson, *Flying in the Face of Competition*.
44. David Gardner, "No Backtracking on 'Open Skies' Policy, Says Brussels," *Financial Times*, 28 September 1993, p.20.
45. Dobson, *Flying in the Face of Competition*, 227.

packages, but underlined the need for further liberalization and market-orientation of air transport operations.

The airlines that did not lobby for further subsidies and protection were a minority in the late 1980s and the 1990s. In 1985, only British Airways had sought to distance itself from conservative AEA policy statements. By the mid-1990s, however, the coalition of supporters of liberalization had grown. The call for state aid in some countries would have severely constrained the expansion of the more successful European airlines, such as KLM, British Airways, Virgin Atlantic, and Finnair. On the road to privatization, Lufthansa also moved away from its earlier reservations about granting market access, especially when Germany was making progress in its talks for a new bilateral with the United States. The ownership structure of the European airlines and the corporate identity they developed as a consequence are thus essential for understanding the evolution of these European calls for protection.

Changes in the identity of firms played a less important role in the United States, because airlines have always evolved in a more or less competitive multicarrier environment, at least in international aviation. Within the domestic market, by contrast, there is a clear dividing line between traditional airlines and low-cost carriers such as Southwest and JetBlue. This became clear when British citizen Richard Branson announced that he wanted to establish a carrier in the United States, Virgin America, which would operate flights from San Francisco to New York. Citing foreign ownership concerns, American Airlines, Continental Airlines, Delta, United Airlines, US Airways, and the pilot unions have lobbied intensively against the granting of the operating license for which Virgin America applied in December 2005. In fact, it is JetBlue Airways, which derives about one-third of its revenue from flying coast-to-coast, that would be the most affected of domestic airlines. But curiously, "JetBlue did not oppose the Virgin America start-up," according to its spokeswoman Jenny Dervin, who adds that "JetBlue welcomed the competition."[46] Like MCI in the telecom sector, the low-cost carriers consider themselves defenders of competition and do not lobby for market barriers, even though they face the strongest economic incentives to do so.

46. Jeff Bailey and Nicola Clark, "American Version of Virgin Atlantic Tentatively Approved," *International Herald Tribune*, 21 March 2007.

Cognitive Shifts: From Reciprocity to Economies of Scale

Moving beyond Reciprocity

Another important element in the evolution of policy stances was the fading possibility of reciprocal air service agreements, which led airlines to start thinking in terms of economies of scale. For the U.S. government, the move toward open skies in the 1990s was tied to consumerism and the logic of international negotiations. A government representative explains:

> The reasons were the following. One, we felt, why should we deny the consumers the benefits? If KLM wants to fly to Atlanta, why should we deny Atlanta this traffic? Second, our ability to get from others what we want is limited if we don't give up something.[47]

Feeling that strict reciprocity had shown its limitations, the U.S. administration adopted a more innovative approach, but many U.S. carriers did not appreciate this new policy orientation. They protested against their government's move toward more "liberal" bilateral agreements, which were "giving away real, hard, intrinsic, measurable values—our geography, if you will—for value that is only nominal at worst and short term at best."[48] United States carriers were worried that their government was offering new market access to American gateways in return for liberal treatments of fares or capacity only. Airlines were used to reciprocal exchanges and had a hard time understanding the benefits of these new negotiations. At the time, the rallying cry of the U.S. industry became "hard rights for hard rights."[49]

The first agreement was negotiated with the Netherlands in 1991, and signed in 1992. A U.S. government official who participated remembers:

> Some airlines asked us, "Why are we are giving away rights to small countries like the Netherlands? We do not want to fly through Amsterdam." They had what they wanted. Pan Am used to fly into Frankfurt and had their hub there. TWA was set up in Paris, Italy, Greece, and Spain. So why should we do this?[50]

The negotiations that followed hardly contributed to convincing doubtful carriers. Since large European countries resisted the United States—

47. Interview with a U.S. government representative, Washington, D.C., 10 April 2003.
48. Former Pan Am executive Willis Player, cited in Jönsson, *International Aviation*.
49. Yergin, Vietor and Evans, *Fettered Flight*, 46.
50. Interview with a U.S. government representative, Washington, D.C., 10 April 2003.

led liberalization, the U.S. government started approaching small ones in order to secure package deals.

> We started negotiating air service agreements with Iceland. Iceland has one national airport and no U.S. carrier flies there. We knew that. We also negotiated with Luxembourg. So their carriers got access to the U.S. market, but what does the U.S. get from a strict air service perspective? . . . So there were carriers that objected.[51]

American carriers were indeed quite critical of the lack of reciprocity. As time moved one, however, they became very intrigued by the new commercial possibilities these agreements offered through the possibility of alliances. In fact, in the years after the Dutch open skies agreement, the KLM/Northwest alliance revealed itself as very beneficial to the carriers involved, and the Amsterdam and Detroit/Minneapolis hub became a model for other carriers.

> They had this huge demand, beyond the people that were flying from Detroit to Amsterdam, because people then connected. It was extraordinary: the carriers were making a lot of money and providing a good service. So other carriers said: "We have got to go do this!"[52]

When the United States finally succeeded in signing an open skies agreement with Germany in 1996, criticism of such agreements on the ground that they were with countries that were too small to bring worthwhile gains was silenced. Naturally, carriers were worried about the shape of things to come. The new agreements had important consequences for the business operations of U.S. carriers. Pan Am and Delta, which had well established hubs in Frankfurt, had to withdraw from there once the Lufthansa-United alliance was put into place. But the U.S.—Germany bilateral nonetheless marked a change in the mind set of most American companies. Carriers which had initially opposed the KLM/Northwest alliance because they did not have the same opportunity realized that there was no use resisting this development:

> We had to change our thinking. We had to realize that it does not matter that there is a very precise exchange as long as we can create this environment where we are allowed to create global entities in strategic positions.[53]

51. Interview with a representative of the U.S. government, Washington, D.C., 16 April 2003.
52. Interview with a U.S. government representative, Washington, D.C., 10 April 2003.
53. Interview with a U.S. airline representative, Washington, D.C., 25 April 2003.

The obvious success of the early alliances set off "a race for everybody to find a suitable alliance partner," explains a U.S. airline representative. The maxim of these years was: "go get a partner and get their government to open their market."[54] Eventually, all international carriers developed "bad cases of alliance envy."[55] This motivation explains the overall airline support the open skies policy enjoys today.

> Antitrust immunity is the biggest thing you can get, because it allows you to become a de facto merged entity. . . . It is a very valuable tool, because you can sit in a room and talk about things you otherwise could not talk about.[56]

With the dangling carrot of alliances, U.S. carriers rallied behind the open skies policy and overcame their initial reservations. In retrospect, all international carriers agree today that the open skies approach has served their interests well.[57]

European Desire to Consolidate

For European airlines, the reasoning was not much different. Many airlines that had taken protectionist stances in the 1980s and early 1990s rethought their policy demands in the wake of the U.S. open skies policy. Like their American counterparts, European carriers began to experience an "alliance fever" in the late 1990s and by 2001 almost all European carriers had American partners.[58] The U.S. partnerships and the open skies agreements raised the interest in the U.S. market and made European carriers familiar with more competitive conditions.

Moreover, European airlines started to feel that a system based on national reciprocity was an impediment to exploiting their economies of scale. They wanted to expand beyond their national markets and realized that European fragmentation hampered cross-national consolidation of European airlines. Initially, national aviation administrations did not share this concern. They felt that existing bilaterals were the best solutions, explains a government official from an EU member state:

54. Ibid.
55. Interviews with U.S. airline and government representatives, Washington, D.C., 24 and 25 April 2003.
56 Interview with a U.S. airline representative, Washington, D.C., 25 April 2003.
57. Interviews with U.S. government and airline representatives, Washington, D.C., 10, 24, and 25 April 2003.
58. A complete list of U.S.-EU alliances can be found in Young, *Extending European Cooperation*, 116.

> We are quite happy about our bilateral agreements, especially with the U.S., and find that they have worked very well. Industry tends to judge this somewhat differently, because large carriers would like to expand.[59]

In the eyes of European carriers, one important disadvantage of bilateral agreements was the impediment to cross-border mergers. To cite the most noted case, over the past decades British Airways and KLM have talked repeatedly about merging. Since British Airways is considerably larger than KLM, the merged carrier would be primarily British. The Dutch open skies agreement with the United States, however, specifies that the Netherlands can only designate a company for U.S. flights that is 51 percent Dutch. The necessary renegotiation of these agreements would mean that such mergers could take place only if the United States approved it, which would often involve other concessions.[60]

After their initial enthusiasm for open skies agreements, European carriers quickly became critical of the U.S. policy and stressed that it impeded further expansion. They call it the "crutch" of the existing system, which is becoming more and more outdated and inappropriate to global airline business operations.[61]

> KLM can fly only from Amsterdam. And in its alliance efforts with Alitalia, one of the things that it would like to do is to be more flexible and operate from Milan as well. But under the present system that is not possible. That's the name of the game: operate a multihub alliance.[62]

In the view of large European carriers, the United States had employed European fragmentation to cement its economic position. Liberalization through open skies will always be limited by the constraints of the bilateral system, Kees Veenstra, at the time public policy manager of AEA, argued:

> Its trade-facilitating effect is limited, as it varies from one bilateral agreement to another, depending on the trade interests and negotiating power of each of the two countries involved. It is therefore not surprising that the United States, as an economic superpower, has been able to conclude more than 50 open sky bilaterals but smaller countries have not. This means that

59. Interview with a government official from an EU member state, 27 November 2002.
60. In this particular case, the United States wanted to use the occasion to renegotiate its access to Heathrow airport in London. The merger finally did not happen because of other problems, but the United States did declare that it would oppose a transfer of the traffic rights.
61. Interviews with EU airline representatives, 27 November and 2 December 2002.
62. Interview with a representative of a European airline, 2 December 2002.

a true "level playing field" can never be established under a bilateral system.[63]

Moreover, the open skies agreements maintained European fragmentation, despite the integration of the intra-European market. They prevented the expansion of business operations, which many European airlines were interested in. Even smaller European carriers, such as TAP Portugal, rallied behind the calls for regulatory reform. Despite a very small stake in the transatlantic market, TAP supported comprehensive liberalization "to end monopolistic situations, where insufficient numbers of operators . . . provide less than satisfactory level of service and to allow more flexibility in terms of resource utilization."[64] The need for reform arose for large and small airlines, either because they wanted to expand or because they wanted to have the opportunity of attracting foreign investment.

The U.S. open skies policy forced American and European airlines alike to stop thinking in terms of reciprocity and to start concentrating on economies of scale that airlines could exploit in a more global aviation market. This cognitive shift in turn, made European airlines acutely aware of the limitations of the existing system for their own expansion.

Strategic Differences: Domestic Protection and European Solutions

The perceived opposition to the United States thus created momentum for a strategic repositioning of EU airlines: instead of continuing to pursue the privileged relationship these carriers had with their national governments, they decided to start working with the European Commission. As a consequence, the strategic contexts for lobbying in the United States and the European Union are quite different. While direct contacts in the United States enabled American carriers to press for their immediate concerns only, EU carriers needed to adopt a pan-European policy approach in order to cooperate successfully with the Commission.

63. Kees Veenstra, "Global Growth Opportunities for the New Millennium," Speech at the 26th Annual FAA Commercial Aviation Forecasting Conference, 14 March 2001 (Washington, D.C., 2001).

64. Presentation of José Guedes Dias, TAP Air Portugal, to a preparatory seminar on "The Future of Liberalization" at the ICAO Conference in Montreal, 23 March 2003.

The United States: Pursuing Immediate Concerns through Direct Contacts

For external aviation, U.S. airlines maintain close ties with the State Department and the Department of Transportation, which are in charge of negotiations in this area.[65] "The airlines are not the bashful types: whatever the negotiation, you would generally hear from them," a government representative stresses.[66] Besides individual contacts, airlines are also represented by an influential association, the Air Transport Association (ATA). Before 1992, the ATA was the representative for all major carriers collectively: it was allowed to sit in on negotiations, and would then report back to the airlines. The inclusion of individual U.S. carriers after 1992 only came about in response to the presence of foreign carriers at bilateral negotiations.

> We would have the airline of the partner country there as well, because it was often owned by the government. So if the foreign airline was allowed to be at the table, our airlines should be allowed to be at the table as well.[67]

Nonetheless, the association still plays an important role as a liaison between the carriers and the government and as a source of expertise on air service provision.[68] "ATA plays when there is a common concern," agree all U.S. carriers, and cite taxation or other costs imposed on airlines.[69] In recent years, the association has been instrumental in organizing the demands of U.S. carriers for government support in the aftermath of 9/11.[70] CEOs of individual airline backed the collective effort through intensive visits to Washington, D.C.[71] On commercial issues, the contact between airlines and the U.S. government is somewhat less close, simply because U.S.

65. The State Department leads the negotiations, while the Department of Transportation has the policy experts. In fact, the Department of Transportation inherited all international responsibilities and portfolios from the CAB when that body ceased operations in 1985. It is therefore also the regulatory agency that grants economic authority and approves antitrust immunity. Only safety and environmental regulation is in the hands of the FAA.

66. Interview with a U.S. official in Washington, D.C., 19 May 2003.

67. Interview in Washington, D.C., 27 March 2003.

68. Interview with an airline representative, Washington, D.C., 27 March 2003.

69. Interviews with U.S. airlines representatives, Washington, D.C., 27 March and 3 April 2003.

70. Air Transport Association, "Airlines in Crisis: the Perfect Economic Storm," ATA Policy Paper (Washington, D.C., 2003).

71. For the example of Delta Airlines, see Marilyn Adams, "Delta CEO Mullin Navigates a Complex, Turbulent Course: 'Last Six Months Or So Have Been Tough,'" *USA Today*, 28 August 2003, 1B.

carriers are in competition with each other and the government is responsible for finding the best possible solution for all stakeholders. These
individual concerns explain why airlines cannot pool their resources
through ATA in order to work effectively on international commercial issues. Personal contact between representatives and public officials then becomes crucial. Nonetheless, whether they lobby individually or through
their association, U.S. carriers maintain successful working relations with
their government. A representative confirms: "The U.S. government does
a very good job in assuring that they are not negotiating away opportunities for U.S. corporate interests."[72]

In many ways, European carriers are not as comfortable in their new
working relationship with the Commission as they were in their old ones
their national administrations. Even large carriers that cooperate quite
successfully with the Commission on a number of issues complain about
difficulties.

> The American interest is American industry. There is no ideology. They are
> for the opening of markets when it suits them only. Their discourse and
> their practices are two different things. We would really like the see the Eu-
> ropean Commission adopt the same intelligent attitude. In Europe, the
> Commission not only holds a liberal discourse, it also applies it! They sys-
> tematically play against their own camp! The Commission does not have a
> policy that corresponds to our interests.[73]

The demands of European airlines receive less attention than those of
their American counterparts. This applies more than anything else to the
granting of government subsidies that used to be quite common in Europe
as recently as fifteen years ago. The airline crisis following 9 / 11 underlined
the differences between the U.S. and the EU approach. While U.S. airlines
received a total of about $15 billion in subsidies, the European Commis-
sion has argued from the beginning that EU carriers should not expect
similar aid. Of course, ailing airlines tried asking for financial aid, but the
Commission resolutely defended its position all the more since Sabena had
already gone bankrupt after the Commission refused to approve further
aid packages. Transport Commissioner Loyola di Palacio emphasized that
she would adopt the same policy with Aer Lingus, Olympic Airways, Alitalia, and Iberia that the Commission had adopted with Sabena. She was

72. Interview with a U.S. airline representative, Washington, D.C., 3 April 2003.
73. Interview with a representative of a European airline, 18 November 2002.

prepared to see many of Europe's flag carriers go bankrupt rather than alter the Commission's rules on state aid.[74]

The United States, for its part, not only granted a first bail-out directly after 9/11, it also agreed to a second aid package in the spring of 2003 with a much larger scope: "we originally did not want to give them as much money as we did, but they convinced us to reimburse them for their forgone revenue."[75]

The attention the U.S. government pays to the concerns of individual carriers also plays out in bilateral negotiations. In particular, U.S. carriers have no incentive to experiment with new solutions like their European competitors, even though they use some of the same arguments. In fact, competitive U.S. carriers feel that the future of air transport will be in a larger, multilateral agreement.

> If we are going to be treated like businesses, we need to start operating like businesses. For years, we wanted to be special. . . . We are special. But do you know what "special education" is or "special Olympics"? It is for people who have problems. And that is how we are treated with investment. We are not in the big leagues and cannot play with the big boys.[76]

Further liberalization, which might be achieved by a U.S.-EU agreement, has two benefits that U,S. carriers are particularly interested in: consolidation and foreign investment opportunities. "Consolidation is needed on both sides," an airline representative stresses, and several colleagues seem to agree.[77] Michael Whitaker of United Airlines recently underlined this diagnosis:

> There are 41 carriers providing scheduled service between the US and Europe. Forty-one! Of the 41 carriers only six are US carriers. The US market has experienced consolidation. 23 are European carriers. The European market is badly in need of consolidation. A US-EU agreement would assist in achieving that.[78]

74. Alistair Osborne, "EU Firm Line on State Aid—Even if Top Airlines Fail," *Daily Telegraph*, 23 November 2001, 35.

75. Interview in Washington, D.C., 19 May 2003.

76. Interviews with U.S. airline representatives, Washington, D.C., 2, 24, and (for the quote) 25 April 2003.

77. Interview with a U.S. airline representative, Washington, D.C., 25 April 2003.

78. Michael Whitaker, "Aviation in Hard Times: Restructuring and Recovery," speech delivered at the Forum on Air and Space Law, American Bar Association, 3 April (Washington, D.C., 2003). The remaining twelve transatlantic carriers come from extra-European countries including New Zealand, Singapore, India, and Pakistan.

Foreign investment, the second advantage of greater liberalization, is also highlighted by the crisis in aviation in the early 2000s. "Today, we have a modern economy, where we allow capital to flow freely," declares an airline representative, "foreign investment is a tool that should be available freely."[79] Yet these theoretical considerations do not weigh strongly enough to convince doubtful carriers that a new solution will necessarily be better than the current situation. With respect to the current requirements of air transport operations, the prospects remain ambiguous.

> From a business standpoint, liberalization is welcomed by any free marketeer. And the airlines definitely are in that camp. But there are some obstacles. Airlines are treated differently. We are the most regulated "deregulated" industry in the world. It is hard to operate purely economically free, when you are so constrained.[80]

In many aspects, the current system has worked well for U.S. carriers. Against the background of huge losses for U.S. airline operation, the transatlantic route has always been the most stable. Traditionally, international routes have been the business area where U.S. airlines could reap the largest profits. In times of economic crisis, they are now the ones where they can at least narrow their losses.[81] This makes experimenting with the transatlantic framework less convincing. More liberal designs are simply "not a priority right now," explains a representative of a U.S. carrier:

> When you are in a hospital, you are not worried about the shape of your garden. We do not know if we will still exist in three years. So once we are no longer concerned with survival, there might be more movement.[82]

United States carriers might be interested in the prospects of a more liberal international architecture, but they are almost certainly not going to drive the process, at least not in the current situation. Although the same liberal ideas exist and find support on both sides of the Atlantic, U.S. car-

79. Interviews with a U.S. airline representative, Washington, D.C., 2 April 2003.

80. Interview with a U.S. airline representative, Washington, D.C., 3 April 2003.

81. In the first three quarters of 2002, major airlines in the United States had a combined operating loss of $5.9 billion on domestic flights, but only $905 million on international flights. On the transatlantic route, U.S. airlines were even able to make a profit: $5.7 million in the second financial quarter of 2002 and $75.4 million in the third. Edward Wong and Micheline Maynard, "Airlines Look for Profits in Overseas Routes," *New York Times*, 29 January 2003.

82. Interview with a U.S. airline representative, Washington, D.C., 25 April 2003. Note that the airline he represented had not filed for bankruptcy after 9/11.

riers have a more comfortable option: their close government contacts allow them to take a more reserved, protectionist stance. European airlines, as we will see below, no longer have this option.

European Union Lobbying and the Aggregation of Individual Concerns

At the national level, European airlines have relationships that are comparable to American business-government relations, in many cases even closer. A business representative confirms: "We always try to be in unison with our national government. It is never useful to not be in unison with our government."[83]

In comparison to tight national business-government relations, airline contacts with the European Institutions are much more distant, explains an official from the European Commission:

> The CEO of a flag carrier can always get the relevant public official of his national government on the phone. They know us less well. . . . The European carriers do not have the same level of intimacy with the Commission that they have with their member states.[84]

European Union contacts are an unfamiliar task for government affairs representatives. Some large European carriers, such as Alitalia, do not even have a Brussels office. As a result, the European flag carrier association AEA has become increasingly important in the preparation of an internal aviation market, especially now that the Community has been granted the competence to negotiate hard traffic rights with the United States.[85] In contrast, individual contacts are difficult, all the more so because the European Commission does not want to give the idea that it privileges carriers over other stakeholders. In the rare bilateral negotiations led by the European Union collectively, the Commission has consequentially found it difficult to constitute its delegation. A Commission official explains with respect to the U.S.-EU talks:

> It is above all the member states that come with their carriers. Certainly, the idea is to work with them, but we have not yet agreed on a formal procedure. In October [2003], they were there. But everybody said "Careful, this might be a precedent!"[86]

83. Interview with a representative of a European airline, 18 November 2002.
84. Interview with an official from the European Commission, 21 October 2003.
85. Interview in Brussels, 21 October 2002.
86. Interview with an official from the European Commission, 21 October 2003.

Indeed, the Commission is not used to having business representatives accompany EU negotiators in any other sector. If air transport were to follow the standard pattern of Commission-led trade negotiations, carriers would not be allowed a seat on the table. However, if the talks were to follow the pattern of bilateral air traffic agreements, carriers would accompany their governments. Airlines feared that this might be changing and complained vigorously that they "were left with very little information during and after negotiations and were not fully debriefed on the outcome, unlike their U.S. counterparts."[87]

Why then did European carriers mobilize to make external negotiations a European issue, even though this implied severing the privileged relationships they maintained with their national governments? According to European airlines, the challenge was twofold. First, the bilateral system had shown its limitations and would need to be reformed in order to permit the expansion of business operations. Second, individual European governments were too weak to negotiate the appropriate conditions bilaterally with the United States.

> EU industry has always been externally looking. For us, those bilateral agreements are of the highest importance, and so we see that the system of bilateral agreements is very limited. . . . That's when you want to bring it to a higher level. And we hope that at least at the EU level, it will bring more, because then we will be like the United States.[88]

Especially carriers interested in expanding became very supportive of a Commission mandate for external negotiations, hoping "that other member states will be persuaded to realize that the best interest for the entire EU is for the Commission to start negotiating with the United States."[89]

> We want to see the Commission to be able to exercise this mandate. We believe it is in the best interests, not just of [ourselves], but of European aviation. They can add value by bring represented as a whole rather than being picked off country by country.[90]

---

87. "European Groups Seek Urgent Meeting with EC on Open Aviation Area Talks," *Air Transport World Daily News,* 28 May 2004, and "European Air Industry Angry about US Talks," *Financial Times,* 27 May 2004, 11.

88. Interview in Brussels, 21 October 2002.

89. Interview with a European airline representative, 13 November 2002; confirmed by the representative of another European airline in an interview on 2 December 2002.

90. Interview with a European airline representive in Brussels, 13 November 2002.

As a result of this opposition to the United States, the group of supporters of an EU mandate expanded to all flag carriers, irrespective of whether their countries had or had not yet concluded an open skies agreement with the United States. For carriers whose countries had not concluded one, most importantly Great Britain, an EU mandate promised to lead to more successful negotiations. For those whose countries already had one, the benefits are similar.

> The logic is simple. We have an open skies agreement with the Americans and we will not achieve a more ambitious negotiation with them, because anything we had to give, we have given. So, we can only win; we have nothing to lose. This is egotistical, but it is pragmatic. It is not an ideological approach.[91]

In the eyes of European observers, the United States had "the political clout to negotiate anything they want."[92] A European airline representative insisted that the European industry needed a more comprehensive liberalization,

> as opposed to the very unbalanced agreements that have been negotiated under the so-called "open skies" label. It is an American label, which they use to describe their version of a liberalized agreement, which is actually extremely unleveled.[93]

The perceived imbalance created by the U.S. open skies policy thus provided a focal point for developing a European strategy. Indeed, few carriers supported an EU mandate in general, but only specifically with respect to the United States, where they saw an added value in a pan-European negotiating position.

> For us, and for all other carriers, it is not evident that external competences necessarily have to be in the hands of the Commission. . . . A transfer of competences is only acceptable when the EU Commission negotiates open skies. We support it when there is a clear added value. That is also the reasoning of AEA. In our opinion, this added value is not the case for [traditional] bilateral negotiation.[94]

---

91. Interview with the representative of a European airline, 18 November 2002.
92. Interview with an airline representative, 21 October 2002.
93. Interview with a European airline representative in Brussels, 13 November 2002.
94. Interview with a European airline representative in Brussels, 5 December 2002.

In fact, the Brussels procedures seemed lengthy and complicated and airlines feared that this might simply result in the Commission negotiating away the larger carrier's interests in bilateral agreements.

> If we wanted more frequencies with Brazil, we would have to pass through the Commission. It would probably take two years, only to find out that we have to split the frequencies that have been negotiated with the Austrians! . . . How do you divide the cake? . . . That is quite a problem.[95]

European Union carriers were concerned about the privileged relationships with their home governments and underlined that there are certain issues that they prefer to bring to these governments only.

> In the end, it is about results. Our government has done this very well in many aspects, especially since we have more influence there. Public officials face fewer stakeholders. On the other hand, the Commission deals well with certain issues where it already has competences: safety, the environment. . . . For us, it is important that the competition quarrels, the lobbying around EU Institutions, will be held to a minimum.[96]

European airlines were interested in working with the Commission, but only to achieve results that they could not achieve otherwise. The disadvantage of working at the Community level was that of being on equal footing with other carriers, a situation that was quite new to many flag carriers. In many respects, the prospect of U.S.-EU negotiations was "a big jump into the unknown."[97]

In particular, working with the Commission necessitated aggregating interests, which meant that the airlines' immediate concerns might not be taken into account. This was unfortunate in their eyes, because European carriers, like their U.S. competitors, did not support liberalization in abstract terms. As one European observer noted, "everybody is for 'opening up, but . . .' "[98] However, at the supranational level the "but" becomes difficult to communicate, if it cannot be transformed into a pan-European demand. As a representative of the European Union as a whole, the Commission has its own agenda: European integration, tied to an increase in community competences if necessary. Working with the Commission thus

95. Interview with a European airline representative, 18 November 2002.
96. Ibid.
97. Interview with an official from the European Commission, 21 October 2003.
98. Interview in Brussels, 21 October 2002

requires keeping this objective in mind. This logic explains the innovative nature of AEA proposals.

> AEA represents very diverse interests. The only agreement that they can find is liberalization. In Europe, what is possible is finding the common good. That is the reason why the position papers of AEA are almost "extremist"—I say this without any negative connotation. They are radical; they push the logic to its very end. That is understandable. When you demand very specific things, you cannot always choose what you will not obtain in the end. And they do not want to give birth to a Frankenstein.[99]

Aggregating policy demands at the European level thus meant that European airlines had to embrace a policy stance centered on liberalization. United States associations certainly represent diverse interests as well, but they simply choose to remain silent when they cannot find a common denominator. In the European Union, moving beyond individual benefits was advantageous, however, because it assured a working relationship with the European Commission, which was the only way carriers could hope to obtain additional market opportunities. This logic has helped large, outward-oriented EU airlines to gather the support of smaller and more reluctant flag carriers, which now all favor liberalization.

Still, the aggregation of interests at the European level had the undesirable effect that defending one's immediate interests became increasingly difficult. British Airways watched with great concern when the European Commission agreed to a U.S.-EU deal that would open Heathrow airport without obtaining changes in U.S. foreign ownership rules.[100] Attacking the deal as a "lousy agreement," British Airways sent letters to UK Transport Secretary Douglas Alexander and EU Transport Commissioner Jacques Barrot, urging them to rethink the deal. CEO Willie Walsh declared that "the EU is naïve to believe that the United States will deliver on the next stage of liberalization without sanctions. Nothing short of an open aviation area by 2010 will be acceptable."[101] Immediately after the an-

99. Interview with an official from the European Commission, 21 October 2003.

100. Only British Airways, Virgin Atlantic, United Airlines, and American Airlines had the right to operate transatlantic flights from Heathrow. British Midland had long been pressing for a deal to obtain valuable slots and has even been accused of running an empty "phantom flight" between Cardiff and London six times a week to retain slots under the "use it or lose it" rule. Dan Milmo, "Phantom Flight Service Grounded," *The Guardian,* 12 March 2007.

101. Marianne Barriaux, "British Airlines Tell EU Ministers: Scrap This Open Skies Agreement," *The Guardian,* 6 March 2007, and Nicola Clark and Dan Bilefsky, "Europe Approves Transatlantic Air Pact," *New York Times,* 23 March 2007.

nouncement of U.S.-EU agreement, British Airways shares dropped 6.6 percent.[102] Yet with all other European airlines supporting the agreement, British Airways eventually resolved to simply insist on the necessity for a successful second phase of negotiations, which also became the official position of AEA.[103]

Summary

Independent of their different levels of competitiveness, European airlines as a whole are much more interested in liberalizing the international aviation architecture than their U.S. counterparts. Furthermore, European airlines that demanded protection as late as in the mid-1990s turned into supporters of liberalization within less than ten years.

The changing identities of European carriers in the course of EU-wide liberalization was a first turning point in this peculiar European evolution. Faced with the U.S.-led policy of open skies, airlines on both sides of the Atlantic also abandoned their previous insistence on reciprocity and started concentrating on expansion in order to exploit their economies of scale. Contrary to the ambiguous stances of U.S. airlines, these new ideas led to quite radical policy demands in the European Union, where protectionist lobbying around the concept of reciprocity was precluded by changes in the political competence division between the supranational institutions and the member states. Furthermore, an additional strategic challenge was the U.S. "divide and rule" strategy, which European carriers could only overcome by adopting a European stance. This in turn meant embracing liberalization. Changing identities and new beliefs provide important insights into the evolution of firm preferences on both sides of the Atlantic, but comparison highlights that their effect is conditioned by the constraints of regulatory reforms and changing political environment in the European Union in particular.

102. Adrian Schofield, "BA: Market Overreacting to Proposed EU-US Deal," *Aviation Week*, 6 March 2007, www.aviationweek.com.
103. "Martial Tardy and Madhu Unnikrishnan, "U.S. and EU Committed to Phase Two of Open-Skies," *Aviation Week*, 23 March 2007, www.aviationweek.com.

6

Who Captures Whom?

The evolution of business preferences in telecommunication services and international air transport displays striking similarities. In both the United States and the European Union, firms that were initially reserved about the prospect of global markets turned supportive and lobbied in favor of ongoing multilateral or bilateral negotiations. While the most competitive and internationalized companies led the way, even smaller home market—centered providers eventually jumped on the bandwagon. The sectoral comparison furthermore shows that telecommunication companies in general were more supportive of full liberalization than international airlines, even though the latter earned a much larger amount of revenue from operations outside of their home markets. If material indicators do not provide a comprehensive explanation of the observed policy stances, does this suggest that ideational elements were behind the changing positions?

From a purely causal perspective, the answer is no. Changing firm identities and changing beliefs about international service operations help to understand the content of the firms' reorientation, but they did not trigger the lobbying behavior. In several cases, firms wavered back and forth between several options until they were forced to assume an unambiguous stance. Government relations, regulatory reform, and user pressures created constraints that eventually caused the reorientation of firm preferences. But this does not mean that trade policy lobbying is nothing more than strategic readjustment. Regulatory changes and political constraints were a necessary but not sufficient determinant of the observed changes. Ideas played a crucial constitutive role that we need to consider in order to understand the full impact of the strategic constraints weighing on service providers. Using translation paths as a heuristic tool, we will see that the strategic realignment triggered by regulatory and political constraints led to a profound readjustment of deep preferences.

In essence, the new political constraints brought about by regulatory reform have transformed what firms wanted. The government activism behind these reforms is especially visible in the European Union, where policymakers have tied international reform strategically to external liberalization in an effort to win support for multilateral talks. Put more bluntly, within certain limits, the European Institutions have the power to reorient business demands. This is not a matter of brute force and goes beyond the traditional rationalist account of strategic interactions. Understanding how this is possible requires considering the constitutive nature of ideas.

This chapter begins by comparing the role of ideas and strategic constraints in the two case studies in order to explain why their causal impact was limited. It then demonstrates how the interests pursued by firms are constituted in order to show when and why regulatory and political constraints had such a profound effect. A third section turns to the European Union to specify the causal mechanism by which the multilevel system affects the preferences of firms: essentially, supranational lobbying puts pressure on firms to support liberalization or European policy solutions such as EU-wide regulation. Finally, extending the EU discussion to the cases of agriculture and textile trade shows that the same mechanisms are at work when firms lobby for protection.

The Causal Role of Ideas

Causation is central to the work of those who seek to address the role of ideas within a rationalist framework, most often as "subjective" motivations alternative to more "objective" factors such as structural or material constraints.[1] Methodologically, causal inference requires verifying whether the content of new ideas becomes indeed part of firm's stances and establishing a time sequence that spells out how these ideas create the observed

---

1. E.g. Odell, *U.S. International Monetary Policy;* Goldstein, *Ideas, Interests, and American Trade Policy;* Goldstein and Keohane, *Ideas and Foreign Policy;* Parsons, *A Certain Idea of Europe.*

effect.[2] Even though the case narratives have revealed the congruency between ideational changes and evolving policy stances and have helped to trace the process through which these have become incorporated in policy demands, ideas are only one of several probable and partial causes of the observed lobbying.

Ideational changes in the two case studies concerned the identity of the firms and the beliefs they held about their international operations. At the level of identity, firms moved from being monopoly providers, as public service companies or regional incumbent operators, to being competitive service companies. Only U.S. telecom providers such as AT&T or MCI did not display any variation in corporate identity, since they were competitive players from the very beginning of negotiations. At the level of beliefs, airlines first evaluated international opportunities in terms of reciprocal market access and later began to focus on economies of scale which disconnected corporate strategies from a strict insistence on reciprocity. Telecom companies shifted from understanding international operations as jointly provided services made possible through interconnection to thinking about foreign direct investment and market access abroad.

In addition, policy stances have a strategic component, which has traditionally been well studied in the rational choice literature: depending on whether certain choices are politically feasible or not, actors will prefer to push for the one that is most likely to be successful. In the United States, firms were confronted with few changes in their political contacts. Only the U.S. government—driven policy of open skies limited airlines' ability to demand market restrictions, while the Telecom Act of 1996 foresaw a future liberalization of the domestic market. In the European Union, the strategic environment evolved considerably. Competence transfer toward the supranational level made the European Institutions one of the new contacts firms had to deal with to voice their demands effectively, and international liberalization profoundly transferred the options open to telecom companies and airlines.

In order to demonstrate the causal impact of ideas, one would have to show that ideational factors created effects that were independent of the strategic realignment. Table 6.1 summarizes the three sources of variation in the case studies and indicates whether each one was responsible for an evolution of the observed policy stances.

---

2. George, "The Causal Nexus Between Cognitive Beliefs and Decision-Making Behavior"; Yee, "The Causal Effects of Ideas on Policies."

Table 6.1. Sources of variation in the case studies

Concept	Case	Variation	Effect on trade stance
Identity	U.S. airlines	None	No
	EU airlines	Monopoly vs. competitive player	Confounded with strategic context
	U.S. telecoms	Service providers: none	No
		Operators: monopoly vs. competitive player	Partial
	EU telecoms	Monopoly vs. competitive player	Confounded with strategic context
Beliefs	U.S. airlines	Reciprocal access vs. economies of scale	Impossible to determine
	EU airlines	Reciprocal access vs. economies of scale	Confounded with strategic context
	U.S. telecoms	Interconnection vs. tradable service	Partial
	EU telecoms	Interconnection vs. tradable service	Confounded with strategic context
Strategic context	U.S. airlines	U.S. government open skies initiative	Yes
	EU airlines	Competence transfer and internal liberalization	Yes
	U.S. telecoms	Telecom Act of 1996	No
	EU telecoms	Internal liberalization	Yes

Changing identities and new beliefs about international operations corresponded to the evolution of policy stances in most cases, but it is very difficult to argue that they did so independently of changes in the strategic
context. In the European Union, service companies appear to have conceived of themselves as competitive players interested in expanding into
new markets and to have adopted the new cognitive framework of service
trade, but they only did so fully once internal liberalization precluded any
alternative possibility of traditional EU protectionism. In the United
States, incumbent operators like NYNEX began to act like competitive
players and to focus on foreign market access long before the Telecom Act
of 1996 opened up the regional market. This might have been induced by
ideational changes, but it only applies to a minority of the Regional Bells.
Finally, U.S. airlines stated that they became interested in exploiting their
economies of scale through open skies once early alliances turned out to
be successful, but that their support for open skies came only after the U.S.
government had already decided to go ahead in order to serve consumer

interests. The airlines' support for open skies therefore does not require that airlines truly changed their preferences; they simply did not have a choice in the matter, so they might as well declare in favor of bilateral liberalization. Let us consider the causal role of ideas and strategic changes in turn.

Ideational Changes

The explanatory power of identity as a sole cause for corporate trade preferences is relatively small. The change from local monopolists to competitive providers has had a slight effect in the case of U.S. network operators and we have evidence that identity has evolved parallel to the policy demands of firms and has facilitated the cooperation of business and government in Europe.

Moreover, one could question whether the effect of changing identity was not simply due to changing material conditions rather than to changes in how companies conceived of themselves and understood their roles and priorities. The transition from public monopolies to competitive players was indeed accompanied by important changes in the ownership and organizational structure of these firms. The field of industrial organization in economics has called attention to the effects of such changes for rent-seeking behavior.[3] In addition, several authors have investigated the effects of ownership on trade preferences. Goodman, Spar and Yoffie, for example, even though they focus on the role of foreign ownership rather than on that of public or private ownership, demonstrate that the ownership structure of firms is an important determinant of their trade preferences.[4] For the firms studied in this book, investment and the transformation of ownership certainly played a central role in shaping their identities. Considering the timing of ownership changes shows, however, that the firms' changing identities were a combination of their changing self-understandings and their changing material characteristics. Tables 6.2 and 6.3 summarize the percentage of public ownership for the European companies.

Even after EU-wide liberalization and privatization, Air France was 55

---

3. See Tirole, *The Theory of Industrial Organization.*

4. Goodman, Spar, and Yoffie, "Foreign Direct Investment and the Demand for Protection in the United States." Foreign-owned firms are more likely to lobby for free trade than local firms. When investment substitutes for imports, however, foreign firms are likely to join forces with local ones in an effort to keep new entrants out of the market. See also Markusen, *Multinational Firms and the Theory of International Trade.*

Table 6.2. Public ownership of European airlines, 1986–2005 (percent)

	1986	1990	1995	2000	2003	2005
Air France (F)	100	100	100	55	55	18.6
Alitalia (I)	86	86	86	62.39	62.39	49.9
British Airways (UK)	50	0	0	0	0	0
Finnair (FN)	70.7	60.0	60.0	59.2	58.0	57.04
Iberia (E)	100	100	100	60	0	0
KLM (NL)	100	100	25	20.6	0	—[a]
Lufthansa (D)	100	54.22	17.84	0	0	0
Olympic (G)	100	100	100	100	100	100
Sabena/SNBA (B)	100	100	56	20.4	0	0
SAS (N, S, DK)	100	100	50	50	50	50
TAP Portugal (P)	100	100	100	100	100	100

Sources: Peter Conway and Giuseppe Nicoletti, "Product Market Regulation in Non-manufacturing Sectors in OECD Countries" and the yearbooks for 1996, 2001, 2004, and 2006 published by the Association of European Airlines.
[a] 2005: see Air France.

percent owned by the French government at the same time as it actively supported further liberalization—about the same percentage as the stake the German government had in Lufthansa when the airline was protectionist in the early 1990s.[5] Changing ownership did not immediately trigger a new corporate strategy of the German carrier prior to the U.S. open skies agreement, nor did continuing government ownership prevent Air France from pushing for liberalization. Even TAP Portugal insisted on the need for transatlantic liberalization and consolidation within Europe despite the fact that its ownership structure has not budged.

The same divergence between actual ownership structure and self-categorization can be observed in telecommunications. Companies that were privatized early, such as British Telecom and Telefónica, had much the same ambitions for their role in the future global market as companies that still had substantial public ownership, such as France Télécom or Deutsche Telekom.

In sum, the self-conception of firms appears to matter independent of the actual material characteristics of the firm. Still, on cannot make a convincing hard case for the causal role of identity. Most importantly, it is impossible to say whether new identities led firms to push for expansion and

5. Conway and Nicoletti, "Product Market Regulation in Non-Manufacturing Sectors in OECD Countries."

Table 6.3. Public ownership of European telecom operators, 1985/90– 2000 (percent)

	1985–90	1992	1994	1996	1998	2000
Belgacom (B)	100	100	100	51	51	50
British Telecom (UK)	50	22	1	1	0	0
Deutsche Telekom (D)	100	100	100	74	63	56
France Télécom (F)	100	100	100	100	62	61
KPN (NL)	100	100	66	45	44	43
PTA (A)	100	100	100	100	100	75
Telecom Italia (I)	100	50	50	50	5	3
Telefónica (E)	35	35	34	21	0	0
Telia (S)	100	100	100	100	100	71

Source: Peter Conway and Giuseppe Nicoletti, "Product Market Regulation in Non-manufacturing Sectors in OECD Countries."

foreign market access and thus to support the efforts to liberalize their markets; or whether regulatory changes at the domestic level forced firms to focus on offensive corporate strategies, which in turn meant embracing liberalization.

The causal role of new beliefs is equally difficult to demonstrate. To be sure, by highlighting particular means-end relationships, beliefs have provided road maps for the lobbying of firms in both the United States and the European Union. Connecting new market access to increasing returns to scale, the new service trade paradigm replaced previous cost-benefit calculations focused on reciprocity in air transport and on interconnection in telecommunications. Furthermore, opposition to the United States created a focal point for European airlines. Bilateral open skies liberalization made EU carriers acutely aware of their own disadvantages as against American competitors. This focus on relative advantage and transatlantic relations, in turn, helped to overcome collective action problems within Europe and led airlines to change strategic contexts by working with the European Commission. Ideational changes in such areas as identity and beliefs thus help to understand *how* preferences evolve, but not necessarily *why*. Searching for causation, even if we admit that causes are most often multiple and probabilistic only, requires looking at strategic constraints.

The Strategic Context

Changes in the strategic environment have had the most visible effect on the lobbying stances adopted by firms on both sides of the Atlantic.

Most importantly, the multilevel system of the European Union turned out to be a particular challenge for lobbyists seeking protectionism. First of all, EU-wide liberalization of the two sectors precluded the traditional national strategies and thus reduced the number of politically viable alternatives service providers could lobby for. Second, the attempt to lobby the European Institutions directly inserted the need for EU-wide preference aggregation into the lobbying process of European firms. In order to maintain contacts with the European Commission, firms and their associations needed to present pan-European policy stances. For U.S. airlines, the government decision to institute an open skies policy was also an important turning point for the policy demands expressed by international carriers.

Does this mean that strategic changes are sufficient for analyzing the evolution of policy demands? Why should we bother to study ideas when strategic changes were the most important trigger of the evolution we are interested in? As Lake and Powell point out, strategic choice approaches recognize that preferences have micro-foundations and may evolve over time.[6] They simply make the bet that preferences will remain constant over one single round of interaction. In their strategic choice approach, problems should be conceived of as "boxes within boxes." What is exogenous in one box may turn into a dependent variable in another box. An analyst can thus study one interaction at a time and proceed to turn to a lower level of explanation if it seems appropriate.

This approach is risky and can lead to flawed conclusions. In many instances, one cannot analyze these boxes separately, because changes in one box may move the parameters of the game to be played in the next one. In many cases, a segmentation of preference formation into separate stable states would obstruct an understanding of the ways in which movements in the different boxes are interconnected. In the air transport example, changes at the strategic level (U.S.-led architecture of open skies and EU liberalization) imposed a cognitive repositioning (from reciprocity to economies of scale) which triggered a new strategic set-up (supranational business-government relations in the European Union). Without studying these connections, there would have been no way of knowing that U.S. liberalization changed the micro-foundations of European airline preferences which led to a transferal of competences and thus a new strategic game in the European Union.

6. Lake and Powell, "Strategic-Choice Approach," 33.

Strategic changes were central to the evolution of policy demands, but not simply because firms adjusted tactically to a new setting. In all of the cases studied, strategic changes put the previous preferences into question. Redefining policy stances then led to more fundamental changes in the beliefs entertained. Sometimes, even the identities of firms had to change before a new policy stance could emerge. If we consider the constitutive nature of ideas, we will see that strategic changes have caused a bottom-up rearrangement of deep preferences.

Comparing the independent effects of ideational factors with strategic changes highlights the fact that ideas and structural constraints work simultaneously. Ideas appear to matter somehow in the case studies, but making a causal argument is largely unconvincing, because it is difficult to show to what extent ideas matter. This is indeed one of the main difficulties of studies on the causal impact of ideas. As Parsons points out, unless scholars can specify how much of an observed change is produced by ideas alone, skeptics can always dismiss them as overemphasized.[7] Without the establishment of a convincing causal mechanism, "ideas can be downplayed as a valuable supplement to interest-based rational actor models."[8] Parsons therefore suggests studying ideas when they cut across material interests. This, however, is oftentimes futile, since in times of uncertainty, it is difficult to establish which material interests ideas should cut across in the first place. The separation of ideas and interests as analytically distinct items is at the root of this confusion. In the case studies, ideas mattered not because they ran counter to the interests of the companies studied, but because they defined what firms considered their interests to be. Nonetheless, ideas did not *cause* reorientations, but only determined the shape of new policy preferences.[9] The trigger that led firms to redefine their interests can be found in the strategic environment.

The Constitutive Role of Ideas

For constructivists, ideas cannot be separated from interests, because they in fact determine how actors perceive and rank what benefits them most.[10]

7. Parsons, "Showing Ideas as Causes," 50.
8. Jacobsen, "Much Ado About Ideas,' 285. See Yee, "The Causal Effects of Ideas."
9. In Alexander Wendt's discussion, this parallels the relationship between the molecular structure H_2O and water. The molecular structure does not cause water; it defines what water actually is. *Causing* water requires an event that leads to the association of two hydrogen atoms and one oxygen atom. Wendt, *A Social Theory of International Relations*, 25.
10. See for example Kratochwil, *Rules, Norms and Decisions*. On the distinction between cognitivists insisting on the causal role of ideas and constructivists interested in their constitutive

In the words of Emmanuel Adler, "the manner in which the material world shapes . . . human interaction depends on dynamic normative and epistemic interpretations of the material world."[11] Interests are embedded in what Clifford Geertz has called a "web of meaning," and need to be understood as the product of an intersubjective social structure.[12] This web of meaning is not immutable, however, and service trade liberalization provides a vivid picture of the ways in which it evolves. In particular, we can see how politics changes acceptable frames for understanding and demanding trade benefits. Reflecting on the link between politics and interpretations, Geertz has noted that "the stream of events that make up political life" seems quite antithetical to "the web of beliefs" that apparently comprise "a vast geometry of settled judgments." He argues:

> What joins such a chaos of incident to such a cosmos of sentiment is extremely obscure. Above all, what the attempt to link politics and culture needs is a less breathless view of the former and a less aesthetic view of the latter.[13]

Studying events helps to avoid the "ideational essentialism" Mark Blyth has warned us against.[14] It is important to trace how political initiatives trigger changes in the ways interests are interpreted. At the same time by emphasizing the effect of new political arrangements for the preference formation of economic actors, the case studies demonstrate that political interactions are more than just strategic games. In the European context, in particular, it becomes possible to show that the transformation of business interests has been consciously pursued by political actors in several instances, above all by the European Commission. In the United States, political changes have had similar effects, but the degree of intentionality is weaker. Appreciating how politics can transform what appear to be evident material interests is crucial for an understanding of the role of firms in economic policymaking.

In the following section, I specify translation paths for the two sectors in order to show how changes at the strategic level are tied to adjustments at

---

nature, see Yee, "The Causal Effects of Ideas"; Bieler, "Questioning Cognitivism and Constructivism in IR Theory." For a similar distinction in French public policy analysis, see Muller, "Esquisse d'une théorie du changement dans l'action publique," 170.

11. Adler, "Seizing the Middle Ground," 322.

12. Geertz himself refers to Max Weber. Geertz, *The Interpretation of Cultures*, 5.

13. Ibid., 311.

14. Blyth, *Great Transformations*, 270. On the study of events, see Sewell, "Historical Events as Transformations of Structures."

the ideational level. In order to construct a preference translation tree, we need to begin with the policy stances observed in the case studies. In telecommunications, policy demands concerning international activities went from ones involving interfirm trade under the traditional ITU regime and subsidies, to high regulation of network access, to market opening with pro-competitive safeguards. None of the carriers supported full MFN liberalization as it would be provided for under the GATS in the absence of the Reference Paper, i.e. unregulated liberalization. In international air transport, policy demands went from restrictions on foreign airlines, such as subsidies and capacity freezes lobbied for in the early 1990s, to the more liberal open skies agreements, which allowed for flexible operations with restrictions on the nationality of carriers. European providers later also lobbied for an open aviation area, with more liberal nationality restrictions. However, none of the carriers demanded full liberalization of international air transport.

In both cases, means preferences seem to have included the maintenance of national monopoly status, protected home markets, even if those were internally deregulated, and expansion. Some policy demands might be relevant for two separate means preferences simultaneously. Subsidies, for example, could be attractive for monopolists or for competitive companies seeking home market protection. Similarly, open skies agreements ensured a certain degree of home market protection for U.S. carriers, but were an equally valid tool for expansion. Other policy demands, in turn, were exclusively connected to one single strategic goal. Multilateral liberalization with pro-competitive regulation, for example, was only attractive for firms pursuing expansion. By specifying logical articulations between the different levels, preference translation paths serve as a heuristic tool for studying the evolution of unobservable deep preferences.

Telecom Companies

The trade policy preference evolution of U.S. telecom companies was somewhat different for competitive service providers, like AT&T and MCI, and for network operators. At the level of identity, telecom firms had very different notions of survival depending on whether they were public or private network operators under universal service obligations fixed by the government, or competitive firms. For all U.S. competitive providers, the identity was stable and stressed the necessity of profitability as a form of economic survival. Likewise a choice between home market protection and expansion did not pose itself for these companies, because their home market had already been opened to competition.

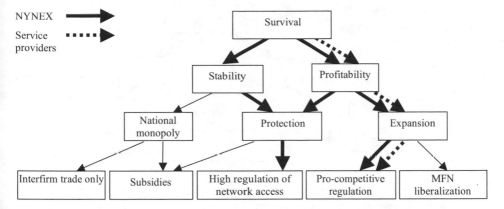

Figure 6.1 Preference evolution in U.S. telecoms

By contrast, home market control was relevant for network operators, which continued to maintain their local monopolies until the mid-1990s. However, during the preparation of the Telecommunications Act of 1996, something fundamental happened for the Regional Bell companies, even though it did not immediately have an impact on their trade policy stance. In 1996, they were to gain access to long-distance markets and would have to open their networks to new entrants, making them competitive players in the long-distance market and privileged, but constrained actors in local markets. For all Regional Bells, profitability became a major factor in the 1990s, as the intense merger wave among telecom companies testifies. While this change did not have an effect on the implicit trade policy stance of most Bell companies, it was crucial for permitting the innovative adjustment of companies like NYNEX or US West, which tried to enhance the value of their foreign direct investment and act as players in the new global marketplace. These former monopolies thus underwent another evolution, not at the level of identity but at the level of beliefs, by framing their business strategies in terms of expansion and not of home market protection. This explains why active Bell companies like NYNEX eventually adopted a policy preference for multilateral liberalization with pro-competitive safeguards. Other Regional Bells, one could argue, did not follow this new interest translation and continued to support more protection or at least did not actively support further liberalization.

The story of most European telecom companies is similar to that of the U.S. Regional Bells, but it is nonetheless distinct due to the particularities of the EU policy process. Unlike their U.S. counterparts, European tele-

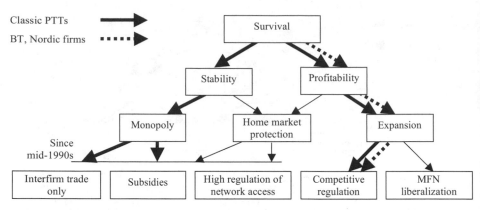

Figure 6.2 Preference evolution in EU telecoms

com administrations (PTTs) were internationally involved, even if they did not act as "companies" but rather as administrative units represented through their governments since in their case telecommunication was a government-owned public service provision. This interfirm cooperation was a natural complement to the strictly national definition and control of telecommunication markets and worked to reinforce it.[15]

However, the internal EU telecom liberalization entirely removed this national demarcation of telecom markets and prevented other forms of national support to individual firms, such as subsidies. In contrast to the U.S. RBOCs, former PTTs could therefore not even insist on home market protection because the very idea of a home market was being put into question. With the European Commission in charge of both internal and multilateral liberalization, European firms not only had to reinvent themselves as competitive players which followed the objective of profitability, they also had to adopt an expansionist understanding of their business strategies, since a protectionist stance was precluded. This movement was a particular task for the formerly state-owned PTTs, while the network operators in the United Kingdom and the Nordic countries had already redefined themselves as competitive players in consequences of national deregulation once European and multilateral liberalization became important.[16]

15. See Cowhey, "Telecommunications."
16. See also Thatcher, *The Politics of Telecommunications,* 199–204.

Airlines

The evolution of preferences of U.S. airlines is not as easy to identify as in the case of U.S. telecom services, because airlines had the option to remain relatively passive. What can be said for sure is that U.S. airlines had been competitive players since the 1980s and those that had established themselves as important international players had to prove a sustained capacity to be profitable. This general competitiveness did not prevent these airlines from trying to protect their domestic markets from new foreign entrants. Like all airlines in the world, U.S. airlines insisted on restrictions on cabotage and foreign ownership, which ensured that competition came only from U.S. carriers and mostly affected national routes.

It is difficult to pinpoint what exactly happened when the U.S. government introduced its policy of open skies. Most probably, the story was not the same for all U.S. airlines. Previously, restrictions on foreign airlines had been fixed through strictly reciprocal agreements. Open skies agreements maintained cabotage and foreign ownership rules, but undid the concept of strict reciprocity. With time, however, most international U.S. airlines started actively supporting the open skies policy framework. With some airlines, this may have been the case because the government was simply determined to institute a more consumer-friendly framework that was beneficial to commercial activity in general and nonetheless sufficiently compatible with home market protection. In the case of other airlines, however, it is more probable that they adjusted their beliefs about how to maintain profitable international operations. Once they saw how beneficial the U.S.-Dutch open skies agreement was for the alliance between KLM and Northwest, they embraced international alliances twinned with open skies as a tool for expanding business. Unfortunately, it is difficult to determine which of the two beliefs actually determined the U.S. airlines' support for open skies since both expansion and home market protection were obtainable through United States-led open skies negotiations.

In the case of European airlines, it is helpful to start with the period when most international airlines in Europe were national flag carriers providing monopoly services to foreign destinations. As public service providers, European airlines were unconcerned with questions of profitability: carriers consistently operated at a loss, but governments tended to treat such losses as public policy expenditures that contributed to regional development, industrial policy, and employment.[17] Until the 1990s, airlines

17. Staniland, *Government Birds*, 93–98.

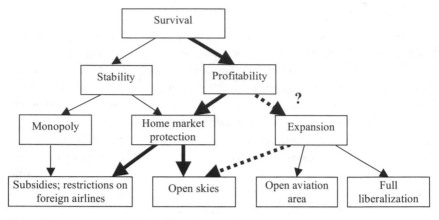

Figure 6.3 Preference evolution in U.S. air transport

demanded subsidies and protection from international competition, even as a "protectionist lobby" at the European level, with the exception of flag carriers from some more liberal-minded countries, like the United Kingdom and the Netherlands.

The boundaries of national markets were eliminated through the internal EU liberalization by 1997. At the same time, all other means of protecting carriers' home market dominance, most notably financial support from their national governments, were precluded by EU competition policy. European carriers had to redefine themselves as competitive airlines in the European market, but also on the international scene. Lacking the political and economic clout of the U.S. government, European countries did not have the possibility to negotiate open skies agreements that effectively protected their respective domestic markets or the European market. European Union carriers nonetheless embraced the open skies model as a useful tool for expanding their operations. Very quickly, however, they grew dissatisfied with the perceived asymmetry of this solution and started developing their own regulatory proposal, an open aviation area.

European Union airlines embraced the ambitious project of transatlantic liberalization for several reasons, despite the fact that it was diametrically opposed to their previous stance as national flag carriers. On the one hand, most of them had little to lose compared to their situation under open skies agreements, with the notable exception of the airlines with a stronghold in Heathrow, British Airways and Virgin Atlantic. But even these two carriers supported the project, out of the same logic that led all

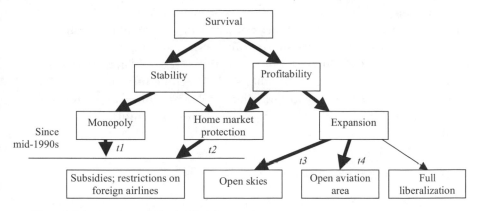

Figure 6.4 Preference evolution in EU air transport

European carriers to adjust their political preferences. They were no longer national service providers with little obligation to be profitable. On the contrary, as experience in the early 2000s demonstrated, flag carriers could simply go bankrupt and disappear. As profitable competitive players, however, EU carriers could not rely on a strategy of home market protection. Their initial home bases had been opened up to European competition, their privileged government ties were put into question by Community legislation, and their governments were increasingly hampered in their ability to negotiate satisfactory external agreements. The strategic environment of EU carriers was severely constrained by U.S. aviation policy, and effectively responding to this challenge meant abandoning the secure relationship they had had with their national governments in order to work with the Commission. This decision, in turn, made lobbying around the concept of national markets impossible. As in the case of EU telecommunications, firms were pushed into an explicitly expansionist strategy for remaining profitable, which was quite different from their earlier protectionist stance as national monopolies. Strategic changes thus explain why airlines abandoned lobbying for national protection (indicated in figure 6.4 as lobbying at times *t1* and *t2*), while U.S. competition explains why airlines were not satisfied with open skies (*t3*) and eventually lobbied for an open aviation area (*t4*).

The feedback effects of strategic changes went beyond a simple re-ordering of ranked preferences once one of the options was no longer feasible. Airlines and telecom companies abandoned old preferences and developed alternative goals by adopting new belief systems and focusing on the survival of different units of analysis. Most of this evolution resulted from social interactions, not just from the updating of information. Power relations are important for understanding business-government relations and the ways in which firms were obliged to adjust to initiatives that were driven by other societal actors. Institutional dynamics, collective devices for formulating a policy response, and emulation informed the ways in which firms anticipated the future and defined their economic interests.

Government Captures Business

In Europe, one institutional dynamic that has had a profound impact on the evolution of business preferences is tied to the role of the European Commission in trade policymaking.[18] As the trade negotiator of the European Communities, the European Commission has made a concerted effort to integrate firms and other private actors into the trade policymaking process.[19] By helping to elaborate policy solutions, interest group participation increases the legitimacy of the Commission on external trade issues. This "reverse lobbying" noted by Gregory Shaffer is not without consequences.[20] While firms do increasingly seize the opportunities available to them at the supranational level, EU trade policy lobbying is marked by a particular logic. Firms face a trade-off between pressing for immediate advantages and responding to the interests of the European Commission, which promises them access to the policymaking process.[21] Since the Commission is not immediately accountable to constituency interests, it can select interest groups and firms that it prefers to work with and ignore others.[22] In selecting private partners, the Commission follows two objectives. First, it requires technical expertise to develop its policy proposals.[23] Second, and on trade issues in particular, it is interested in finding pan-European solutions to prevent disputes between the member states that

18. The argument in this section is developed in greater detail in Woll, "Trade Policy Lobbying in the European Union."

19. Elsig, *EU's Common Commercial Policy;* Van den Hoven, "Interest Group Influence on Trade Policy"; Shaffer, *Defending Interests.*

20. Shaffer, *Defending Interests, 66.*

21. Broscheid and Coen, "Insider and Outsider Lobbying."

22. Grande, "The State and Interest Groups in a Framework of Multilevel Decision-Making."

23. Bouwen, "Corporate Lobbying in the European Union"; Mahoney, "The Power of Institutions."

would risk stalling trade negotiations.[24] When protectionist measures depend on national boundaries, industry privileges are likely to conflict with the Commission's goals. Firms therefore have to decide between lobbying for their immediate advantage at the risk of being ignored, and framing their demands in terms of a pan-European interest even if they are not certain of obtaining an advantage.

This mechanism does not imply that the EU Institutions brainwash firms to love free trade or that they insert new interests into unwilling societal actors. However, it does create selective incentives for formulating business demands and creates a two-way logic for trade policy lobbying in the European Union. A firm or industry interested in classic protection is most successful when it uses a national lobbying strategy directed at the member states and thus ultimately the Council of Ministers. After all, it is the Council of Ministers that grants the European Commission its trade mandate, and the member states' control over the mandate's execution is very tight.[25] Supranational lobbying, in turn, requires framing demands to include European dimensions. Lobbyists thus have to find ways of proposing pan-European protection, most commonly in the form of EU-wide regulation.[26] Alternatively, they can lobby for trade liberalization in order to establish or maintain contacts with the European Commission and then hope to integrate more precise demands into the details of trade regulation or the implementation of agreements.

The following section demonstrates how this logic operates. In service trade, supranational lobbying opportunities have indeed provided strong incentives for firms to embrace liberalization in order to ensure stable working relations with the European Commission. In textiles and clothing, industry tried unsuccessfully to pursue protectionist lobbying at the supranational level, and eventually had to reinvent its strategy. On agricultural issues, interest groups focus on exerting pressure on their home governments to maintain traditional protection.

---

24. Shaffer, *Defending Interests*, 78–79. For the Commission, maintaining the authority to negotiate on behalf of the EU member states is "a day-to-day struggle," as Meunier stresses, even once an official negotiating mandate has been granted. Meunier, "What Single Voice?" 111.

25. Meunier and Nicolaïdis, "Who Speaks for Europe?"; De Bièvre and Dür, "Constituency Interests and Delegation."

26. Young, "The Incidental Fortress."

Support for Liberalization in Service Trade

As we have seen in the previous chapters, service trade lobbying in the European Union is intimately tied to the lobbying efforts mounted by U.S. industry. During the Uruguay Round and the sectoral negotiations in the 1990s, American firms determined the parameters of trade talks and European negotiators grew quite frustrated with the lack of business input on their side, especially when talks collapsed due to the resistance of American industry, as was the case in basic telecommunication services and financial services.[27] In the mid-1990s, the European Commission went out of its way to gain the support of European financial service firms so that it could counter the influence of the U.S. private sector. For the European Commission, working with these private sector associations was crucial, because it felt that it was actual European firms that could best engage the U.S. private sector in a continued dialogue. U.S. and European financial services representatives met in the office of British Invisibles and eventually formed the Financial Leaders Group to promote the interests of the affected firms on both sides of the Atlantic.[28] The European Trade Commissioner, Sir Leon Brittan, worked closely with the group's European chair, Andrew Buxton of Barclays Bank. and encouraged or created similar business associations such as TABD and the ESF. In contrast to the aggressive lobbying of U.S. financial service firms, European firms entered negotiations not so much on their own initiative but in response to the active encouragement of the European Commission. The close business—government relationship in financial services that developed in the European Union in the mid-1990s was based on the shared aim of liberalizing the sector. Today, the ESF provides continued support for the liberalization of service industries and consequentially benefits from privileged access to trade policymaking at the supranational level. Had European firms not supported liberalization, it is highly unlikely that they would have been able to work so closely with EU policymakers.

Indeed, the behavior of telecommunication operators shows that policy demands contrary to liberalization can inhibit supranational lobbying. The European association ETNO affirms that it was unable to develop a common stance prior to European telecommunication reform, because its members were not ready to support the multilateral talks. In the absence

27. Woolcock, "Liberalisation of Financial Services," 33.
28. Sell, "Big Business," 178.

of an agreement on liberalization, there is simply no supranational lobby-ing. But even in 1996, when network operators decided that they wanted to benefit from foreign market access, firms maintained close links to their national governments to be able to counter harmful aspects of liberaliza-tion. For example, Telefónica, the Spanish operator, insisted on restricting non-EU investment in the Spanish market, despite the fact that it had be-come an important overseas investor in Latin America. When the United States criticized the Spanish position, negotiations over the case turned into bilateral talks between the European Commission and the Spanish government, which had taken up the highly politicized issue.[29] Similarly, network operators in other countries tried to guarantee national privileges in the course of implementation of the EC regulatory framework in their home countries. Indeed, member states and their regulatory agencies en-joyed immense freedom to determine interconnection terms and tariffs between networks or to impose universal service conditions. In contrast to British Telecom, which received no extra funding for universal service, France Télécom demanded and obtained considerable compensation.[30] At the same time that ETNO was lobbying for reciprocal liberalization of basic telecommunication services through the WTO, national operators were seeking to maintain advantages and restrictions on foreign market ac-cess through their national governments.

The same two-way logic operates in air transport. Airlines that had tried to obtain subsidies and restrictions on their home markets in the early 1990s had learned that protectionist lobbying at the supranational level was doomed to fail. The close contacts between the Association of Euro-pean Airlines and the European Commission in the late 1990s grew out of the common attempt to create a more liberal transatlantic architecture. Still, airlines insisted on the importance of ties with their national govern-ments to ensure that their advantages would not be negotiated away by the European Commission. When the negotiators finally agreed to a poten-tially insufficient open skies deal, British Airways considered appealing to the British government to veto the agreement in the Council of Ministers. Again, restrictions on free trade were pursued through national contacts while supranational business-government relations required that firms support liberalization of their sectors. Because the European Commission is actively soliciting business participation in the policymaking process,

29. Niemann, "Between Communicative Action and Strategic Action."
30. Thatcher, "The Europeanisation of Regulation."

firms have a strong incentive to frame their demands in ways that suit the Commission's objectives. Failure to do so can lead to being sidelined in the informal consultation process, as we will see below in two cases where protectionist demands are central.

Reframing Protectionist Demands in Textiles and Clothing

Textiles and clothing have long been considered an industry that requires special treatment. Protectionism was enshrined multilaterally in four successive Multifiber Arrangements (MFAs) from 1974 to 1994 and ended with a Uruguay Round Agreement on Textiles and Clothing, which stipulated that the MFA will be phased out over a ten-year period.[31] In Europe, protectionism in textiles and clothing was achieved through national strategies. Conversely, when interest groups had to start interacting with the European Commission, lobbying for protectionism became increasingly difficult.

Throughout the MFA period, the orientation of the respective arrangements resulted from intense intergovernmental bargaining. The relatively moderate EC policy on MFA I (1974–76) was influenced by the liberal German and Dutch approach, which resisted U.S. calls for strict protectionism. Since the European industry had not yet lost its comparative advantage, the Commission did not want to intervene. Once the textiles and clothing trade balance deteriorated, the Committee for the Textile Industries in the European Community (COMITEXTIL) lobbied heavily in Brussels to draw attention to the dramatic fall in employment in the sector. Unimpressed and doubting the reliability of the figures, the Commission maintained that it would be wrong to give in to these protectionist demands. But things were different in the Council of Ministers. Member states felt concerned about the health of their textiles and clothing industries and announced that Community policy should be centered on voluntary export restraints.[32] In the difficult economic times of the late 1970s, the United Kingdom had joined France and Ireland's strict protectionist demands, supported also in Italy. Moderate countries seeking a simple renewal of the MFA were eventually outnumbered.[33] Faced with insistent member states determined to protect what they considered to be their na-

31. For a historical overview, see Aggarwal, *Liberal Protectionism;* Hoekman and Kostecki, *Political Economy of the World Trading System.*

32. Ugur, "Explaining Protectionism and Liberalization in European Union Trade Policy," 660.

33. Aggarwal, *Liberal Protectionism,* 146.

tional interests, the Commission had to switch to a protectionist trade policy during MFA II and MFA III (1977–85).

The shift toward gradual liberalization under MFA IV (1986–94) was tied to the desire of developed countries to open up trade in services and other new issues. Yet protectionist lobbying at the European level had not ceased in 1985. COMITEXTIL worked hard to draw attention to the difficult situation in the sector. In spite of this tactic's previous success, the industry's difficulties were seized on by opponents of textile protection to show that earlier measures had not left the industry better off. As European countries turned away from Keynesian demand management, member state support faded. Despite intense lobbying from COMITEXTIL, trade unions, and other textile associations, national representatives on the Article 133 Committee and the Committee of Permanent Representatives (COREPER) were able to work out a compromise in favor of gradual liberalization. In 1989, moreover, the Commission accepted the midterm review of the Uruguay Round, against the insistence of the textile industry association.[34] The Commission later issued a communication stressing that restructuring was appropriate for the industry and Sir Leon Brittan announced to a shocked industry audience that "the textile industry is a normal industry."[35] Without the backing of the member states, protectionist lobbying in textiles and clothing at the EU level was a failure.

In a last attempt to secure special treatment in EU trade policy, in the early 1990s industry representatives formed a new coalition, the European Textile and Clothing Coalition, to avert the dangers of the new policy orientation. Simultaneously, the European Trade Union Committee for Textiles began to organize meetings and demonstrations. All of these efforts were largely ignored by the Commission, which insisted that the industry's problems had to be resolved by securing market openings in third countries.[36] At the conclusion of the Uruguay Round, the European Union endorsed the WTO's Agreement on Textiles and Clothing, which was to phase out all protection by January 2005.

Faced with this new reality, the textile industry had to reorganize. COMITEXTIL, together with other textile associations, founded a new European group in 1995: the European Apparel and Textile Organization (EURATEX). Needing to work with the Commission in order to influence or delay the integration of sensitive categories into the WTO agreement, EU-

---

34. Ugur, "Explaining Protectionism and Liberalization," 663.
35. Brittan quoted in Scheffer, "Textiles."
36. Ugur, "Explaining Protectionism and Liberalization," 664–65.

RATEX launched a review of its strategy.[37] In contrast to the unsuccessful pressure lobbying that had characterized earlier protectionist demands, European industry representatives decided to engage in a more cooperative manner with the European Institutions.

Dominique Jacomet, a board member of EURATEX, declares that the new "interactive lobbying" during the WTO negotiations in the early 1990s differed sharply from previous activities because lobbyists had to accept a "trade-off" in the policy demands they could voice: they exchanged the elimination of the MFA for market access in third countries.[38] Only by embracing a policy stance centered on market access did textile lobbyists maintain their contacts with the European Institutions. Indeed, the selection logic of the EU Institutions forcing European industry representatives to reframe their demands helps to explain why the EU textile industry became supportive of foreign market access while its American counterpart continued to press for strict protection. The need to supply a specific kind of lobbying at the supranational level also becomes clear in the reorganization of EURATEX. As a result of its internal review, EURATEX decided to develop a more comprehensive policy "in order to be seen as relevant partners for policymakers."[39] Faced with very heterogeneous demands from its national associations, EURATEX now aims not to counteract national lobbying, but to promote synergies between domestic and European efforts. After the lobbying failures of the past, EURATEX's approach today is to focus on pan-European stances to maintain its leadership role at the EU level.

At the end of the Agreement on Textiles and Clothing's transition period in 2005, European companies complained vigorously about Chinese competition. Still, they acknowledged that the abandonment of the quota system was beyond their control. Whether they liked it or not, "the affected companies had to accept the new logic in order to be able to influence the calendar, the modalities of the new measures, or the transition aid."[40] In the absence of member state pressure for protection, successful business—government relations at the supranational level required going along with the liberalization objective of the European Commission.

---

37. Scheffer, "Textiles."
38. Jacomet, "Les stratégies d'entreprises face aux politiques publiques," 307.
39. Scheffer, "Textiles," 108.
40. Jacomet, "Les changements induits par l'intégration européenne et la mondialisation sur la stratégie d'influence des entreprises."

National Pressure in Agriculture

The agricultural market, one of the most integrated in the European Union, is characterized by a highly centralized structure of interest representation at the supranational level: the Comité des organisations professionnelles agricoles (COPA), founded in 1958. Despite the close, traditionally quasi-corporatist relations between COPA and the EU on the Common Agricultural Policy (CAP), lobbying on multilateral trade issues has mainly passed through national channels. Starting in the 1980s, the crisis of the CAP dissolved the consensus between national agricultural organizations and left space for a more pluralist organization of agricultural interest groups. Several combined demonstrations in Brussels notwithstanding, the diversity of interest representation implies that interest representation on external trade is mediated by the member states.[41]

Indeed, during the first years of the Uruguay Round, national farmer organizations, most notably in France and Germany, lobbied heavily to ensure that their governments did not cede ground on agricultural liberalization. In December 1990, deep divisions among the EU member states led to a rejection of the settlement on agriculture that was supposed to conclude the Uruguay Round.[42] The Commission hoped to strike a compromise by tying the multilateral negotiations to a reform of the CAP. At the beginning of the CAP reform process, the Commission had tried to consult with national farmers' unions, but eventually abandoned its contacts when it realized that farmers were not willing to move away from the status quo.[43] As a consequence, the Commission negotiated directly with the member states and isolated itself from the critical farmers' unions. In reaction, "farmers' unions simply intensified their lobbying activities at the member state level" to block CAP reform and concessions in the GATT negotiations.[44] Once the Commission succeeded in negotiating a compromise with the United States at Blair House in Washington in 1992, it was again the French government which threatened to veto the agreement. Violent protests from angry farmers in the context of a crucial national election made opposition to the agreement a priority for French politicians and the center-right government elected in March 1993.[45] Once Germany

41. Delorme, "Les agriculteurs et les institutions communautaires."
42. For a detailed discussion of the agricultural negotiations during the Uruguay round, see Meunier, *Trading Voices,* chap. 4.
43. Vahl, *Leadership in Disguise,* 149.
44. Van den Hoven, "Interest Group Influence on Trade Policy," 11.
45. Meunier, *Trading Voices,* 114.

had shifted its position to support the Blair House accord, however, France ended up in an isolated position.[46] In the end, France accepted the agricultural agreement but not without tightening member state control over the Commission during the remaining Uruguay negotiations and demanding new EC instruments against unfair trading practices.[47]

During the new round of trade talks, opposition to liberalization was also channeled through national routes. France and Ireland publicly criticized the Commission's negotiating position during the Doha ministerial meeting, arguing that the defense of the CAP ought to be the European Union's priority for negotiations.[48] Throughout the 2000s, member state disagreement has severely constrained the Commission's room for maneuver in the current negotiations. It is thus member state opposition, not agricultural lobbying, that explains developments in agricultural trade negotiations. For the Commission, successful negotiations require neutralizing this opposition, not resisting protectionist lobbyists at the supranational level.

The comparison between service trade, textiles and clothing, and agriculture shows that the EU trade policy process shapes the ways in which economic actors can lobby on multilateral issues. Protection is best defended through the national route (as in agriculture), while lobbying in support of liberalization happens at the supranational level, in particular through contacts with the European Commission (as in financial services and air transport). Companies that seek both foreign market access and restrictions on competition in their home markets therefore tend to adopt an ambiguous position: they choose to support liberalization "in general" in order to stay in contact with the European Commission, but they also work through their member states to maintain national restrictions (as in telecommunications). Without the backing of home governments, protectionist lobbying that impedes European market integration is unsuccessful at the supranational level (as in textiles and clothing). In trade policy, firms thus face a trade-off. If they want to maintain good relations with the European Commission, they have to voice their demands in European terms, which often implies adapting to the frame of reference employed by the European Commission.

---

46. Balaam, "Agricultural Trade Policy," 60.
47. Meunier, *Trading Voices*, 122.
48. Van den Hoven, "Interest Group Influence on Trade Policy," 19–20.

Conclusion

The preference translation paths presented in this chapter clarify why strategic constraints have such a profound effect on the trade preferences of firms. Over the course of political interactions with government representatives, competitors, and user groups, businesses constantly refined their understanding of their own interests. In particular, they adopted new beliefs about means-end relationships and reevaluated their corporate identity. However, in very few cases did these changes trigger a radical repositioning of firms in the ongoing trade talks in their sectors. Simultaneous strategic changes were necessary to make firms privilege new preference translations over previous ones.

In the European Union in particular, political constraints implied that firms chose the political level most appropriate for the pursuit of their interests. At the continued insistence of the European Commission, telecommunication firms and airlines engaged in supranational political activities, once they were willing to go beyond purely national policy demands. Embracing liberalization became more than just a rhetorical commitment when regulatory reform within Europe made national political activities increasingly difficult. The constraints of multilevel political arrangements and internal reform put pressure on firms to redefine their interests in terms of the new trade beliefs and to focus on their roles as competitive players. In the United States, similar pressure was put on several local network operators, which emulated service providers like AT&T and MCI in order to not lose out in anticipated future competition. All in all, however, strategic changes able to exert upward pressure on preference translation of American firms were less radical and did not have the profound effects they have had in Europe.

The role of ideas in the lobbying of service firms is thus constitutive, not causal. New identities and beliefs shaped *how* firms redefined their economic interests, while strategic changes explain *when* and *why* they abandoned their traditional demands. Still, considering merely the causal mechanisms would only tell us half of the story. In particular, the nature of these changes would be quite indeterminate. Understanding how a European network operator can move from demanding monopoly rights to lobbying for multilateral liberalization requires paying attention to the ways in which the self-conceptions of firms evolved and their beliefs about international trade changed. As the cases have shown, many of the new ideas were promoted by governments in both the United States and

Europe, which sheds doubt on policy models that start with business interests as objective external elements. Put differently, the liberalization of service trade was a profoundly political issue, not simply an economic necessity demanded by profit-seeking firms that reacted to the pressures of globalization.

7

Business Influence and Democratic Decision-Making

Service trade liberalization is intimately tied to the political activities of firms that proposed, reacted to, elaborated, and supported the ideas of trade in this formerly "invisible" domain. American companies such as AIG, American Express, Citigroup, and Time Warner contributed immensely to the promotion of service trade prior to and during the Uruguay Round, and continue to push for further liberalization both individually and through various associations. Sectoral liberalization since the mid-1990s happened in close consultation with the affected companies, in financial services, professional services, and basic telecommunications, but also in international air transport through the regional liberalization conducted outside of the WTO. By the late 1990s, even European companies spoke out in favor of the liberalization project, despite the fact that it affected their previously protected home markets. Business support was crucial for government representatives in both the United States and the European Union. It gave legitimacy to their ambitious trade agendas and helped negotiators to sway opponents in Congress and among European member states.

The case analyses show that firms did not simply dictate their preferred policy solutions to passive governments willing to execute these demands in international trade talks. On the contrary, a qualitative study of business-government interactions suggests that firms adapted their lobbying demands over time in order to make them fit with government objectives. In the United States, companies such as AIG and American Express expanded their demands for financial service liberalization to all other services, because a broad-ranging agreement was more interesting for the U.S. Trade Representative. The costly and lengthy lobbying necessary to achieve such a general objective thus responded to government imperatives as much as it was designed to further the economic interests of the companies. In the European Union, firms had to adapt the content of demands to the logic of the multilevel trade policy process. The reason for this is that negotiators who are institutionally removed from electoral pressure, as is the case with the European Commission, provide selective incentives for those interest groups that help them to further their own political agenda and ignore others that do not.

The interactive process that leads to corporate trade policy demands may turn out to be nothing more than firms' strategic adaptation to political opportunities. In many cases, firms know what they want and simply choose the strategy that is most likely to lead to positive results, even if they would have preferred another outcome that is not politically feasible. In times of uncertainty, however, business-government interactions not only affect the strategic context, they also shape the beliefs firms hold about their activities and sometimes even the ways in which they conceive of themselves. Moreover, which of these new ideas eventually turn out to be decisive depends on the regulatory decisions and the political constraints imposed by governments. Firms pursuing political benefits intend to further what they consider to be their economic interests, but the meaning of these interests is shaped and redefined in social interactions.

It is an empirical question whether firms active on international economic issues have complete information about future benefits or whether the stakes are sufficiently unique to make it possible to speak of Knightian uncertainty. By comparing service trade liberalization to tariff negotiations, I have shown that uncertainty is common in trade negotiations that seek to harmonize domestic regulation or establish new supranational regulatory standards. When new frameworks go beyond a reproduction of national standards at the international level, governments and societal actors form coalitions to learn about the potential risks and benefits of these frameworks. These instances of international bargaining and deliberation do provide occasions for the powerful to impose their preferred standards, but they also create the need for collective deliberation, which can have important feedback effects on the demands made by economic actors.[1]

---

1. Powerful actors will insist on their own national standards as a guideline for international regimes, which explains why many of these negotiations turn into a "battle of the systems," as

Trade negotiations that deal with the reciprocal reduction of tariff barriers continue to play an important role in multilateral talks and dispute settlement. To dismiss the findings of the research presented here as a marginal phenomenon, however, underestimates the increasingly regulatory nature of trade. Not only the GATS, but also the agreements on Trade-Related Aspects of Intellectual Property Rights and Trade-Related-Investment Measures, on Technical Barriers to Trade, on Sanitary and Phytosanitary Measures, as well as the increasing importance of social and environmental standards are evidence of this development.

In the analysis of such issues, the constructed rationality perspective proposed in this book sheds a new light on questions of business power and democratic decision-making. Traditionally, the participation of economic actors in political affairs has been lamented as harmful to the public interest. Especially firms were considered to simply capture governments, reducing trade policy to "a tragedy in the making."[2] If this demand-side conception turns out to be inaccurate and if firms affect government objectives to the same extent that governments affect business objectives, we need to ask different kinds of questions about power and political influence. First of all, who contributes to the ideas that constitute the economic interests pursued by firms and defended by governments in international trade negotiations? Is the process by which new objectives get defined open to all societal actors or does it happen behind closed doors? If firms are constrained by governments, their mere participation in the definition of objectives might not be problematic, but their exclusive presence would be. Second, if governments have room for maneuver in the selection and incorporation of societal demands, who controls this selection process? Is consultation with interest groups an arbitrary bureaucratic process with only limited transparency or are administrators accountable to electors or other branches of the government? Both of these questions bring us to a normative debate about democratic decision-making and accountability in international diplomacy.

Power, Ideas, and Access

Ideas matter in international politics, not necessarily independent of material considerations, but because they define which elements constitute

---

the recent internet standard dispute between the United States and the rest of the world during the World Summit on the Information Society in 2003 and 2005 illustrates.

2. Krueger, *American Trade Policy: A Tragedy in the Making.*

economic interests. New beliefs affect not only state interests, as several authors have shown for international economic policy, they also trickle down to societal actors and reshape how they think about their individual advantages.[3] Although firms might push for new ideas, perhaps as a shield to screen the selfish pursuit of private benefits, they are most often part of a larger and less linear process of deliberation. Instead of starting all investigations into international political economy by looking at the demands made by economic actors, scholars would do better to begin with the political setting.

This is particularly true for comparative analysis and refers to both institutional and informal constraints that societal actors have to take into account. As Ngaire Woods reminds us by citing Robert Bates's work on agricultural policy in Africa, rational choice perspectives on political economy all too often neglect the role of the state in setting the agenda for interest groups. In rural Africa, governments uphold policies that discriminate against farmers, because they are able to create at will and maintain political coalitions between farmers who can benefit from market alternatives and other societal actors.[4] Similarly, Yves Tiberghien demonstrates that one needs to study how states and in particular political entrepreneurs responded to the emergence of global equity markets in order to understand the role interest groups played in the reform of corporate governance systems in France, Japan, and Korea.[5]

> It is within options set out by the state that interest groups organize and influence policies. Ideas play a critical role in defining social categories and social expectations, [while] institutions play an important role in defining such ideas. Crucial among these institutions is the bureaucracy of the state.[6]

In trade, as in other economic domains, the state circumscribes, enables, and conditions not only the activities, but also the content of the demands made by business lobbies. An analysis of the political settings has to precede the study of interest groups, if we want to understand the parameters within which groups try to exert pressure on government representatives.[7]

3. On state interests, see Odell, *U.S. International Monetary Policy;* Abdelal, *Capital Rules.*
4. Bates, *Markets and States in Tropical Africa.*
5. Tiberghien, *Entrepreneurial States.*
6. Woods, "Economic Ideas and International Relations," 170.
7. See the essays in B. Evans, Rueschemeyer, and Skocpol, *Bringing the State Back In;* Evans, "The Eclipse of the State?"

We may find that governments have little autonomy from societal demands, as with the U.S. Congress—a fact that perhaps explains why interest groups have become the starting point for political economy analyses in American research. In international relations, however, the room for maneuver of the state vis-à-vis societal actors increases, because governments can use their two-level commitments strategically.[8]

The particularity of international settings can have two consequences. In a pessimistic version, multinational firms will be the only ones that can continue to bargain with their governments, while other groups such as trade unions and public interest groups will increasingly ignored. The reason for this is that economic interdependence gives an exit option to firms, which allows them to put pressure on governments wanting to keep firms within their national boundaries. This account, which is commonly followed by critics of globalization and by economic analysts, points to important dynamics, but underestimates the role of deliberation in global public policymaking. In a more optimistic version, governments will try to consult with a variety of public and private actors and contribute to the dissemination of new ideas that result from these negotiations. The analysis in this book reveals that firms do occupy a central place in these negotiations, but that they are not the only participants.

The question that imposes itself then becomes: Who contributes to these deliberations over global economic governance? A burgeoning literature has drawn attention to the rise of global epistemic communities, the role of international organizations, in particular the International Monetary Fund, the World Bank, and the Organization for Economic Cooperation and Development, but also social movements and diverse advocacy coalitions.[9] Indeed, many have shown that the ideas advanced by economists within these communities have had a more profound effect than the lobbying of self-interested firms.[10] Still, certain biases seem to exist that favor multinational corporations over smaller firms, nongovernmental organizations (NGOs), and social movements. First of all, participation in global public policy deliberations requires important resources for transnational lobbying and the production of expertise.[11] Second, multinational policy-

---

8. Putnam, "Diplomacy and Domestic Politics"; Evans, Jacobson, and Putnam, *Double-Edged Diplomacy.*

9. Haas, "Introduction"; Keck and Sikkink, *Activists Beyond Borders;* Woods, *The Globalizers.*

10. E.g. Chwieroth, "Neoliberal Economists and Capital Account Liberalization in Emerging Markets."

11. Woll, "Leading the Dance?"

making favors universally applicable policy solutions and disadvantages particularistic demands. Recent studies show that NGOs are beginning to master these challenges and to organize in ways that are highly professional.[12] Susan Sell and Aseem Prakash show, for example, that both business lobbying for the Agreement on Trade-Related Intellectual Property Rights and the NGO campaign against enforcing that agreement so as to ensure universal access to HIV/AIDS medicines used essentially the same techniques.[13] Both business groups and NGOs contributed to the construction of normative frames: business by grafting intellectual property rights onto free trade prior to 1994, the NGO campaign by tying intellectual property rights to public health in the 1990s and early 2000s. Within only a few years, NGOs succeeded in redefining the issues of the debate and effectively countered business demands to have the U.S. government aggressively pursue violations by developing countries such as Thailand, South Africa, and Brazil.

As international economic issues move into the public sphere, a more and more diverse set of actors participates in the debates surrounding negotiations. For the proponents of pluralist policy processes, this development is a good thing. Representatives of developing countries, by contrast, tend to regret the participatory nature of global economic governance, arguing that the great majority of nongovernmental actors come from developed countries and cannot address the concerns of developing countries.[14] To counter the agenda-setting power of well-informed negotiators and groups, developing countries would need to develop capacities to obtain societal information about their own interests. Without such capacity building, the North-South gap will continue to hamper trade negotiations, not only at the bargaining level, but also at the deliberation level.

Democratic Accountability

At present, the equitable representation of societal interests is still most capably ensured at the level of the nation-state. In the multilevel system, the EU Institutions are collectively accountable for the trade policy decisions of the European Communities. As the recent U.S. scandal involving Jack

---

12. See, for example, Della Porta and Tarrow, *Transnational Protest and Global Activism.* Outside of the economic sphere, the international campaign against landmines is a testament to the skill of NGOs in influencing international cooperation in the highly sensitive military domain. Price, "Reversing the Gun Sights."

13. Sell and Prakash, "Using Ideas Strategically."

14. Zammit, *Development at Risk.*

Abramoff has demonstrated, regulating lobbying is not an easy task. Still, public and institutional scrutiny of the ways in which government representatives consult with private actors are essential elements of democratic decision-making. While U.S. lawmakers have responded to apparent abuses by developing an ever tighter lobbying regulation, EU-wide regulation on the subject is still in its infancy.[15]

The debate about the democratic deficit has highlighted that electoral control over EU decision-making is hampered by the secondary role of the national parliaments and the often incomplete control of the European Parliament over the European Commission. The indirect control of the European Commission by national governments through the Council of Ministers only partially ensures that voter preferences affect legislative decisions, especially under qualified majority voting rules.[16] Some authors argue that the delegation from national governments to the supranational institutions results from governmental decisions to achieve more efficient collective results. Since governments are accountable to their electorates, the multilevel process is therefore unproblematic.[17] Moreover, EU legislation is often highly technical and does not require political debates; in fact, electoral control would only hinder efficient problem-solving.[18] The study of trade policymaking sheds doubt on this optimistic perspective.[19] Trade policy has clear distributional consequences that are wrapped in technical language and hidden behind the veil of negotiating secrecy. If only a select group of economic actors has access to the policy process, both formal and informal political contestation becomes impossible. In this context, the reverse lobbying of the European Commission is disconcerting. While it reinforces the capacity of European negotiators to bargain with their U.S. counterparts, thus contributing to the output legitimacy of EU trade policy, it aggravates the undemocratic nature of trade policymaking and leads to a diminished input legitimacy.[20]

Quite unsurprisingly, the entrepreneurial role of the European Commission in soliciting business input has been strongly criticized by societal

15. In the United States, the Lobbying Disclosure Act of 1995 was modified in 1998 and supplemented by the 2006 Legislative Transparency and Accountability Act. In the European Union, the European Commission launched a Transparency Initiative in 2005. Currently, regulation exists only for the European Parliament or in the form of voluntary codes of conduct.

16. See Schäfer, "Nach dem permissiven Konsens."

17. See Moravcsik, "In Defence of the 'Democratic Deficit.'"

18. See Majone, "The Credibility Crisis of Community Regulation."

19. For a more general critique, see Follesdal and Hix, "Why There Is a Democratic Deficit in the EU."

20. On the distinction between output and input legitimacy, see Scharpf, *Governing in Europe*.

groups that feel that the European Union ignores other public concerns.[21] Aware of the accusation, the European Commission has therefore made a particular effort to consult with societal actors from a wide variety of backgrounds to increase its legitimacy and work toward a policy consensus.[22] Still, firms remain the principal source of expertise on trade barriers and come into their own whenever the European Union seeks to increase its leverage vis-à-vis trading partners such as the United States. To be sure, the growing importance of NGO consultation on trade issues obliges firms to work on their public image. Yet while NGOs may affect the atmosphere of trade negotiations, it is important not to overestimate the direct influence of public interest groups, even though the Commission tries to take their opinion into account through the Civil Society Dialogue.[23] The four transatlantic dialogues created for business, labor, environment, and consumers in the 1990s are an instructive example: despite equal institutional opportunities, the Transatlantic Business Dialogue is arguably the most successful of these.[24]

Good intentions on the part of the European Commission are thus insufficient to convince skeptics that the EU policy process is equitable and open to all societal actors. ALTER-EU, a newly formed coalition of EU-critical NGOs, has made the open and transparent regulation of lobbying activities its primary cause and urges the European Union to impose restrictive regulation on the participation of interest groups.[25] At a greater distance, European citizens seem to share some of these apprehensions. Euroskepticism and the "No" votes on the European constitution indicate that citizens feel that multilevel decision-making is an elitist and often bureaucratic process removed from direct democratic control.[26] Resolving some of the tensions between efficient policy production and equal participation will remain a challenge for the European Union in the decades to come. As much as a complete solution to the democratic deficit of the European Union is unlikely, formal and transparent rules on interest group participation, in trade as in other policy areas, are urgently needed.

21. E.g. Balanyá et al., *Europe Inc.;* Van der Stichele, Bizzarri, and Plank, *Corporate Power over EU Trade Policy.*

22. Woolcock, "European Trade Policy."

23. Dirk De Bièvre and Andreas Dür, "Inclusion without Influence?"

24. The Transatlantic Environment Dialogue was suspended in 2001 because the U.S. government failed to provide its share of the funding.

25. "Stakeholder Consultation: A Voice for Civil Society in Europe?" *EurActiv.org,* 16 June 2006.

26. Schäfer, "Nach dem permissiven Konsens."

Inside the Firm

In drawing attention to these large political issues, I have so far omitted to speak to some of the more particular questions that remain at the end of this book. The mesolevel analysis presented in this study set out to bridge the gap between accounts that aim at predicting economic policy developments and those that seek to understand them. My focus on the constitutive role of ideas suggests that traditional trade models work best in areas where identities and ideas are stable. When we have reason to believe that they are fluid and can evolve, we need to study the social surroundings in which firms are embedded to find indications about the most likely future orientation of business demands. The lesson of this study is that we must be wary of mechanical transferring business-government models that have worked well in the study of trade in goods to other trade issues and to political settings outside of the United States.

Yet beyond calling attention to fact that social settings shape corporate responses, I have not provided a very detailed account of the ways in which this happens at the microlevel. My method of surveying all firms active on issues of service trade liberalization in two sectors and two political settings has obliged me to deal with the firm as a unitary actor. This obscures the actual negotiation processes inside the firm that are crucial to understanding how political constraints are mediated and translated into policy positions. From the perspective of both management science and the sociology of organizations, the account presented in this book is thus largely incomplete. For the sake of parsimony, I have accepted to reify a single corporate rationality, a procedure that is in many ways as problematic as accounts of the unitary state in international politics. Differences in corporate governance, in the ways in which government affairs departments within firms report to the executive officers, and in the organizational structures of firms most certainly contributed to the interfirm variation we have observed in the case studies.

By insisting on the need to consider the paradoxical ways in which firms adapt to governments in the making of international trade, I hope to have at least justified why trade scholars can learn from managerial and sociological studies of corporate decision-making. As much as they may focus on a different set of questions, trade scholars need to take seriously the construction of economic rationality within the firm.

Appendix: Interviews Conducted

International Organizations and Associations

IATA (Richard Smithies)
ICAO (Magda Boulos, e-mail contact only)
OECD (Wolfgang Hübner)
WTO (Bernard Kuiten, Pierre Latrille, Lee Tuthill)

United States

GOVERNMENT

Service trade. Department of Commerce (Sara E. Hagigh)
Air transport. State Department (John R. Byerly, Allan I. Mendelsohn); Department of Transportation (John H. Kiser); Department of Commerce (Eugene Alford); White House (former advisor on aviation Dorothy Robyn); Senate (Democratic senior counsel Sam Whitehorn).
Telecommunications. U.S. Trade Representative (Kenneth A. Schagrin); FCC (Donald Abelson); State Department (Timothy C. Finton); Department of Commerce (Dan Edwards).

ASSOCIATIONS

Service trade. U.S. Council of Service Industries (Harry L. Freeman, J. Robert Vastine); Representation of German Industry and Trade (Gert-M. Gerecht).

Air transport. Air Transport Association (Rhett D. Workman); Airline Pilots Association (R. Russell Bailey).

Telecommunications. United States Council for International Business (David A. Fares); Telecommunications Industry Association (Jason Leuck).

COMPANIES

Air transport. American Airlines (Dan Elwell); Delta Airlines (John M. Moloney); Northwest Airlines (Cecilia Bethke); United Airlines (Michael G. Whitaker).

Telecommunications. AT&T (Doug Schoenberger); Cable & Wireless USA (Joanne S. Lowry, Cathy Slesinger); ComSat (Beverly Andrews); MCI (Scott Shefferman); Squire, Sanders & Dempsey (Herbert E. Marks); Verizon/NYNEX (Karen Corbett-Sanders).

European Union

EUROPEAN INSTITUTIONS

Service trade. Council Secretariat (Dirk Hellwig); DG Trade (Karl-Friedrich Falkenberg).

Air transport. DG TREN (Hubert Beuve-Méry); DG Trade (Soeren Jakobsen); DG Competition (Joos Stragier); European Commission Delegation to the United States (Lars-Olof Hollner, Christopher Ross).

Telecommunications. DG Trade (Philippe Chauve); DG Info Society (Alison Birkett, Svend Kraemer); DG Competition (Dr. Herbert Ungerer).

NATIONAL GOVERNMENTS

Service trade. France: Ministère de l'Economie, des Finances et de l'Industrie (Frank Supplisson); United Kingdom: Department of Trade and Industry (Malcolm McKinnon).

Air transport. Germany: Bundesministerium für Verkehr, Bau- und Wohnungswesen (Dieter Bartkowski, Sabine Dannelke, Marina Köster); United Kingdom: Department for Transport (Tony Baker), British Embassy in the United States (Simon Knight).

Telecommunications. France: Ministère de l'Economie, des Finances et de l'Industrie (Christophe Ravier); Germany: Bundesministerium für Wirtschaft und Arbeit (Dr. Wilhelm Eschweiler, Eckart Lieser), Regulierungsbehörde für Telekommunikation und Post (Dr. Annegret Gröbel); United Kingdom: Office of Telecommunications (Vincent Affleck).

ASSOCIATIONS

Service trade. European Services Forum/Transatlantic Business Dialogue (Pascal Kerneis).
Air transport. Association of European Airlines (Dr. René Fennes).
Telecommunications. European Telecommunications Network Operators' Association (Fiona Taylor); European Information and Communication Technology Association (Ana Garcia).

COMPANIES

Air transport. Air France (Arnaud Camus); British Airways (John Wood); KLM (Rutger Jan toe Laer); Lufthansa (Jan Philipp Görtz); Virgin Atlantic (Chris Humphrey).
Telecommunications. British Telecom (Tilmann Kupfer); Deutsche Telekom (Wolfgang Jakubek, Dr. Jan Krancke); France Télécom (Jean-Louis Burillon, Alain-Louis Mie); Portugal Telecom (Pedro V. Goncalves— e-mail contact only); TDC Denmark (Allan Bartroff); Telefónica (Carlos Rodríguez Cocina); TeliaSonera (Olof Nordling).

OTHERS

Corporate Europe Observatory (Erik Wesselius); France: Direction Générale de l'Aviation Civile (Didier Jacquot); Union des Industries Textiles (Dominique Jacomet); Weber Shandwick (Marc Taquet-Graziani).

Bibliography

Abdelal, Rawi. *Capital Rules: The Construction of Global Finance*. Cambridge, Mass.: Harvard University Press, 2007.

Abdelal, Rawi, Mark Blyth, and Craig Parsons. "Constructivist Political Economy." Unpublished manuscript (2005).

Abdelal, Rawi, Yoshiko M. Herrera, Alastair Iain Johnston, and Rose McDermott. "Identity as a Variable." Unpublished manuscript (2005).

Abeyratne, Ruwantissa. "Trade in Air Transport Services: Emerging Trends." *Journal of World Trade* 35, 6 (2001): 1133–68.

Adler, Emmanuel. "Seizing the Middle Ground: Constructivism in World Politics." *European Journal of International Relations* 3, 3 (1997): 319–63.

——. "Constructivism and International Relations." 95–118, in *Handbook of International Relations*, ed. Walter Carlsnaes, Thomas Risse, and Beth A. Simmons. London: Sage, 2002.

Aggarwal, Vinod K. *Liberal Protectionism: The International Politics of Organized Textile Trade*. Berkeley: University of California Press, 1985.

Alesina, Alberto, and Eliana La Ferrara. "Preferences for Redistribution in the Land of Opportunities." *NBER Working Paper* 8267 (2001).

Alleman, James H., Paul N. Pappoport, and Kenneth B. Stanley. "Alternative Settlement Procedures in International Telecommunication Service." 129–60, in *Communications Policy in Europe*, ed. Dieter Elixmann. Heidelberg: Springer Verlag, 1990.

Alt, James E., Jeffry Frieden, Michael J. Gilligan, Dani Rodrik, and Ronald Rogowski. "The Political Economy of International Trade: Enduring Puzzles and an Agenda for Inquiry." *Comparative Political Studies* 29, 6 (1996): 689–717.

Alt, James E., and Michael J. Gilligan. "The Political Economy of Trading States: Factor Specificity, Collective Action Problems, and Domestic Political Institutions." *Journal of Political Philosophy* 2, 2 (1994): 165–92.

Arkell, Julian. "Lobbying for Market Access for Professional Services." 173–89, in *Marketing Strategies for Services*, ed. Michel M. Kostecki. Oxford: Pergamon Press, 1994.

Aronson, Jonathan David, and Peter Cowhey. *When Countries Talk: International Trade in Telecommunication Services*. Washington, D.C.: American Enterprise Institute, 1988.

Austen-Smith, David. "Information and Influence: Lobbying for Agendas and Votes." *American Journal of Political Science* 37, 3 (1993): 799–833.

Balaam, David N. "Agricultural Trade Policy." 52–66, in *Trade Politics: International, Domestic and Regional Perspectives*, ed. Brian Hocking and Steven McGuire. London: Routledge, 1999.

Balanyá, Belén, Ann Doherty, Olivier Hoedeman, Adam Ma'anit, and Erik Wesselius. *Europe Inc.: Regional and Global Restructuring and the Rise of Corporate Power.* Brussels: Pluto Press, 1999.

Balbus, Isaac D. "The Concept of Interest in Pluralist and Marxian Analysis." *Politics and Society* 1, 2 (1971): 151–77.

Baldwin, Robert E., Colin Scott, and Christopher Hood, eds. *A Reader on Regulation.* Oxford: Oxford University Press, 1998.

Banks, Howard. *The Rise and Fall of Freddie Laker.* London: Faber and Faber, 1982.

Bartkowski, Dieter, and John Byerly. "Forty Years of U.S.-German Aviation Relations." *Zeitschrift für Luft- und Weltraumrecht* 46, 1 (1997): 3–45.

Barton, John H., Judith L. Goldstein, Timothy E. Josling, and Richard H. Steinberg. *The Evolution of the Trade Regime: Politics, Law, and Economics of the GATT and the WTO.* Princeton, N.J.: Princeton University Press, 2006.

Bates, Robert H. *Markets and States in Tropical Africa: The Political Basis of Agricultural Policies.* Berkeley: University of California Press, 1981.

Bauer, Raymond A., Ithiel De Sola Pool. and Lewis Anthony Dexter. *American Business and Public Policy: The Politics of Foreign Trade.* Chicago: Aldine, 1963.

Beaulieu, Eugene. "Factor or Industry Cleavages in Trade Policy? An Empirical Analysis of the Stolper—Samuelson Theorem." *Economics and Politics* 14, 2 (2002): 99–131.

Becker, Gary S. "A Theory of Competition among Pressure Groups for Political Influence." *Quarterly Journal of Economics* 98, 3 (1983): 371–400.

Beckert, Jens. "What Is Sociological about Economic Sociology? Uncertainty and the Embeddedness of Economic Action." *Theory and Society* 25, 6 (1996): 803–40.

——. *Beyond the Market: The Social Foundations of Economic Efficiency.* Princeton, N.J.: Princeton University Press, 1997.

——. "The Great Transformation of Embeddedness: Karl Polanyi and the New Economic Sociology." in *Market and Society: The Great Transformation Today,* ed. Christ Hann and Keith Hart. Forthcoming.

Berger, Peter L., and Thomas Luckmann. *The Social Construction of Reality: A Treatise in the Sociology of Knowledge.* New York: Anchor Books, 1990 [1966].

Berman, Sheri. *The Social Democratic Moment.* Cambridge, Mass.: Harvard University Press, 1998.

Bieler, Andreas. "Questioning Cognitivsm and Constructivism in IR Theory: Reflections on the Material Structure of Ideas." *Politics* 21, 2 (2001): 93–100.

Blyth, Mark. *Great Transformations: Economic Ideas and Institutional Change in the Twentieth Century.* Cambridge, UK: Cambridge University Press, 2002.

——."Great Punctuations: Prediction, Randomness, and the Evolution of Comparative Political Science." *American Political Science Review* 100, 4 (2006): 493–98.

Borrmann, Christine. "Corporate Strategies in the Telecommunications Sector in an Environment of Continuing Liberalization." 53–84, in, *Trade, Investment and Competition Policies in the Global Economy: The Case of the International Telecommunications Regime,* ed. Paolo Guerrieri and Hans-Eckart Scharrer. Baden-Baden: Nomos, 2002.

Bouwen, Pieter. "Corporate Lobbying in the European Union: The Logic of Access." *Journal of European Public Policy* 9, 3 (2002): 365–90.

Braithwaite, John, and Peter Drahos. *Global Business Regulation.* Cambridge, UK: Cambridge University Press, 2000.

Brittan, Leon. "European Service Leaders' Group." Speech at the launching meeting of the ESF (Brussels, 1999). http://www.esf.be/pdfs/documents/speeches/splb0199.pdf.

Bronckers, M. C. E. J., and P. Larouche. "Telecommunication Services and the World Trade Organisation." *Journal of World Trade* 31, 3 (1997).

Broscheid, Andreas, and David Coen. "Insider and Outsider Lobbying in the European Commission." *European Union Politics* 4, 2 (2003): 165–89.

Buchanan, James, R. D. Tollison, and Gordon Tullock, eds. *Towards a Theory of the Rent-Seeking Society.* College Station: Texas A&M University Press, 1980.

Campbell, John L. *Institutional Change and Globalization.* Princeton, N.J.: Princeton University Press, 2004.

Campbell, John L., John A. Hall, and Ove Kaj Pedersen, eds. *National Identity and the Varieties of Capitalism: The Danish Experience.* Montreal: McGill-Queen's University Press, 2006.

Casella, Alessandra. "Large Countries, Small Countries, and the Enlargement of Trading Blocs." *European Economic Review* 40, 2 (1996): 389–415.

Chase, Kerry A. "Economic Interests and Regional Trading Arrangements: The Case of NAFTA." *International Organization* 57, 1 (2003): 137–74.

Chwieroth, Jeffrey. "Neoliberal Economists and Capital Account Liberalization in Emerging Markets." *International Organization* 61, 2 (2007): 443–63.

Codding, George A. *The International Telecommunication Union: An Experiment in International Cooperation.* Leiden: E. J. Brill, 1952.

Coen, David. "Business-Regulatory Relations: Learning to Play Regulatory Games in European Utility Markets." *Governance* 18, 3 (2005): 375–98.

Coglianese, Cary, Richard Zeckhauser, and Edward Parson. "Seeking Truth for Power: Informational Strategy and Regulatory Policymaking." *Minnesota Law Review* 89, 2 (2004): 277–341.

Cohen, Jeffrey E. *The Politics of Telecommunications Regulation: The States and the Divestiture of AT&T.* Armonk, N.Y.: M. E. Sharpe, 1992.

Connolly, William E. "On 'Interests' in Politics." *Politics and Society* 2, 4 (1972): 459–77.

Conway, Peter, and Giuseppe Nicoletti. "Product Market Regulation in Non-Manufacturing Sectors in OECD Countries: Measurement and Highlights." *OECD Economics Department Working Paper* 530 (2006).

Cowhey, Peter. "Telecommunications: Market Access Regimes in Services and Equipment." 133–70, in *New Challenges to International Cooperation,* ed. Peter Gourevitch and Paolo Guerrieri. San Diego: University of California Press, 1993.

———. "FCC Benchmarks and the Reform of the International Telecommunications Market." *Telecommunications Policy* 22, 11 (1998): 899–911.

Cowhey, Peter, and Jonathan David Aronson. *Managing the World Economy: The Consequences of Corporate Alliances.* New York: Council on Foreign Relations, 1993.

Cowhey, Peter, and John Richards. "Dialing for Dollars: Institutional Designs for the Globalization of the Market of Basic Telecommunication Services." 148–69, in *Coping with Globalization,* ed. Aseem Prakash and Jeffrey A. Hart. London: Routledge, 2000.

Cowhey, Peter, and John E. Richards. "Deregulating and Liberalizing the North American Telecommunications Market: Explaining the U.S. Approach." 85–118, in *Trade, Investment and Competition Policies in the Global Economy: The Case of the International*

Telecommunications Regime, ed. Paolo Guerrieri and Hans-Eckart Scharrer. Baden-Baden: Nomos, 2002.

Cowles, Maria Green. "The Transatlantic Business Dialogue and Domestic Business-Government Relations." 159–79, in *Transforming Europe: Europeanization and Domestic Change,* ed. James Caporaso, Maria Green Cowles, and Thomas Risse. Ithaca, N.Y.: Cornell University Press, 2001.

Crandall, Robert W. "Telecom Mergers and Joint Ventures in an Era of Liberalization." 107–24, in *Unfinished Business: Telecommunications after the Uruguay Round,* ed. Gary Clyde Hufbauer and Erika Wada. Washington D.C.: Institute for International Economics, 1997.

Croome, John. *Reshaping the World Trading System: A History of the Uruguay Round.* Geneva: World Trade Organization, 1995.

Crouch, Colin, and Wolfgang Streeck, eds. *The Political Economy of Modern Capitalism: Mapping Convergence and Diversity.* London: Sage, 1997.

Crystal, Jonathan. "Bargaining in the Negotiations over Liberalizing Trade in Services: Power, Reciprocity and Learning." *Review of International Political Economy* 10, 3 (2003): 552–78.

———. "What Do Producers Want? On the Origins of Societal Policy Preferences." *European Journal of International Relations* 9, 3 (2003): 407–39.

Cusack, Thomas, Torben Iversen, and David Soskice. "Economic Interests and the Origins of Electoral Systems." *American Political Science Review* 101 (forthcoming 2007).

De Bièvre, Dirk, and Andreas Dür. "Constituency Interests and Delegation in European and American Trade Policy." *Comparative Political Studies* 38, 10 (2005): 1271–96.

———. "Inclusion without Influence? Civil Society Involvement in European Trade Policy." *Journal of Public Policy* 27, 1 (2007): 79–101.

Della Porta, Donatella, and Sidney G. Tarrow. *Transnational Protest and Global Activism.* Lanham, Md.: Rowman & Littlefield, 2005.

Delorme, Hélène. "Les agriculteurs et les institutions communautaires: Du corporatisme agricole au lobbyisme agro-alimentaire." 313–46, in *L'action collective en Europe,* ed. Richard Balme, Didier Chabanet, and Vincent Wright. Paris: Presses de Sciences Po, 2002.

Dienel, Hans-Liudger, and Peter Lyth, eds. *Flying the Flag: European Commercial Air Transport since 1945.* New York: St. Martin's Press, 1998.

DiMaggio, Paul J. "The New Institutionalisms: Avenues of Collaboration." *Journal of Institutional and Theoretical Economics* 154, 4 (1998): 696–705.

DiMaggio, Paul J., and Walter W. Powell. *The New Institutionalism in Organizational Analysis.* Chicago: University of Chicago Press, 1989.

Dobson, Alan P. *Flying in the Face of Competition: The Policies and Diplomacy of Airline Regulatory Reform in Britain, the USA and the European Community 1968–94.* Aldershot: Avebury Aviation, 1995.

Doganis, Rigas. *Flying Off Course: The Economics of International Airlines.* London: Harper Collins, 1991.

Doremus, Paul N., William W. Keller, Louis W. Pauly, and Simon Reich. *The Myth of the Global Corporation.* Princeton, N.J.: Princeton University Press, 1999.

Drake, William J. "The Rise and Decline of the International Telecommunications Regime." 124–77, in *Regulating the Global Information Society,* ed. Christopher T. Marsden. London: Routledge, 2000.

Drake, William J., and Kalypso Nicolaïdis. "Ideas, Interests, and Institutionalization: Trade in Services and the Uruguay Round." *International Organization* 46, 1 (1992): 37–100.

Drake, William J., and Eli Noam. "The WTO Deal on Basic Telecommunications: Big Bang or Little Whimper." *Telecommunications Policy* 21, 9/10 (1997): 799–818.

Drezner, Daniel W. *All Politics is Global: Explaining International Regulatory Regimes.* Princeton, N.J.: Princeton University Press, 2007.

Duina, Francesco. *The Social Construction of Free Trade: The European Union, NAFTA, and Mercosur.* Princeton, N.J.: Princeton University Press, 2005.

Dunning, John H., ed. *Governments, Globalization, and International Business.* Oxford: Oxford University Press, 1997.

Dutheil de la Rochère, Jacqueline. *La politique des Etats-Unis en matière d'aviation civile.* Paris: Librairie de droit et de jurisprudence, 1971.

Elsig, Manfred. *The EU's Common Commercial Policy: Institutions, Interests and Ideas.* Aldershot: Ashgate, 2002.

Elster, Jon. *Sour Grapes.* Cambridge, UK: Cambridge University Press, 1983.

Engelmann, Stephen G. *Imagining Interest in Political Thought: Origins of Economic Rationality.* Durham, N.C.: Duke University Press, 2003.

Ergas, Henry. "International Trade in Services: An Economic Perspective." 89–106, in *Unfinished Business: Telecommunications after the Uruguay Round,* ed. Gary Clyde Hufbauer and Erika Wada. Washington D.C.: Institute for International Economics, 1997.

Ergas, Henry, and Paul Paterson. "International Telecommunications Settlement Arrangements: An Unsustainable Inheritance?" *Telecommunications Policy* 15 (1991): 29–48.

Esping-Andersen, Gøsta. *Politics Against Markets: The Social Democratic Road to Power.* Princeton, N.J.: Princeton University Press, 1985.

European Commission. *European Governance: A White Paper.* COM (2001) 428 final, Brussels: 2001.

Evans, David S., ed. *Breaking Up Bell: Essays on Industrial Organization and Regulation.* New York: North Holland, 1983.

Evans, Peter B. "The Eclipse of the State? Reflections on Stateness in an Era of Globalization." *World Politics* 50, 1 (1997): 62–87.

Evans, Peter B., Harold Karan Jacobson, and Robert D. Putnam. *Double-Edged Diplomacy: International Bargaining and Domestic Politics.* Berkeley: University of California Press, 1993.

Evans, Peter B., Dietrich Rueschemeyer, and Theda Skocpol. *Bringing the State Back In.* Cambridge, UK: Cambridge University Press, 1985.

Faulhaber, G. R. *Telecommunications in Turmoil: Technology and Public Policy.* Cambridge, Mass.: Ballinger, 1987.

Feketekuty, Geza. *International Trade in Services: An Overview and Blueprint for Negotiations.* Cambridge, Mass.: Ballinger, 1988.

——. "Regulatory Reform and Trade Liberalization in Services." 225–40, in *GATS 2000: New Directions in Service Trade Liberalization,* ed. Pierre Sauvé and Robert M. Stern. Washington D.C.: Brookings Institution, 2000.

Feldman, Stanley. "Economic Self-Interest and Political Behavior." *American Journal of Political Science* 26, 3 (1982): 446–66.

Finnemore, Martha. *National Interest in International Society.* Ithaca, N.Y.: Cornell University Press, 1996.

Finnemore, Martha, and Kathryn Sikkink. "International Norm Dynamics and Political Change." *International Organization* 52, 4 (1998): 887–917.

——. "Taking Stock: The Constructivist Research Program in International Relations and Comparative Politics." *Annual Review of Political Science* 2001, 4 (2001): 391–416.

Fligstein, Neil. *The Architecture of Markets: An Economic Sociology of Twenty-First-Century Capitalist Societies.* Princeton, N.J.: Princeton University Press, 2002.

Follesdal, Andreas, and Simon Hix. "Why There Is a Democratic Deficit in the EU: A Response to Majone and Moravcsik." *Journal of Common Market Studies* 44, 3 (2006): 533–62.

Ford, Jane. *A Social Theory of the WTO: Trading Cultures.* Houndmills: Palgrave, 2003.

Frankel, Jeffrey A. "Measuring International Capital Mobility: A Review." *American Economic Review* 82, 2 (1992): 197–202.

Freeman, Harry L. "A Pioneer's View of Financial Services Negotiations in the GATT and in the World Trade Organization: 17 Years of Work For Something or Nothing." 12th International Seminar of Progress, Geneva, 1996.

Frieden, Jeffry. "Actors and Preferences in International Relations." 39–76, in *Strategic Choice in International Relations,* ed. David A. Lake and Robert Powell. Princeton, N.J.: Princeton University Press, 1999.

Frieden, Jeffry, and Lisa L. Martin. "International Political Economy: Global and Domestic Interactions." 118–46, in *Political Science: The State of the Discipline,* ed. Ira Katznelson and Helen Milner. New York: Norton, 2002.

Friedman, Milton. "The Methodology of Positive Economics." 3–43, in *Essays in Positive Economics,* ed. Friedman, Milton. Chicago: University of Chicago Press, 1953.

Froot, Kenneth A., and David B. Yoffie. "Strategic Trade Policies in a Tripolar World." *International Spectator* 26, 3 (1991): 3–28.

Ganghof, Steffen. "Promises and Pitfalls of Veto Player Analysis." *Swiss Political Science Review* 9, 2 (2003): 1–25.

Garrett, Geoffrey, and Barry Weingast. "Ideas, Interests and Institutions: Constructing the European Communities Internal Market." 173–206, in *Ideas and Foreign Policy: Beliefs, Institutions, and Political Change,* ed. Judith Goldstein and Robert Keohane. Ithaca, N.Y.: Cornell University Press, 1993.

Geertz, Clifford. *The Interpretation of Cultures.* New York: Basic Books, 1973.

George, Alexander L. "The Causal Nexus Between Cognitive Beliefs and Decision-Making Behavior: The 'Operational Code' Belief System." 95–124, in *Psychological Models in International Politics,* ed. Lawrence S. Falkowski. Boulder, Colo.: Westview Press, 1979.

Gidwitz, Betsy. *The Politics of International Air Transport.* Boston: Lexington Books, 1980.

Gilpin, Robert. *Global Political Economy: Understanding the International Economic Order.* Princeton, N.J.: Princeton University Press, 2001.

Goldstein, Judith. *Ideas, Interests, and American Trade Policy.* Ithaca, N.Y.: Cornell University Press, 1993.

Goldstein, Judith, and Robert Keohane, eds. *Ideas and Foreign Policy: Beliefs, Institutions, and Political Change.* Ithaca, N.Y.: Cornell University Press, 1993.

Goodman, John B., Debora Spar, and David B. Yoffie. "Foreign Direct Investment and the Demand for Protection in the United States." *International Organization* 50, 4 (1996): 565–91.

Grande, Edgar. "The State and Interest Groups in a Framework of Multi-Level Decision-Making: The Case of the European Union." *Journal of European Public Policy* 3, 3 (1996): 318–38.

Granovetter, Mark. "Economic Action and Social Structure: The Problem of Embeddedness." *American Journal of Sociology* 91, 3 (1985): 481–510.

Grossman, Emiliano. "Bringing Politics Back In: Rethinking the Role of Economic Interest Groups in European Integration." *Journal of European Public Policy* 11, 4 (2004): 637–54.

Grossman, Gene, and Elhanan Helpman. "Protection for Sale." *American Economic Review* 84, 4 (1994): 833–50.

——. *Special Interest Politics*. Cambridge, Mass.: MIT Press, 2001.

Grossman, Gene, and James A. Levinsohn. "Import Competition and the Stock Market Return to Capital." *American Economic Review* 79, 5 (1989): 1065–87.

Haas, Peter M. "Introduction: Epistemic Communities and International Policy Coordination." *International Organization* 46, 1 (1992): 1–35.

Hainmueller, Jens, and Michael J. Hiscox. "Learning to Love Globalization: The Effects of Education on Individual Attitudes Toward International Trade." *International Organization* 60, 2 (2006): 469–98.

Hall, Peter A. "Institutions, Interests and Ideas in the Comparative Political Economy of the Industrialized Nations." 174–207, in *Comparative Politics: Rationality, Culture and Structure*, ed. Mark Lichbach and Alan Zuckerman. New York: Cambridge University Press, 1998.

——. "Aligning Ontology and Methodology in Comparative Research." 373–404, in *Comparative Historical Research in the Social Sciences*, ed. James Mahoney and Dieter Rueschemeyer. New York: Cambridge University Press, 2002.

——. "Preference Formation as a Political Process: The Case of European Monetary Union." 129–60, in *Preferences and Situations: Points of Intersection Between Historical and Rational Choice Institutionalism*, ed. Ira Katznelson and Barry Weingast. New York: Russell Sage Foundation, 2005.

——. "Stabilität und Wandel in den Spielarten des Kapitalismus." 181–204, in *Transformationen des Kapitalismus*, ed. Jens Beckert, Bernard Ebbinghaus, Anke Hassel, and Philip Manow. Frankfurt a. M.: Campus, 2007.

——, ed. *The Political Power of Economic Ideas: Keynesianism Across Nations*. Princeton, N.J.: Princeton University Press, 1989.

Hall, Peter A., and David Soskice. *Varieties of Capitalism: Institutional Foundations of Comparative Advantage*. Cambridge, UK: Cambridge University Press, 2001.

Helpman, Elhanan, and Paul R. Krugman. *Market Structure and Foreign Trade: Increasing Returns, Imperfect Competition, and the International Economy*. Cambridge, Mass.: MIT Press, 1985.

Hirschman, Albert O. *The Passions and the Interests*. Princeton, N.J.: Princeton University Press, 1977.

——. "The Concept of Interest: From Euphemism to Tautology." 35–55, in *Rival Views of Market Society and Other Recent Essays*, by Albert O. Hirschman. New York: Viking Penguin, 1986.

Hirshleifer, Jack, and John G. Riley. *The Analytics of Uncertainty and Information*. Cambridge, UK: Cambridge University Press, 1992.

Hiscox, Michael J. "Class Versus Industry Cleavages: Inter-Industry Factor Mobility and the Politics of Trade." *International Organization* 55, 1 (2001): 1–46.

——. *International Trade and Political Conflict: Commerce, Coalitions, and Mobility*. Princeton, N.J.: Princeton University Press, 2002.

——. "Through a Glass and Darkly: Framing Effects and Individuals' Attitudes Towards International Trade." *International Organization* 60, 3 (2006): 755–80.

Hiscox, Michael J., and Brian Burgoon. "The Mysterious Case of Female Protectionism: Gender Bias in Attitudes Toward International Trade." Unpublished manuscript (2005).

Hoekman, Bernard M., and Michel M. Kostecki. *The Political Economy of the World Trading System*. Oxford: Oxford University Press, 2001.

Hollingsworth, J., and R. Boyer, eds. *Contemporary Capitalism: The Embeddedness of Institutions*. Cambridge, UK: Cambridge University Press, 1997.

Holmes, Peter, and Francis McGowan. "The Changing Dynamic of EU-Industry Relations: Lessons from the Liberalization of European Car and Airline Markets." 159–84, in *Participation and Policy-Making in the European Union*, ed. Helen Wallace and Alasdair Young. Oxford: Clarendon Press, 1997.

Holmes, Peter, and Alasdair Young. "Liberalizing and Reregulating Telecommunications in Europe: A Common Framework and Persistent Differences." 119–58, in *Trade, Investment and Competition Policies in the Global Economy: The Case of the International Telecommunications Regime*, ed. Paolo Guerrieri and Hans-Eckart Scharrer. Baden-Baden: Nomos, 2002.

Hopf, Ted. "The Promise of Constructivism in International Relations Theory." *International Security* 23, 1 (1998): 171–200.

———. *Social Construction of International Politics: Identities and Foreign Policies, Moscow, 1955 and 1999*. Ithaca, N.Y.: Cornell University Press, 2002.

Hübner, Wolfgang, and Pierre Sauvé. "Liberalization Scenarios for International Air Transport." *Journal of World Trade* 35, 5 (2001): 973–87.

Immergut, Ellen M. "The Theoretical Core of the New Institutionalism." *Politics and Society* 26, 1 (1998): 5–34.

Iversen, Torben, and David Soskice. "An Asset Theory of Social Policy Preferences." *American Political Science Review* 95, 4 (2001): 875–93.

Jabko, Nicolas. "The Importance of Being Nice: An Institutionalist Analysis of French Preferences on the Future of Europe." *Comparative European Politics* 1, 2 (2004): 282–301.

———. *Playing the Market: A Political Strategy for Uniting Europe, 1985–2005*. Ithaca, N.Y.: Cornell University Press, 2006.

Jacobsen, John Kurt. "Much Ado About Ideas: The Cognitive Factor in Economic Policy." *World Politics* 47, 2 (1995): 283–310.

Jacomet, Dominique. "Les stratégies d'entreprises face aux politiques publiques: Le lobbying des producteurs occidentaux et la politique commerciale internationale dans le textile-habillement." Ph.D. diss. Université Paris IX Dauphine, 2000.

———. "Les changements induits par l'intégration européenne et la mondialisation sur la stratégie d'influence des entreprises: le cas de l'Union des Industries Textiles (UIT)." Paper presented at "Interest groups in the 21st century in France and Europe," Paris, 2004.

Jones, R. J. Barry. "International Political Economy." 813–29, in *Routledge Encyclopedia of International Political Economy*, ed. R. J. Barry Jones. London: Routledge, 2001.

Jönsson, Christer. *International Aviation and the Politics of Regime Change*. New York: St. Martin's Press, 1987.

Jordan, William A. *Airline Regulation in America: Effects and Imperfections*. Baltimore: Johns Hopkins University Press, 1970.

Jordana, Jacint, and David Levi-Faur. "The Politics of Regulation in the Age of Governance." 1–28, in *The Politics of Regulation: Institutions and Regulatory Reforms for the Age of Governance*, ed. Jacint Jordana and David Levi-Faur. Cheltenham: Edward Elgar Publishing, 2004.

Kasper, Daniel M. *Deregulation and Globalization: Liberalizing International Air Services*. Cambridge, Mass.: Ballinger, 1988.

Kassim, Hussein. "Air Transport." 106–31, in *The European Union and National Industrial Policy*, ed. Hussein Kassim and Anand Menon. London: Routledge, 1996.

Katzenstein, Peter J. *Cultural Norms and National Security: Police and Military in Postwar Japan*. Ithaca, N.Y.: Cornell University Press, 1996.

———. *The Culture of National Security: Norms and Identity in World Politics*. New York: Columbia University Press, 1996.

Katznelson, Ira, and Barry Weingast. "Intersections Between Historical and Rational Choice Institutionalism." 1–26, in *Preferences and Situations: Points of Intersection Between Historical and Rational Choice Institutionalism,* ed. Ira Katznelson and Barry Weingast. New York: Russell Sage Foundation, 2005.

——, eds. *Preferences and Situations: Points of Intersection Between Historical and Rational Choice Institutionalism.* New York: Russell Sage Foundation, 2005.

Keck, Margaret E., and Kathryn Sikkink. *Activists Beyond Borders: Advocacy Networks in International Politics.* Ithaca, N.Y.: Cornell University Press, 1998.

Keohane, Robert O. *After Hegemony: Cooperation and Discord in the World Political Economy.* Princeton, N.J.: Princeton University Press, 1984.

Kitschelt, Herbert P. "Political Opportunity Structures and Political Protest: Anti-Nuclear Movements in Four Democracies." *British Journal of Political Science* 16, 1 (1986): 57–85.

Kitschelt, Herbert, Peter Lange, Gary Marks, and John D. Stephens, eds. *Continuity and Change in Contemporary Capitalism.* Cambridge, UK: Cambridge University Press, 1999.

Knight, Frank H. *Risk, Uncertainty and Profit.* Boston, Mass.: Houghton Mifflin, 1921.

Korpi, Walter. *The Working Class in Welfare Capitalism: Work, Unions, and Politics in Sweden.* London: Routledge, 1978.

——. *The Democratic Class Struggle.* London: Routledge, 1983.

——. "Contentious Institutions: An Augmented Rational-Action Analysis of the Origins and Path Dependency of Welfare State Institutions in the Western Countries." *Rationality and Society* 13, 2 (2001): 235–83.

Kratochwil, Friedrich. *Rules, Norms and Decisions: On the Conditions of Practical and Legal Reasoning in International Relations and Domestic Affairs.* Cambridge, UK: Cambridge University Press, 1989.

Krehbiel, Keith. *Information and Legislative Organization.* Ann Arbor: University of Michigan Press, 1992.

Krueger, Anne O. *American Trade Policy: A Tragedy in the Making.* Washington, D.C.: American Enterprise Institute, 1995.

Lake, David A., and Robert Powell. "A Strategic-Choice Approach." 3–38, in *Strategic Choice in International Relations,* ed. David A. Lake and Robert Powell. Princeton, N.J.: Princeton University Press, 1999.

——, eds. *Strategic Choice in International Relations.* Princeton, N.J.: Princeton University Press, 1999.

Larouche, Pierre. "Relevant Market Definition in Network Industries: Air Transport and Telecommunications." *Journal of Network Industries* 1 (2000): 407–45.

Linos, Katerina, and Martin West. "Self-Interest, Social Beliefs, and Attitudes to Redistribution: Readdressing the Issue of Cross-national Variation." *European Sociological Review* 19, 4 (2003): 393–409.

Lohmann, Susanne, and Sharyn O'Halloran. "Divided Government and US Trade Policy: Theory and Evidence." *International Organization* 48, 4 (1994): 595–632.

Magee, Stephen P., William A. Brock, and Leslie Young. *Black Hole Tariffs and Endogenous Policy Theory: Political Economy in General Equilibrium.* Cambridge, UK: Cambridge University Press, 1989.

Mahoney, Christine. "The Power of Institutions: State and Interest Group Activity in the European Union." *European Union Politics* 5, 4 (2004): 441–66.

Majone, Giandomenico. "The Credibility Crisis of Community Regulation." *Journal of Common Market Studies* 38, 2 (2000): 273–302.

Mansbridge, Jane J. *Beyond Adversary Democracy.* New York: Basic Books, 1980.

March, James G., and Johan P. Olsen. *Rediscovering Institutions: The Organizational Basis of Politics*. New York: Free Press, 1989.

Mares, Isabela. *The Politics of Social Risk: Business and Welfare State Development*. Cambridge, UK: Cambridge University Press, 2003.

Markusen, James R. *Multinational Firms and the Theory of International Trade*. Cambridge, Mass.: MIT Press, 2002.

Mattoo, Aaditya, and Pierre Sauvé, eds. *Domestic Regulation and Service Trade Liberalization*. Washington, D.C.: World Bank and Oxford University Press, 2003.

Mawson, J. "Air Transport Liberalization in the European Union: An Assessment." *Regional Studies* 31, 8 (1997): 807–22.

Mayntz, Renate, and Fritz W Scharpf, eds. *Gesellschaftliche Selbstregelung und politische Steuerung*. Frankfurt a.M.: Campus, 1995.

McGuire, Steven. "Firms and Government in International Trade." in *Trade Politics: International, Domestic and Regional Perspectives*, ed. Brian Hocking and Steven McGuire. London: Routledge, 1999.

McNamara, Kathleen. *The Currency of Ideas*. Ithaca, N.Y.: Cornell University Press, 1998.

Messerlin, Patrick, and Karl Sauvant. *The Uruguay Round: Services in the World Economy*. Washington, D.C.: World Bank, 1990.

Meunier, Sophie. "What Single Voice? European Institutions and EU-U.S. Trade Negotiations." *International Organization* 54, 1 (2000): 103–35.

——. "EU Trade Policy: The 'Exclusive' versus Shared Competence Debate." 325–46, in *The State of the European Union: Risks, Reform, Resistance, and Revival*, ed. Maria Green Cowles and Michael Smith. Oxford: Oxford University Press, 2000.

——. *Trading Voices: The European Union in International Commercial Negotiations*. Princeton, N.J.: Princeton University Press, 2005.

Meunier, Sophie, and Kalypso Nicolaïdis. "Who Speaks for Europe? The Delegation of Trade Authority in the European Union." *Journal of Common Market Studies* 37, 3 (1999): 477–501.

Milner, Helen V. *Resisting Protectionism: Global Industries and the Politics of International Trade*. Princeton N.J.: Princeton University Press, 1988.

——. *Interests, Institutions, and Information*. Princeton, N.J.: Princeton University Press, 1997.

——. "The Political Economy of International Trade." *Annual Review of Political Science* 1999, 2 (1999): 91–114.

Milner, Helen V., and David B. Yoffie. "Between Free Trade and Protectionism: Strategic Trade Policy and a Theory of Corporate Trade Demands." *International Organization* 43, 2 (1989): 239–72.

Moravcsik, Andrew. "In Defence of the 'Democratic Deficit': Reassessing Legitimacy in the European Union." *Journal of Common Market Studies* 40, 4 (2002): 603–24.

Moselle, Boaz, James Reitz, Dorothy Robyn, and John Horn. *The Economic Impact of an EU-US Open Aviation Area*. Washington, D.C.: The Brattle Group, 2002.

Muller, Pierre. "Esquisse d'une théorie du changement dans l'action publique: Structures, acteurs et cadres cognitifs." *Revue française de science politique* 55, 1 (2005): 155–87.

Narlikar, Amrita. *International Trade and Developing Countries: Bargaining Coalitions in the GATT and WTO*. London: Routledge, 2003.

Nicolaïdis, Kalypso, and Joel P. Trachtman. "Liberalization, Regulation, and Recognition for Services Trade." 43–58, in *Services Trade in the Western Hemisphere: Liberalization, Integration and Reform*, ed. Sherry M. Stephenson. Washington, D.C.: Brookings Institution, 2000.

Niemann, Arne. "Between Communicative Action and Strategic Action: The Article 113 Committee and the Negotiations on the WTO Basic Telecommunications Agreement." *Journal of European Public Policy* 11, 3 (2004): 379–407.

Noam, Eli. *Telecommunications in Europe*. New York: Oxford University Press, 1992.

North, Douglas. *Institutions, Institutional Change and Economic Performance*. New York: Cambridge University Press, 1990.

Oatley, Thomas. *International Political Economy: Interests and Institutions in the Global Economy*. New York: Pearson Longman, 2004.

Odell, John S. *U.S. International Monetary Policy: Markets, Power, and Ideas as Sources of Change*. Princeton, N.J.: Princeton University Press, 1982.

O'Reilly, Dolores, and Alec Stone Sweet. "The Liberalization and Reregulation of Air Transport." *Journal of European Public Policy* 5, 3 (1998): 441–66.

Palier, Bruno. "Ambiguous Agreement, Cumulative Change: French Social Policy in the 1990s." 127–44, in *Beyond Continuity: Institutional Change in Advanced Political Economies*, ed. Wolfgang Streeck and Kathleen Thelen. Oxford: Oxford University Press, 2005.

Parsons, Craig. "Showing Ideas as Causes: The Origins of the European Union." *International Organization* 56, 1 (2002): 47–84.

——. *A Certain Idea of Europe*. Ithaca, N.Y.: Cornell University Press, 2003.

Pauly, Louis W., and Simon Reich. "National Structures and Multinational Corporate Behavior: Enduring Differences in the Age of Globalization." *International Organization* 51, 1 (1997): 1–30.

Peltzman, Sam. "Towards a More General Theory of Regulation." *Journal of Law and Economics* 19 (1976): 211–40.

——. "The Economic Theory of Regulation after a Decade of Deregulation." *Brookings Papers on Economic Activity, Microeconomics* (1989): 1–41.

Peterson, Barbara S., and James Glab. *Rapid Descent: Deregulation and the Shakeout in the Airlines*. New York: Simon and Schuster, 1994.

Petrazzini, Ben. *Global Telecom Talks: A Trillion Dollar Deal*. Washington, D.C.: Institute for International Economics, 1996.

Pickrell, Donald. "The Regulation and Deregulation of U.S. Airlines." 5–47, in *Airline Deregulation*, ed. Kenneth Button. New York: New York University Press, 1991.

Pierson, Paul. "Not Just What, but When: Timing and Sequence in Political Processes." *Studies in American Political Development* 14, 1 (2000): 72–92.

Pierson, Paul, and Theda Skocpol. "Historical Institutionalism in Contemporary Political Science." 693–721, in *Political Science: The State of the Discipline*, ed. Ira Katznelson and Helen Milner. New York: Norton, 2002.

Polsby, Nelson W. *Community Power and Political Theory: A Further Look at Problems of Evidence and Inference*. New Haven, Conn.: Yale University Press, 1980.

Potters, Jan, and Frans Van Winden. "Modelling Political Pressure as Transmission of Information." *European Journal of Political Economy* 6, 1 (1990): 61–88.

Powell, Robert. "Anarchy in International Relations Theory: The Neorealist-Neoliberal Debate." *International Organization* 48, 2 (1994): 313–44.

Price, Richard. "Reversing the Gun Sights: Transnational Civil Society Targets Land Mines." *International Organization* 52, 3 (1998): 613–44.

Putnam, Robert. "Diplomacy and Domestic Politics: The Logic of Two-Level Games." *International Organization* 42 (1988): 427–60.

Radaelli, Claudio. "The Role of Knowledge in the Policy Process." *Journal of European Public Policy* 2, 2 (1995): 159–83.

Ricardo, David. *The Principles of Political Economy and Taxation.* London: J. M. Dent, 1992 [1817].

Richards, John. "Towards a Positive Theory of International Institutions: Regulation of Postwar International Aviation Markets." *International Organization* 53, 1 (1999): 1–37.

———. "Institutions for Flying: How States Built a Market in International Aviation Services." *International Organization* 55, 4 (2001): 993–1017.

Rogowski, Ronald. *Commerce and Coalition: How Trade Affects Domestic Political Alignments.* Princeton, N.J.: Princeton University Press, 1989.

Rugman, Alan M., and Alain Verbeke. *Global Corporate Strategy and International Trade Policy.* London: Routledge, 1990.

Sandholtz, Wayne. "The Emergence of a Supranational Telecommunications Regime." 134–63, in *European Integration and Supranational Governance,* ed. Wayne Sandholtz and Alec Stone Sweet. Oxford: Oxford University Press, 1998.

Schäfer, Armin. "Nach dem permissiven Konsens: Das Demokratiedefizit der Europäischen Union." *Leviathan* 34, 3 (2006): 350–76.

Scharpf, Fritz W. *Games Real Actors Play: Actor-Centered Institutionalism in Policy Research.* Boulder, Colo.: Westview Press, 1997.

———. *Governing in Europe: Effective and Democratic?* Oxford: Oxford University Press, 1999.

Schattschneider, E. E. *Politics, Pressures and the Tariff: A Study of Free Private Enterprise in Pressure Politics, as Shown in the 1929–1930 Revision of the Tariff.* New York: Prentice-Hall, 1935.

Scheffer, Michiel. "Textiles." 103–14, in *The Challenge of Change in EU Business Associations,* ed. Justin Greenwood. New York: Palgrave, 2003.

Scheve, Kenneth, and Matthew Slaughter. "What Explains Individual Trade-Policy Preferences?" *Journal of International Economics* 54, 2 (2001): 267–92.

Schimmelfennig, Frank. "The Community Trap: Liberal Norms, Rhetorical Action, and the Eastern Enlargement of the European Union." *International Organization* 55, 1 (2001): 47–80.

———. *The EU, NATO and the Integration of Europe: Rules and Rhetoric.* Cambridge, UK: Cambridge University Press, 2003.

Schmidt, Susanne K. "Commission Activism: Subsuming Telecommunication and Electricity under European Competition Law." *Journal of European Public Policy* 5, 1 (1998): 169–84.

Schneider, Volker. *Staat und technische Kommunikation: Die politische Entwicklung der Telekommunikation in den USA, Japan, Grossbritannien, Deutschland, Frankreich und Italien.* Opladen: Westdeutscher Verlag, 1999.

———. *Die Transformation der Telekommunikation: Vom Staatsmonopol zum globalen Markt (1800–2000).* Frankfurt a. M.: Campus, 2001.

Sell, Susan K. "Big Business and the New Trade Agreements: The Future of the WTO." 174–83, in *Political Economy and the Changing Global Order,* ed. Richard Stubbs and Geoffrey R. D. Underhill. Oxford: Oxford University Press, 2000.

Sell, Susan K., and Aseem Prakash. "Using Ideas Strategically: The Contest Between Business and NGO Networks in Intellectual Property Rights." *International Studies Quarterly* 48, 1 (2004): 143–75.

Sen, Amartya K. "Rational Fools: A Critique of the Behavioral Foundations of Economic Theory." *Philosophy and Public Affairs* 6, 4 (1977): 317–44.

Sewell, William H. "Historical Events as Transformations of Structures: Inventing Revolution at the Bastille." *Theory and Society* 25, 6 (1996): 841–81.

Shaffer, Gregory C. *Defending Interests: Public-Private Partnerships in WTO Litigation.* Washington, D.C.: Brookings Institution, 2003.

Sherman, Laura B. "'Wildly Enthusiastic' About the First Multilateral Agreement on Trade in Telecommunications Services." *Federal Communications Law Journal* 51, 1 (1998): 61–110.

Sikkink, Kathryn. *Ideas and Institutions: Developmentalism in Brazil and Argentina.* Ithaca, N.Y.: Cornell University Press, 1991.

Simon, Herbert Alexander. *Models of Bounded Rationality.* Cambridge, Mass.: MIT Press, 1982.

Smith, Edward W. "Re-Regulation and Integration: The Nordic States and the European Economic Area." Ph.D. diss. University of Sussex, 1999.

Snape, Richard. "Principles in Trade in Services." 5–11, in *The Uruguay Round: Services in the World Economy,* ed. Patrick Messerlin and Karl Sauvant. Washington, D.C.: The World Bank, 1990.

Sochor, Eugene. *The Politics of International Aviation.* Iowa City: University of Iowa Press, 1991.

Soskice, David. "Varieties of Capitalism and Cross-National Gender Differences." *Social Politics* 12, 2 (2005): 170–79.

Staniland, Martin. *Government Birds: The State and Air Transport in Western Europe.* Lanham, Md.: Rowman & Littlefield, 2003.

Steinmo, Sven, Kathleen Thelen, and Frank Longstreth, eds. *Structuring Politics: Historical Institutionalism in Comparative Analysis.* Cambridge, UK: Cambridge University Press, 1992.

Stewart, Terence P. *The GATT Uruguay Round: A Negotiating History (1986–1992).* Deventer: Kluwer, 1993.

———. *The GATT Uruguay Round: The End Game (1993–1994).* Deventer: Kluwer, 1994.

Stigler, George. "The Theory of Economic Regulation." *Bell Journal of Economics and Management Science* 2 (1971): 3–21.

———. "Economic Competition and Political Competition." *Public Choice* 13 (1972): 91–107.

Stigler, George J., and Gary S. Becker. "De gustibus non est disputandum." *American Economic Review* 67 (1977): 76–90.

Stopford, John M. and Susan Strange, eds. *Rival States, Rival Firms: Competition for World Market Shares.* Cambridge, UK: Cambridge University Press, 1991.

Streeck, Wolfgang, Jürgen R. Grote, Volker Schneider, and Jelle Visser, eds. *Governing Interests: Business Associations Facing Internationalization.* London: Routledge, 2006.

Swedberg, Richard. *Max Weber and the Idea of Economic Sociology.* Princeton, N.J.: Princeton University Press, 1998.

———. "Can There Be a Sociological Concept of Interest?" *Theory and Society* 34, 4 (2005): 359–90.

Swenson, Peter. *Capitalists Against Markets: The Making of Labor Markets and Welfare States in the United States and Sweden.* Oxford: Oxford University Press, 2002.

Tarry, Scott E. "Globalization and the Prospect of Policy Convergence in Air Transport." *Global Society* 14, 2 (2000): 279–96.

Thatcher, Mark. "The Europeanisation of Regulation: The Case of Telecommunication." *EUI Working Papers* 99, 22 (1999).

———. *The Politics of Telecommunications: National Institutions, Convergence, and Change in Britain and France.* Oxford: Oxford University Press, 1999.

———. "The Commission and National Governments as Partners: EC Regulatory Expansion in Telecommunications 1997–2000." *Journal of European Public Policy* 8, 4 (2001): 558–84.

Thelen, Kathleen. "Beyond Corporatism: Towards a New Framework for the Study of Labor in Advanced Capitalism." *Comparative Politics* 27, 3 (1994): 107–24.

Tiberghien, Yves. *Entrepreneurial States: Reforming Corporate Governance in France, Japan, and Korea.* Ithaca: Cornell University Press, 2007.

Tirole, Jean. *The Theory of Industrial Organization.* Cambridge, Mass.: MIT Press, 1988.

Tullock, Gordon. "The Welfare Costs of Tariffs, Monopolies, and Theft." *Western Economic Journal* 5 (1967): 224–32.

Tuthill, Lee. "The GATS and New Rules for Regulators." *Telecommunications Policy* 21, 9/10 (1997): 783–98.

Ugur, Mehmet. "Explaining Protectionism and Liberalization in European Union Trade Policy: The Case of Textiles and Clothing." *Journal of European Public Policy* 5, 4 (1998): 652–70.

United Nations, et al. "Manual on Statistics of International Trade in Services." *Statistical Papers Series* ST/ESA/STAT/SER.M/86 (2002).

Vahl, Remco. *Leadership in Disguise: The Role of the European Commission in EC Decision-Making on Agriculture in the Uruguay Round.* Aldershot: Ashgate, 1997.

Van den Hoven, Adrian. "Interest Group Influence on Trade Policy in a Multilevel Polity: Analyzing the EU Position at the Doha WTO Ministerial Conference." *EUI Working Papers* 2002, 67 (2002).

Van der Stichele, Myriam, Kim Bizzarri, and Leonard Plank. *Corporate Power over EU Trade Policy: Good for Business, Bad for the World.* Policy report, Brussels: Seattle to Brussels Network, 2006.

Vogel, David. *Trading Up: Consumer and Environmental Regulation in a Global Economy.* Cambridge, Mass.: Harvard University Press, 1995.

Vogel, Steven K. *Freer Markets, More Rules: Regulatory Reform in Advanced Industrial Countries.* Ithaca, N.Y.: Cornell University Press, 1996.

———. "When Interests Are Not Preferences: Ehe Cautionary Tale of Japanese Consumers." *Comparative Politics* 31, 2 (1999): 187–207.

Wæver, Ole. "The Sociology of a Not So International Discipline: American and European Developments in International Relations." *International Organization* 52, 4 (1998): 687–727.

Waltz, Kenneth. *Theory of International Politics.* New York: Random House, 1979.

Warren, Tony, and Christopher Findlay. "Competition Policy and International Trade in Air Transport and Telecommunications Services." *The World Economy* 21, 4 (1998): 445–56.

Watson, Matthew. *Foundations of International Political Economy.* Houndmills: Palgrave, 2005.

Weber, Max. *Wirtschaft und Gesellschaft.* Frankfurt a. M.: Zweitausendeins, 2005 [1922].

Welfens, Paul, and C. Yarrow. *Telecommunications and Energy in Transforming Economies: International Dynamics, Deregulation and Adjustment in Network Industries.* Heidelberg: Springer, 1996.

Wendt, Alexander. "Anarchy Is What States Make of It: The Social Construction of Power Politics." *International Organization* 46, 2 (1992): 391–425.

———. "Collective Identity Formation and the International State." *American Political Science Review* 88, 2 (1994): 384–96.

Wendt, Alexander. *A Social Theory of International Relations.* Cambridge, UK: Cambridge University Press, 1999.

Wesselius, Erik. "Behind GATS 2000: Corporate Power at Work." *Transnational Institute Briefing Series* 2002, 6 (2002).

Williamson, O. E. "Comparative Economic Organization: The Analysis of Discrete Structural Alternatives." *Administrative Science Quarterly* 36, 2 (1991): 269–96.

Willman, Paul, David Coen, David Currie, and Martin Sinner. "The Evolution of Regulatory Relationships: Regulatory Institutions and Firm Behavior in Privatized Industries." *Industrial and Corporate Change* 12, 1 (2003): 69–89.

Wilts, Arnold. "Identities and Preferences in Corporate Political Strategizing." *Business and Society* 45, 4 (2006): 441–63.

Woll, Cornelia. "The Politics of Trade Preferences: Business Lobbying on Service Trade in the United States and the European Union." Ph.D. diss. Paris/Cologne: Institut d'Etudes Politiques de Paris/Universität zu Köln, 2004.

——. "The Road to External Representation: The European Commission's Activism in International Air Transport." *Journal of European Public Policy* 13, 1 (2006): 52–69.

——. "Leading the Dance? Power and Political Resources of Business Lobbyists." *Journal of Public Policy* 27, 1 (2007): 57–78.

——. "Trade Policy Lobbying in the European Union: Who Captures Whom?" In *Lobbying in the European Union: Institutions, Actors and Issues,* ed. David Coen and Jeremy Richardson. Oxford University Press, forthcoming.

Woodruff, David M. "Commerce and Demolition in Tsarist and Soviet Russia: Lessons for Theories of Trade Politics and the Philosophy of Social Science." *Review of International Political Economy* 12, 2 (2005): 199–225.

Woods, Ngaire. "Economic Ideas and International Relations: Beyond Rational Neglect." *International Studies Quarterly* 39, 2 (1995): 161–80.

——. *The Globalizers: The IMF, the World Bank, and Their Borrowers.* Ithaca, N.Y.: Cornell University Press, 2006.

Woolcock, Stephen. "Liberalisation of Financial Services." Unpublished manuscript (1998). www.lse.ac.uk/collections/internationalTradePolicyUnit/pdf/liberalisation OfFinan

——. "European Trade Policy: Global Pressures and Domestic Constraints." 373–99, in *Policy-making in the European Union,* ed. Helen Wallace and William Wallace. Oxford: Oxford University Press, 2000.

Yee, Albert S. "The Causal Effects of Ideas on Policies." *International Organization* 50, 1 (1996): 69–108.

——. "Thick Rationality and the Missing 'Brute Fact': The Limits of Rationalist Incorporations of Norms and Ideas." *Journal of Politics* 59, 4 (1997): 1001–39.

Yergin, Daniel, Richard H. K. Vietor, and Peter C. Evans. *Fettered Flight: Globalization and the Airline Industry.* Cambridge Mass.: Cambridge Energy Research Associates, 2000. www.air-transport.org/econ/files/FetteredFlight.pdf.

Yoffie, David B., ed. *Beyond Free Trade: Firms, Governments, and Global Competition.* Boston, Mass.: Harvard Business School Press, 1993.

Yoffie, David B., and Sigrid Bergenstein. "Creating Political Advantage: The Rise of the Corporate Political Entrepreneur." *California Management Review* 28, 1 (1985): 124–39.

Young, Alasdair. *Extending European Cooperation: The European Union and the "New" International Trade Agenda.* Manchester: Manchester University Press, 2002.

——. "The Incidental Fortress: The Single European Market and World Trade." *Journal of Common Market Studies* 42, 2 (2004): 393–414.

Zacher, Mark, and Brent Sutton. *Governing Global Networks: International Regimes for Transportation and Communications.* New York: Cambridge University Press, 1996.

Zammit, Ann. *Development at Risk: Rethinking UN-Business Partnerships.* Geneva: South Centre and UNRISD, 2003. www.globalpolicy.org/reform/business/2003/risk.pdf.

Zehfuss, Maja. "Constructivism and Identity: A Dangerous Liaison." *European Journal of International Relations* 7, 3 (2001): 315–48.

Ziegler, J. Nicholas. *Governing Ideas: Strategies for Innovation in France and Germany.* Ithaca, N.Y.: Cornell University Press, 1997.

Zukin, Sharon, and Paul DiMaggio. "Introduction." 1–36, in *Structures of Capital: The Social Organization of the Economy,* ed. Paul DiMaggio and Sharon Zukin. Cambridge, UK: Cambridge University Press, 1990.

Index